Business Result

SECOND EDITION

Pre-intermediate *Student's Book*  with Online practice

David Grant, Jane Hudson & John Hughes

Contents

Contents

Introduction

Welcome to *Business Result Second Edition Pre-intermediate*. In this book you will find:

- 15 units
- 5 Viewpoint video lessons
- Practice files
- Communication activities
- Audio scripts
- Access to the Online practice

What's in a unit?

Starting point
- an introduction to the theme of the unit
- discussion questions

Working with words
- reading and listening about a work-related topic
- focus on key words and phrases
- practise the new words in speaking activities

Language at work
- grammar presented in authentic work contexts
- *Language point* box focuses on the key grammar points
- practise using the language in real work situations

Practically speaking
- focus on an aspect of everyday communication at work
- helps you to sound more natural when speaking
- practise speaking in real work situations

Business communication
- key expressions for authentic work contexts
- improve your communication skills for meetings, presentations, socializing, and phone calls
- *Key expressions* list in every unit

Talking point
- focus on interesting business topics and concepts
- improve your fluency with *Discussion* and *Task* activities
- *Discussion* and *Task* allow you to apply the topic to your own area of work

What's in the *Communication activities*?

- roles and information for pair and group activities
- extra speaking practice for the main sections of each unit

What's in the *Viewpoint* lessons?

The *Viewpoints* are video lessons, which appear after every three units. The topics of the *Viewpoint* lessons relate to a theme from the main units and include:
- interviews with expert speakers
- case studies of real companies

Each *Viewpoint* is divided into three or four sections, with a number of short video clips in each lesson. A *Viewpoint* lesson usually includes:
- A focus to introduce the topic. This contains a short video showing people discussing the topic.
- Key vocabulary and phrases which appear in the videos.
- Main video sections which develop listening and note-taking skills, and build confidence in listening to authentic language in an authentic context.
- Activities which provide speaking practice about the topic of the lesson.

All of the videos in the *Viewpoint* lessons can be streamed or downloaded from the *Online practice*.

What's in the *Practice files*?

Written exercises to practise the key language in:
- *Working with words*
- *Business communication*
- *Language at work*

Use the *Practice files*:
- in class to check your understanding
- out of class for extra practice or homework

The *Practice files* include a *Grammar reference* section with more detailed explanations of the grammar from each unit.

Follow the links (as shown below) to the *Practice file* in each unit.

>> For more exercises, go to **Practice file 6** on page 116

>> For more information, go to **Grammar reference** on page 117

What's in the *Online practice*?

- practice exercises for each *Working with words*, *Language at work*, and *Business communication* section
- unit tests
- email exercises for each unit
- automatic marking for instant answers
- gradebook to check your scores and progress

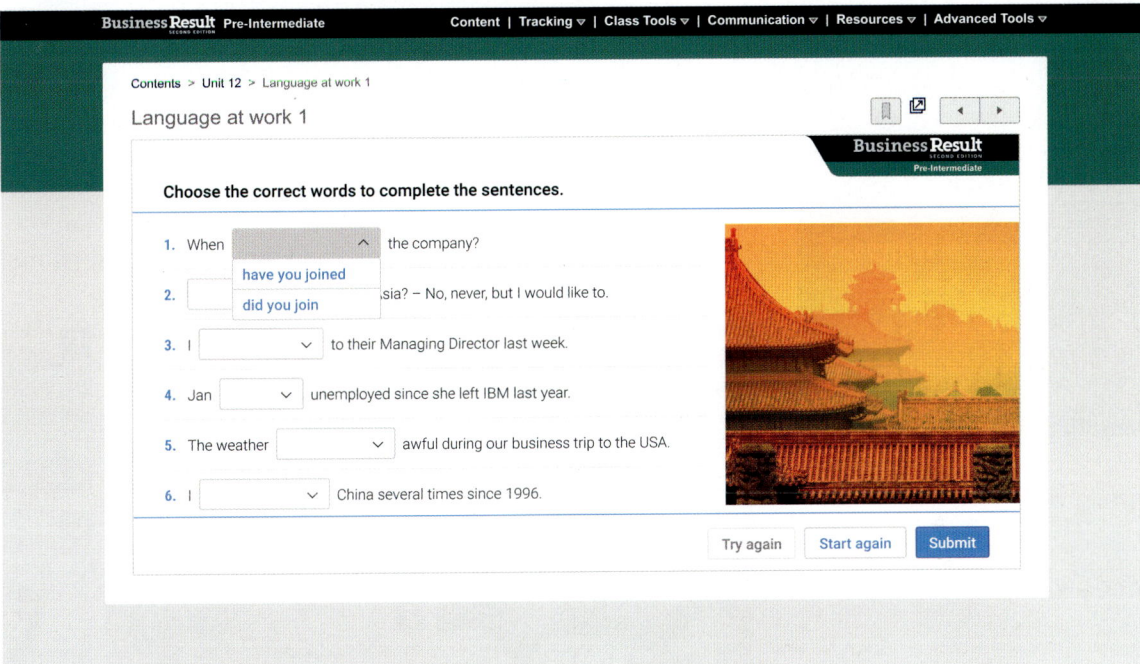

Additional resources

- watch and download all of the *Viewpoint* videos
- listen to and download all of the class audio
- sample emails for each unit

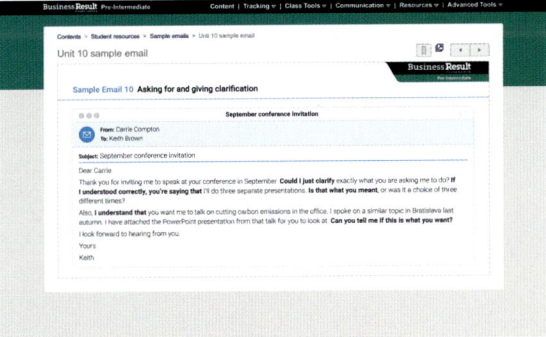

How to access your *Online practice*

To access your *Online practice*, you will find an access card on the inside cover of your Student's Book. This contains an access code to unlock all the content in the *Online practice*.

Go to **www.oxfordlearn.com** and activate your code, and then follow the instructions online to access the content.

1 Companies

Starting point

1 What kind of company do you work for?

2 Do you think it's better to work for a large or a small company?

Working with words | Company facts

1 Work with a partner. What do you know about these companies?

Ben and Jerry's   Michelin   Yahoo!   Samsung   Ikea

2 Read this text. Match descriptions 1–5 to the companies in 1.

1 This company **provide**s many different Internet services, including news, online shopping and email. Most of its **revenue** comes from advertising on its website. Its head office is in Sunnyvale, California. _____

2 This company makes tyres for cars and other vehicles. It is **based** in France, but it has more than 111,000 **employee**s all over the world. It is also well known for its red and green travel guides. _____

3 It's a Swedish company and it **operates** in 37 countries. It **specialize**s in low-price household products, including furniture, bathrooms and kitchens. _____

4 It's a **subsidiary** of Unilever. The company makes ice cream and frozen yoghurt, and its main **competitor** is Häagen-Dazs. _____

5 This company **produce**s many different electrical and electronic products, such as TVs, computers and mobile phones. It's South Korea's largest company and **exporter**. _____

3 Work with a partner. Which companies in 2 do you know well? Do you use any of the companies or their products? What do you think of them?

4 Complete these sentences with the words in **bold** from **2**.

1 Some companies make or _____ goods.
2 Other companies _____ or offer services.
3 If you _____ in a product or service, it's your main activity.
4 If you work for a company, you are an _____.
5 Your company is _____ in the town or city where it has its head office.
6 If you work in a _____, your company is part of a bigger group.
7 Your company _____ in a country where it sells or makes its products.
8 A company in the same business as you is your _____.
9 A company that sells its products in other countries is an

   _____.
10 Your _____ is the money you receive for your products or services.

5 How many syllables are there in the words in **4**? Where is the stress?

6 Complete this text with words from **4**. Sometimes you need to change the form.

> Skoda ¹_____ cars and other vehicles. It is a
> ²_____ of Volkswagen (VW) Group and it is the third
> oldest car maker in the world. It's ³_____ in the
> Czech Republic, but it is a global company. It ⁴_____
> in 103 markets and has more than 25,000 ⁵_____
> worldwide.
>
> Skoda has the advantages of a central European location and technology
> from the VW Group. For this reason, its costs are lower than many of
> its ⁶_____, and it ⁷_____ in cars
> which offer good value for money.
>
> When the company started, it produced bicycles. Today, it continues to
> ⁸_____ support services to the Tour de France and
> Tour of Britain cycle races.

» For more exercises, go to **Practice file 1** on page 106.

7 Name three big companies in your country. What do they do?

8 ▶ 1.1 Listen and complete the information about the ASSA ABLOY Group.

Name of group	ASSA ABLOY
Products	¹l_____ and ²s_____ s_____
Competitors	³E_____ C_____, Ingersoll-Rand, and Master Lock
Nationality	⁴S_____
Number of employees	⁵_____,000
Revenue	⁶€_____ billion
International operations	⁷over _____ countries, ⁸_____ companies
Name of the subsidiary	⁹B_____

9 Make sentences about the employee and her company, using the information in **8** and some or all of the words in **4**.

> *Example:* *She works for ASSA ABLOY.*
>   *It produces locks and security systems.*

10 Work with a partner. Talk about your company or organization.

Tip | Word stress

To pronounce a longer word correctly, you need to know (a) the number of syllables (b) which syllable has the main stress or accent.

company (3 syllables)
country (2 syllables)
activity (4 syllables)

Language at work | Present simple

1 Work with a partner. Ask and answer questions 1–5.
 1 Which company do you work for?
 2 Is it a new company?
 3 What does it do?
 4 Do you work at the head office?
 5 Does the company have offices in other countries?

2 Work with a partner. Are these sentences about *Gazprom*, *Nestlé* and *Toyota* true (*T*) or false (*F*)?
 1 Gazprom produces energy.
 2 The companies aren't competitors.
 3 Nestlé provides services but it doesn't produce anything.
 4 Two of the companies produce cars.
 5 Toyota isn't Russian.
 6 Nestlé and Gazprom don't have their head office in Japan.

3 Find examples from **1** and **2** for descriptions 1–5 in the *Language point*. Then choose the correct words in *italics* to complete sentences a–c.

LANGUAGE POINT

 1 Verbs with *-s* or *-es* at the end   _____
 2 A negative sentence using the verb *do*   _____
 3 A negative sentence using the verb *be*   _____
 4 A question using the verb *do*   _____
 5 A question using the verb *be*   _____

 a We use the present simple to talk about *something happening now* / *facts or regular actions*.
 b We add *-s* or *-es* to the end of the verb in the *second* / *third* person singular.
 c We use *be* / *do* for questions with adjectives, and we use *be* / *do* for questions with verbs.

>> For more information, go to **Grammar reference** on page 107.

4 Choose the correct words in *italics* to complete the text.

You probably ¹*know* / *knows* that Nestlé ²*produce* / *produces* Nespresso machines and Nescafé instant coffee. And many people ³*see* / *sees* the Nestlé name on their breakfast cereal packet every morning. But what else ⁴*do* / *does* you know about the company? What other products ⁵*is* / *does* it sell, and where? And the food industry ⁶*isn't* / *doesn't* always green, so what does the company ⁷*do* / *does* to protect the environment?

Our reporter Rosa Manning ⁸*talk* / *talks* to employees of Nestlé and discovers what they do. She ⁹*learn* / *learns* why most employees ¹⁰*are* / *do* happy to work there and why most of Nestlé's employees ¹¹*isn't* / *don't* want to leave.

Listen to Nestlé in Focus tonight at 8 p.m. to learn more about one of the world's biggest food companies.

5 ▶ 1.2 Listen and make a note of three interesting facts about Nestlé. Compare with your partner.

6 ▶ 1.2 Listen again and answer questions 1–9.
1 How old is the company?
2 What products does it produce?
3 What is its annual revenue?
4 Where is the head office?
5 How many factories does it have?
6 How many employees does it have?
7 Is employee training important for the company?
8 Does the company help local communities?
9 Is it a green company?

7 Use the information from **6** to make sentences about Nestlé.
Example: *The company is over 150 years old.*

» For more exercises, go to **Practice file 1** on page 107.

8 Work with a partner. Ask and answer the questions in **6** about your company or a company you know well.

9 Work with a different partner. Tell them about your first partner's company.

Practically speaking | How to ask somebody to repeat information

1 Somebody speaks to you at a conference but you don't hear them. How can you ask the person to repeat the information?
*Hi. My name's **** and I work for **** in ****.*

2 ▶ 1.3 Listen to the conversation. Write the information about the company.
Number of countries: _____
Number of factories: _____
Number of employees: _____
Annual sales: _____

3 ▶ 1.3 Listen again and complete the expressions for asking somebody to repeat the information.
1 Sorry, can you _____?
2 Sorry, can you _____ a bit _____?
3 Sorry, _____ employees do you have?
4 And _____ your annual sales _____?

4 Which two questions in **3** ask the speaker to repeat only part of the information? What similar questions can you ask in response to the person in **1**?

5 Write five facts about yourself or your company, but replace certain words with ****. Read your sentences to your partner. Take turns asking them to repeat the missing information.

Tip | Intonation in questions

In a *Wh* question (*What, Where, Why,* etc.), your voice normally goes down at the end. When you ask a person to repeat certain information, your voice goes up:

What's your name?
Mika Krzyzewski

Sorry, what's your name (again)?
Just call me Mika.

Business communication | Making introductions

1 What do you talk about when you meet someone at a conference for the first time?

2 ▶ 1.4 Listen to Gianluca introducing himself to Carmen at a conference. Make notes about:
1 Carmen's nationality
2 her job
3 why she's at the conference

3 ▶ 1.4 Complete what Gianluca says. Then listen again and check your answers.
1 Excuse me. _____ this seat free?
2 Thanks very much. Can I _____ myself? I'm Gianluca Donatelli.
3 Nice to meet you _____, Carmen. Where are you _____?
4 And _____ do you work for?
5 Oh really? And what do you _____?
6 So _____ are you at this conference?
7 That's interesting. A friend of mine works for an Italian service provider. Can I introduce _____ to _____?
8 Roberto. Can you come here a minute? This is … Sorry, what's your name _____?
9 Roberto. _____ is Carmen. She's writing an article on Internet service providers.

4 ▶ 1.4 Match questions 1–8 in **3** to Carmen's responses a–h. Then listen and check.
1 _c_   a I'm a journalist.
2 ___   b Carmen. Carmen Sanchez.
3 ___   c ~~Yes, it is. Go ahead.~~
4 ___   d Nice to meet you. I'm Carmen Sanchez.
5 ___   e I'm here to research an article on Internet service providers.
6 ___   f I don't work for a company. I'm self-employed.
7 ___   g Yes, of course. That would be nice.
8 ___   h I'm from Argentina.

5 Practise the conversation with a partner.

6 ▶ 1.5 Listen to another extract of the conversation between Gianluca and Carmen. Underline the stressed words in Carmen's questions. Why does she stress these words?
1 **Gianluca:** What do you do? **Carmen:** What about you? What do you do?
2 **Gianluca:** Why are you here at this conference? **Carmen:** How about you? Why are you here?

>> For more exercises, go to **Practice file 1** on page 106.

7 Work with a partner. Have short conversations using the prompts below.
- Name
- Job
- Company
- Reason for being here
- Country

   Example: A *Can I introduce myself? I'm Felipe.*
           B *Nice to meet you. My name's Juan.*
           A *Where are you from, Juan?*
           B *I'm from Spain. What about you? Where are you from?*
           A *I'm from Brazil.*

8 Work in small groups. You are at a conference. Introduce yourself to another person. Then introduce this person to other people in the group.

Key expressions

Introducing yourself
Can I introduce myself?
My name's / I'm …

Introducing others
Can I introduce you to …?
This is …

Responding
Nice to meet you. / How do you do?
Nice to meet you, too.

Asking about person/job/company
What's your name (again)?
Where are you from?
Who do you work for?
What do you do?
Why are you here?
What/How about you?

Make that contact!

▶ **1.6** Work with a partner. You are both at a conference. You are competing for a big customer. The first person to finish is the winner. Turn to **page 136** for the rules of the game.

PLAYER A Start here			**PLAYER B** Start here	
Where are you from?	I'm a sales manager.	Who are your main competitors?	Yes, I am. Nice to meet you.	Is this seat free?
We make car windows.	Who do you work for?	JOKER	Sorry, what's your name (again)?	No, it's a French company.
Can I introduce you to my boss?	It's 1263 Gray Rd, Carmel.	Does your company operate in Europe?	Italy	I'm Spanish. What about you?
You, too.	JOKER	Olsen. Jan Olsen.	JOKER	Yes, it is.
What is your annual revenue?	In Milan.	How many employees does your company have?	We operate in Europe and North America.	What does your company do?
No, I work in one of our subsidiaries.	What services do you provide?	JOKER	Do you use English in your job?	Yes, I am.
Where's your head office?	No, we don't. We're a service company.	I'm here to look at new products. What about you?	Fifteen	What does your company specialize in?
No, I'm from South America.	JOKER	I work for Goodyear.	JOKER	No, I'm not. Just today.
I'm in room 356. How about you?	My husband/wife? He's/She's a journalist.	Sorry, what's your company again?	That's a very personal question!	Do you do any business in Asia?
Yes, we do.	Do you come here every year?	JOKER	Why is your English so good?	No, it doesn't.

Congratulations! You made contact with the customer first!

2 Contacts

Starting point

1 At work, who do you usually speak to …?
- by phone
- face-to-face

2 How much time do you spend …?
- speaking with people inside your company
- speaking with people outside your company
- working alone

Working with words | Describing your job and contacts

1 What do these people do?
- A retail buyer
- A public relations officer
- A business psychologist

2 Read the texts and compare your answers to 1.

My name's Sara Prentiss. I'm a retail buyer and I work for a supermarket chain. My main job is to buy salads and vegetables from **suppliers**. I research the kind of products that our **customers** want. I also work on logistics projects. For example, at the moment I'm working with an external **consultant**. He's advising me on how to get our products to the supermarkets more quickly.

Hi, I'm Ben Davidson. I work for the police, but I'm not a police officer. I'm a public relations officer, so I answer questions from journalists when the police are in the news. I'm currently working on a new project to attract new people to the police force. For this, I'm working with senior police officers and an outside **employment agency**.

I'm Heidi Johnson and I'm a business psychologist. I'm self-employed, so I work on projects for various **clients** and companies. Basically, I deal with problems at work and help **staff** develop good relationships. At the moment, I'm helping a local team to communicate better with their **colleagues** abroad.

3 Read the texts in **2** again. Which person or people …?
1 work(s) on problems of communication
2 work(s) with people outside the company
3 work(s) with products
4 work(s) *with* companies, but not *for* a company

4 Match the words in **bold** in the text in **2** to definitions 1–7.
  1 These companies sell their products to retailers _____
  2 This organization finds new employees for you _____
  3 These people work with you _____
  4 These people pay for the services of a professional person or organization _____
  5 This expert outside the company helps you with problems _____
  6 These people buy your products _____
  7 These people are the employees of a company _____

5 Work with a partner. Which people in **4** do you work with?

6 ▶ **2.1** Listen to Simon Faubert talk about his job and answer questions 1–4.
  1 What's Simon's main job?
  2 Which department does he work in?
  3 Who does he work with?
  4 What is his main problem at work?

7 ▶ **2.1** Complete the sentences about Simon Faubert. Then listen again and check your answers.
  1 I work for a company that _____ software.
  2 They use our software to _____ the cost of making a _____ in different countries.
  3 Then they choose the _____ with the best price.
  4 My company only _____ 12 people.
  5 I _____ the _____ courses.

8 Complete the table with the correct words from **4** and **7**.

Verb	Nouns
_____	producer, _____
supply	_____, supplies
_____	calculator, calculation
_____	employer, _____, employment
_____	organizer, organization
train	trainer, trainee, _____
consult	_____, consultation

Tip | Word families
When you learn a new word, try and find other words in the same 'family' and note how to use them. We often use -er for people, e.g. *employer*, and -ation for things, e.g. *organization*.

>> For more exercises, go to **Practice file 2** on page 108.

9 Complete questions 1–5 with prepositions *with, on, for* or *in*.
  1 Which company do you work _____?
  2 Which department/area do you work _____?
  3 Who do you work _____ inside and outside of the company?
  4 What sort of projects do you work _____?
  5 What problems do you deal _____?

10 Work with a partner. Ask and answer the questions in **9**.

Language at work | Present continuous

1 Look at the people in the pictures and answer the questions.
   1 Where are they?
   2 What are they talking about?

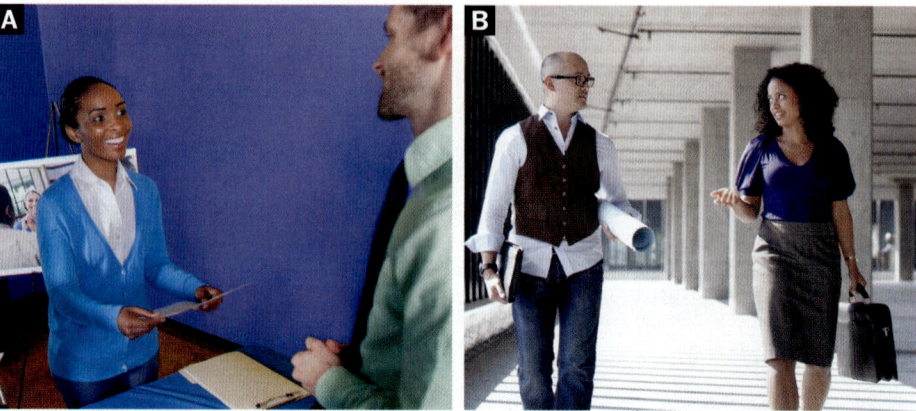

2 ▶2.2 Listen to three conversations. Write the answer to the question for each conversation.
   Conversation 1   What do you do? _____
   Conversation 2   What are you doing these days? _____
   Conversation 3   What are you doing? _____

3 Look at your answers in **2** and complete the explanations and examples in the *Language point*.

LANGUAGE POINT

1 We use the *present simple / present continuous* to talk about an action happening at the moment of speaking.
   Example: _____
2 We use the *present simple / present continuous* to talk about an action happening around the present time.
   Example: _____
3 We use the *present simple / present continuous* to talk about a fact or regular action.
   *Example:*_____
4 We form the present continuous with _____ + -*ing* form of the verb.
5 We form questions in the present continuous with (question word) + _____ + subject + _____ .

》 For more information, go to **Grammar reference** on page 109.

4 Work with a partner. Tell your partner three things you do regularly at work and three things you are working on at the moment.

5 ▶2.3 Listen to two conversations and answer the questions.
Conversation 1: 1 What's Nadira trying to do?
                 2 What's her log-in?
                 3 What's the problem?
Conversation 2: 1 What's Johann doing this week?
                 2 Who with?
                 3 Who's going for lunch?

6 ▶2.3 Complete Conversation 1 with the present continuous form of the verbs from the list. Then listen again and check.

have   speak   try   accept   work

A Who ¹_____ I _____ to?
B Sorry, this is Nadira. I ²_____ _____ to access my customer files, but the computer ³_____ _____ my log-in.
A … There's a problem with the server.
B ⁴_____ somebody _____ on it at the moment?
A Yes, I am. But it's not easy, because I'm on my own here. Everybody else ⁵_____ _____ lunch.

7 ▶2.3 Make sentences from the prompts using the present continuous or present simple. Then listen to Conversation 2 again and check.

    Example: A *Are you staying here all week?*
A You / stay / here all week?
B Yes / I / give / training course.
A Who / train / this time?
B Group / six people. They / all work / telesales.
A I / know / Sonya / her team. It / go / well?
B Yes / they / make / good progress. You / work / with / telesales team?
A No / we / have / lunch / from time to time.
B I / go / restaurant / them / now. You / want / come?
A Sorry / I / always / go / to the gym / Wednesdays.

8 Work with a partner. Practise the conversation in **7**.

»For more exercises, go to **Practice file 2** on page 109.

9 Work with a partner. Look again at pictures A and B in **1**. Have a conversation for each situation using information about you and your job.

Practically speaking | How to say phone numbers and spell names

1 Look at the post-it. How do you say the phone number?

> Hans-Peter,
>
> Can you call Myra Tully on 01865 556767
>
> Or if not, on her mobile: _____
>
> (code for UK _____)

2 ▶2.4 Listen and complete the missing numbers on the post-it in **1**. Did you say the phone number in **1** correctly?

3 Work with a partner. Say your home, work and mobile phone numbers to your partner. Write down what your partner says.

4 ▶2.5 Listen to two more conversations and write the names.

5 Work with a partner. Spell your first name, last name and the name of your company to your partner. Write down what your partner says.

Tip | Saying phone numbers

We usually say each number separately, except when two numbers are the same:
The code for Thailand is double oh double six (00 66).
In American English, we say *zero* and not *oh* for *0*.

Business communication | Making and receiving phone calls

1 What do you say or do in the following situations?
  a Somebody calls and asks to speak to your colleague who isn't there.
  b Somebody calls trying to sell you something.

2 ▶ 2.6 Listen and match the two conversations to the situations in **1**.

3 ▶ 2.6 Match sentences 1–5 with responses a–e. Then listen to Conversation 1 again to check.

  1 Is Mrs Ackers there, please? ___
  2 Who's calling, please? ___
  3 What can I do for you? ___
  4 Can I call you back tomorrow? ___
  5 Thanks for calling. ___

  a This is Simon Ilago from AOS.
  b I'm calling to offer you a special price on printers.
  c Speaking.
  d You're welcome. Goodbye.
  e Sorry, but I'm out of the office tomorrow.

4 Which sentences and responses in **3** are said by the caller and which by the receiver?

5 Work with a partner. Take turns to be the caller. Have similar conversations using your own names.
  Call 1: You want to organize a company visit for a group of foreign business students.
  Call 2: You are offering in-company training courses.

6 ▶ 2.6 Make five questions with the words in the table. Listen to Conversation 2 again to check and write down the responses. Then practise the questions and responses.

Could	I you	speak	Leo to call me back?
		leave	me what it's about?
		have	your name, please?
		ask	to Leo Keliher, please?
		tell	a message?

》 For more exercises, go to **Practice file 2** on page 108.

7 Work with a partner. Have two phone conversations.
  Student A
  1 Ask to speak to Alex. You're an ex-colleague. You want to meet him/her for lunch or dinner tomorrow. You're only in town for one day.
  2 Alex calls you back.
  Student B
  1 You work with Alex. He/she is very busy and wants you to answer all phone calls. Ask who's calling and why, and take a message.
  2 Now you are Alex. Your colleague gave you the message. Call Student A.

Key expressions

Asking to speak to someone
Could I speak to (name)?
Is (name) there, please?

Identifying the caller / person called
Could I have your name, please?
A Who's calling, please?
B This is (your name).

Giving a reason for the call
I'm calling about …
I'm phoning to …

Saying the person is/isn't free
I'm sorry, but (I'm busy at the moment).
I'm afraid (he's out of the office).
Can I take a message?

Leaving a message
Can/Could I leave a message?
Can/Could you ask him/her to call me back?

Finishing
I'll give him/her the message.
Thanks for your help/for calling.
Speak to you later/tomorrow.

TALKING POINT

Do you work too much?

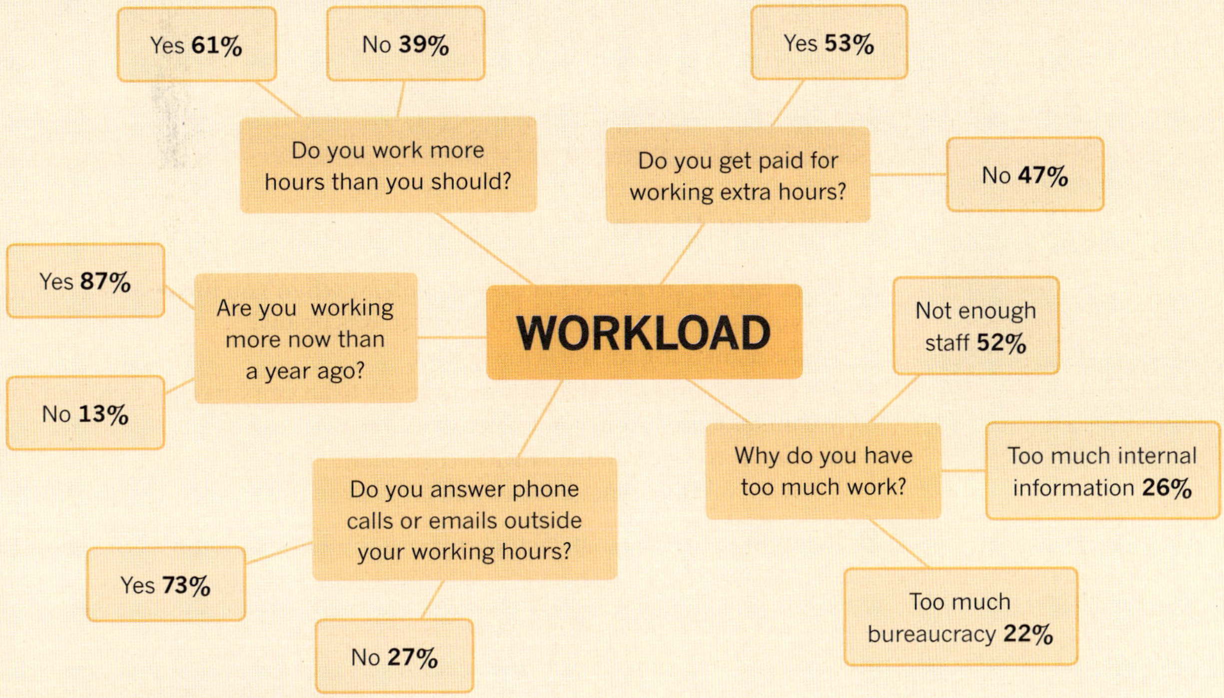

Yes **61%** No **39%**	Yes **53%**
Do you work more hours than you should?	Do you get paid for working extra hours? No **47%**

Yes **87%**

Are you working more now than a year ago?

WORKLOAD

Not enough staff **52%**

No **13%**

Why do you have too much work?   Too much internal information **26%**

Do you answer phone calls or emails outside your working hours?

Yes **73%**

No **27%**

Too much bureaucracy **22%**

Discussion

1 Look at the infographic from a recent work survey. Do you think any of the answers are surprising?

2 What is similar in your country or company? What is different? How?

3 What would you change in your present job to reduce your workload?

4 Ask the questions in the survey to others in your class. Are your results similar to the survey?

Task

1 Your boss is offering you a part-time assistant for 15 hours a week. Make notes about these questions.
   • What parts of your job do you want to give to your new assistant?
   • Who and what does your new assistant need to know?
   • What hours do you want him/her to work?
   • How will you use the extra time you now have?

2 Your partner is your new assistant. Use your notes in 1 to explain the job to your partner and answer any questions he/she has. Then switch roles.

3 Products & services

Starting point

1 What products or services are very popular at the moment where you live?

2 Why are they popular?

Working with words | Describing products and services

1 Work with a partner. What do you look for when you buy a new product? Do you agree or disagree with the opinions below?
1 The main thing for me is low prices.
2 I think it's important to be able to speak to an employee for help and advice.
3 I prefer to buy from companies that I know.
4 For me, a good product always costs more.
5 I want products and services that are easy to use.

2 Read this text. Do most customers have the same opinion as the people in 1?

WHAT CUSTOMERS WANT

Shopping for new products is a very personal thing. Some of us are looking for **original** products that nobody else will have. Others want to have the same things as everybody else, so they are more attracted by **popular** products.

But it seems that we all have the same reasons for choosing one product or service over another. A recent online survey showed that the top five priorities for customers were:

1 VALUE

Most people want to be sure that they are getting **good value** when they buy a product. This doesn't always mean that the product is cheap; it means that it is the product we want and that we are happy with the price we are paying.

2 SERVICE

Most of us want to talk to people who know their job and can give us good advice. We want **helpful** staff who can deal with problems quickly and efficiently. This is true not only in shops, but also when we order by phone or online.

3 TRUST

Most customers want to buy from **reliable** companies that give them what they promise, every time. Companies that deliver late or that sell faulty products will soon lose our business.

4 QUALITY

We know that a Cartier watch is a quality product, but quality isn't only about price and expensive materials. A cheap watch that looks good and still tells us the right time after ten years is also a **high-quality** product.

5 SIMPLICITY

Most people want **user-friendly** products and services. We don't want to read a 200-page manual before we can use our mobile phone or other **high-tech** gadget.

3 Work with a partner. The five reasons in the survey are in order of importance for customers. Do you agree with the order? Would it change for different types of product?

Tip | Adjective position
Adjectives usually go before the noun in English:
*It's a **high-tech** product.*
NOT ~~*It's a product high-tech*~~.
We can put the adjective after the noun with the verb *be*:
*The computer is very **user-friendly**.*
*Our staff are **helpful**.*

4 Complete descriptions 1–8 with the adjectives in **bold** from the text in **2**.
1 We deliver the right product at the right time. We are _____.
2 You will learn to use it very quickly. Our product is _____.
3 We offer a great product at the right price. Our products are _____.
4 Our products never break. They are _____.
5 Today everyone wants one. It's a very _____ product.
6 We use the latest technology. Our products are _____.
7 No other company makes a product like this. It's really _____.
8 We are here to answer all your questions. Our staff are _____.

5 Work with a partner. Which adjectives in **4** do we often use to describe these products and services?

6 ▶ **3.1** Listen and match each extract to the pictures in **5**. Which adjectives does each speaker use?

7 ▶ **3.1** Listen again and complete these sentences with a word from the list.
very   totally   pretty   really   extremely   quite
1 We've added a _____ new high-definition camera.
2 I love the material. It's _____ high quality.
3 Your things are always _____ original.
4 It's an _____ reliable product.
5 It's a _____ user-friendly site.
6 The accommodation was _____ good value, too.

8 Work with a partner. Which sentences in **7** would describe products and services that you use?

>> For more exercises, go to **Practice file 3** on page 110.

9 Work with a partner. Recommend a company, shop or product you know well.
1 Make a list of words from this section to describe the company, shop or product.
2 Use your list to recommend it to your partner. Explain *why* your statements are true.
   Example: *It offers a very reliable service. The products always arrive on time and they never make a mistake.*

Language at work | Past simple

1 Look at the list of inventions below. Which ones are the most important to you today? Why?

Twitter   *Mobile phone*   *World Wide Web*   *Smart cards*

2 Try to match the inventions in **1** to their inventors and the year you think they were invented.

Twitter	Tim Berners-Lee	1973
Mobile phone	Jack Dorsey	1991
World Wide Web	Roland Moreno	2006
Smart cards	Martin Cooper	1974

3 ▶ 3.2 Listen to the beginning of a radio programme about inventors and check your answers.

4 Match sentences 1–4 to explanations a–d in the *Language point*.

> **LANGUAGE POINT**
>
> 1 He launched his popular social networking service in 2006. ___
> 2 Many people didn't know him before 2012. ___
> 3 When did mobile communications begin? ___
> 4 Martin Cooper made the first mobile phone call. ___
>
> **We use the past simple to talk about finished actions in the past.**
> a The past simple form of regular verbs ends in *-ed*.
> b The past simple form of irregular verbs does not end in *-ed*.
> c The negative is formed by using *didn't* + the infinitive of the main verb.
> d In questions we generally use *did* + subject + infinitive of the main verb.

» For more information, go to **Grammar reference** on page 111.

5 ▶ 3.3 Listen to the story of Jack Dorsey and Twitter and put the events in the right order.

___ People don't understand why Twitter is necessary
___ Starts a new company with two other people
___ Goes to New York University
___ Doesn't finish his studies
_10_ Presidential candidates use Twitter
___ Studies in Missouri
___ Sells software online
___ Moves to California
_1_ Produces software for taxi drivers
___ Creates a website in two weeks

6 Use the information in **5** to tell the story of Jack Dorsey. Change the verbs to the past simple and add any other details you remember.
   Example: *He produced software for taxi drivers.*

» For more exercises, go to **Practice file 3** on page 111.

7 Read about Roland Moreno or Martin Cooper and write notes in the table. Student A, turn to **page 136**. Student B, turn to **page 141**.

	Roland Moreno	Martin Cooper
Main invention		
School/Education		
Job(s)		
Launch date of invention		
First success		
Other inventions		

8 Ask your partner questions about Roland/Martin and complete the information in the other column in **7**. Use these prompts to help you with the questions.

What / invent?   When / launch / invention?
Where / go to school?   When / invention / become / a success?
Who / work for?   Invent / other products?

9 Work with a partner. Talk about your experience of using the inventions in **1** using the questions below.
When did you start using them?
Was it for work or for personal use?
What did you think of them at first?
How are they different now compared with before?

Practically speaking | How to show interest

1 ▶ 3.4 Tick (✓) four phrases which we use to show interest in what another person is saying. Then listen and check your answers.

___ Oh   ___ Oh really?
___ Did you?   ___ No, it wasn't.
___ Yes, I did.   ___ Thanks.
___ That's interesting! ___ Was it?

2 ▶ 3.4 Listen again and complete extracts 1–4 with an expression showing interest from **1**.

1 **A** I went on a trip for a change.
  B _____? Where did you go?
2 **A** We went to Monte Carlo.
  B _____! Why did you go there?
3 **A** It was really exciting!
  B _____? I don't know Monte Carlo.
4 **A** The weather was fantastic.
  B _____? It rained here all week.

3 Work with a partner. Practise the sentences and responses in **2**.

4 Write down four things you did last week or last weekend. Then have a conversation with a partner. Use the expressions in **2** and ask questions to continue the conversation.

Tip | Intonation

Notice the intonation in the expressions in ▶ 3.4. To show you are really interested, your voice needs to go up and down.

If your voice doesn't change, people will think you aren't interested at all.

21

Business communication | Giving a research report

1 Work with a partner. Look at the picture of a podpad. Where do you think they are used? Would you stay in this type of accommodation?

2 ▶ 3.5 Listen to someone giving a research report into the use of podpads at a festival. Make notes in the table:

Why did they do the research?	
How did they do it?	
What were the results?	
What were the conclusions?	

3 ▶ 3.5 Work with a partner. Match 1–10 to a–j to make sentences. Then listen again and check your answers.

1 The purpose of our research was ___
2 We wanted to find out ___
3 We did this by ___
4 Then we ___
5 We asked ___
6 We found that ___
7 75% of visitors said that ___
8 Our research showed that ___
9 Our conclusion is ___
10 We recommend ___

a they would pay to use them.
b interviewing 50 visitors to the festival.
c podpads were popular with visitors and farmers.
d using them at our next festival.
e them for their opinion of the podpads.
f to find the best accommodation for visitors.
g the podpads were a big success.
h if people would pay to rent a podpad.
i that they are a great choice of accommodation.
j interviewed them about their experience.

» For more exercises, go to **Practice file 3** on page 110.

4 Answer the questions with a partner.
1 Have you done any research studies?
 • What was the purpose? • How did you do it? • What were the results?
2 Have you taken part in any research studies? What were they for?

5 Work with a partner. Your company has asked you to research places where employees can have a short sleep after lunch. Give a report on your results. Student A, turn to **page 136**. Student B, turn to **page 141**. Then decide which one is better.

Key expressions

Stating aims
The purpose of this research was …
We wanted to find out …

Explaining the process
We did this by (+ -ing).
First, we contacted/offered them …
Then we visited/interviewed/asked them …
Finally, we …

Reporting on results
They said/thought that …
We found that …
Seventy five per cent/The majority said that …
Our research showed that …

Concluding
Our conclusion is that …
We recommend (+ -ing)

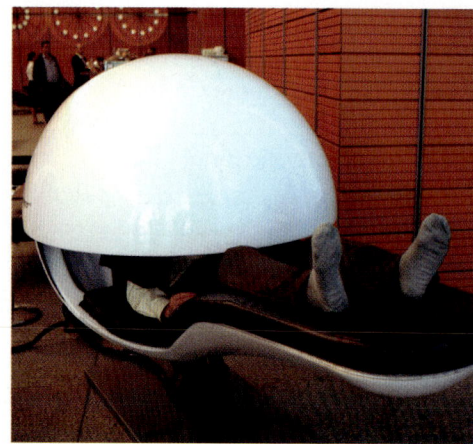

Products you can't live without

Discussion

1 ▶ 3.6 Listen to the description of the four products above. Why did each person decide to buy the product? What advantages does each product have?

2 Do you use the products in the pictures? Why?

3 Can you live without them?

4 Can you live without the products they're compared to: mobile phone, books, maps, gas (or electric) cookers?

Task

1 Work in groups. You are going to choose 'the greatest product of all time' in these categories.
   • Traditional products   • Modern-day products

2 Agree on a list of three products for each category.

3 Make a list of criteria for evaluating the products in each category.
   Example: *easy to use, saves time*

4 Decide on the best product in each category.

Preview

In this video lesson, different people talk about their company. You will also watch a video about a German company and an interview with its company director.

Focus

1 ▶01 Watch four people talking about their companies. What questions do you think they are answering? Complete the questions below.

Who …?	*Who do you work for?*
Which …?	_____
What …?	_____
Where …?	_____
How …?	_____
How …?	_____

2 ▶02 Watch the video again, this time with the questions included. Check your answers in **1**.

3 Work with a partner and interview each other. Ask and answer the questions from the video.

First impressions of a company

4 ▶03 Watch part of a video (with only pictures). As you watch, answer the questions in the table.

From watching the video, do you think the company …?	
makes a product or provides a service	
is a modern or traditional company	
employs lots of people	
works with international clients	
is specialized and technical	

5 Work with a partner. Compare your answers in **4** and give reasons for your opinions.

An interview with the company director

6 ▶04 Now watch the full video. It is an interview with Till Hahn, the company director of Glasbau Hahn. Check your answers in **4** and add more information about the company to the table.

7 ▶04 Watch the interview again. Complete these sentences about the company.

1 The company is based in the city of _____.
2 Till Hahn's great grandfather started the business in _____.
3 The company is divided into _____ sections and operates mainly in the _____ business.
4 Most of the company's _____ are museums in England, USA, and the rest of the world.
5 The company has _____ offices representing them.
6 In Frankfurt, there are about _____ employees, _____ in Stockstadt, and another _____ people in various offices.
7 They didn't have any _____ in 1935. Nowadays they have competitors in Italy and _____.
8 They are very successful in England, the United States, Japan, _____ and _____.

Comparing your company

8 Work with a partner. What are the similarities and differences between Glasbau Hahn and your company? Compare:
- the types of business (e.g. manufacturing or service, family-owned)
- the sizes of the companies (e.g. number of employees)
- the clients and competitors (e.g. regions, nationalities)

9 In the interview, Till Hahn talks about his main competitors. He says:

"Usually we are the most expensive [company], but fortunately our clients rank quality highest and the price tag is not the only decision factor."

Work with a partner and talk about the following:
- Is your company usually more expensive or less expensive than its competitors?
- Do clients buy from your company because of price, quality or other decision factors?

4 Visitors

Starting point

1 Which department do you work in?

2 What is the main purpose of your department?
- To make money for the company
- To save money for the company
- To keep customers happy
- To keep other colleagues happy
- Something else

Working with words | Company structure

1 Make a list of the different departments in a company.

2 Where would you rank your department in terms of its importance to the company? Where would you rank the other departments?

3 Read this article. Which departments are mentioned? Which department is the most important for the writer?

What's the most important department in your company?

This is the question I love to ask new clients. Management often focus their energy on the Sales and Marketing departments, because they **generate** money for the company. But many employees believe that it is their own department that is the most important.

Two departments point out that they save money for the company: the Finance Department, because it **controls** the spending of all the other departments, and the Purchasing Department, because it **buys** products at low prices. But in Accounts they say

> Many employees believe that it is their own department that is the most important

that money in the bank is more important: it is their department that **invoices** customers and collects the money.

The Production Department points out that if there is nobody to **manufacture** the products, there is nothing to sell. The Quality Control Department says that they **check** that every product leaves in perfect condition, and mistakes can be expensive. Two other departments think that they are important because they are in contact with customers all the time: Logistics, which has to **dispatch** and deliver products on time; and Customer Service, which has to **resolve** all kinds of problems to keep customers happy. The Human Resources Department highlights that their job is to **recruit** the best employees for all departments, and IT has to **maintain** the computer systems and IT infrastructure within the company.

The best answer, of course, is that all departments are equally important. Each department has to work *with* and *for* the others. If one department isn't working correctly, it can have a negative effect on everybody.

by Deanne Goforth, Management Consultant

4 Work with a partner. Answer questions 1–3.

1 Do you agree with the reasons for each department?

2 Would you change the ranking that you chose in **2**?

3 Do you think that all departments are equally important?

5 Complete these sentences with the words in **bold** from the text in **3**.

1 The Logistics Department _____es the products to the customer.

2 The IT Department _____s the computer systems and software.

3 The Purchasing Department _____ products from suppliers.

4 The Sales Department _____s new business with customers.

5 The Customer Service Department _____s customer problems when they call.

6 The Quality Control Department _____s that there are no problems with the products.

7 The Production Department _____s the products in the factory.

8 The Accounts Department _____ customers for products that they have bought.

9 The Finance Department _____ budgets and other costs.

10 The HR Department _____s new people to work in the company.

6 Work with a partner. Draw an organization chart of your company and tell your partner about the different departments.

» For more exercises, go to **Practice file 4** on page 112.

7 ▶ 4.1 Listen to three people receiving visitors from other departments in their company. Complete the table with the names of the departments.

Person	A	B	C
Works in			
Usually works with			
Meeting today with			

8 ▶ 4.1 Listen again and complete sentences 1–5.

1 We _____ closely _____ the Accounts Department.

2 I have a meeting today with Anna Neves in IT, who's _____ _____ all our software.

3 He's the person in _____ _____ purchasing for the whole company.

4 I have frequent _____ _____ all the different departments.

5 I _____ _____ the HR Director.

9 Work with a partner. Ask and answer questions about your own job.

1 What exactly does your department do?

2 What are you responsible for in your department?

3 Who is in charge of your department?

4 Who do you report to?

5 Which department(s) do you have the most contact with? Why?

Language at work | Asking questions

1 Complete these questions with words from the list. Then ask and answer questions 1–7 with a partner.

Who   Did   When   Is   How often   How many   Which

1 _____ did your company start?
2 _____ people work for your company?
3 _____ department do you work in?
4 _____ manages your department?
5 _____ do visitors come to your department?
6 _____ you work for a different department before this one?
7 _____ your job difficult?

2 Look at the question forms in **1** and answer the questions in the *Language point*.

LANGUAGE POINT

1 Which questions have the following word order?

> *Question word/phrase + auxiliary verb + subject + main verb*

2 Which verb changes depending on the tense: the auxiliary verb or the main verb?

3 Which questions can you answer with 'yes' or 'no'?

4 Which *yes/no* question does not have an auxiliary verb *and* a main verb? Why not?

5 Why do questions 2 and 4 have no auxiliary verb?

» For more information, go to **Grammar reference** on page 113.

3 Choose the correct option in *italics* to complete the questions. Then answer questions 1–5 with a partner.

1 *Are / Do* you start work early in the morning?
2 Who *leaves / does leave* work last in your office?
3 How many hours a week *you / do you* work?
4 *Is / Does* your department big or small?
5 Where did you *work / worked* before your current job?

4 ▶4.2 An employee is showing a visitor around her company. Listen to extracts 1–4 and say which department they are visiting in each extract.

Extract 1 _____
Extract 2 _____
Extract 3 _____
Extract 4 _____

5 ▶4.2 Put the words in the correct order to make questions. Then listen again and answer the questions.

1 this / often / work / How / does / office / he / in ?
2 from / does / he / come / Where ?
3 long / are / here / staying / How / you ?
4 work / many / in / Resources / How / Human / people ?
5 this / open / did / building / you / When ?
6 all / English / in / staff / fluent / Are / the ?
7 sales / Who / your / markets / chooses ?
8 your / Which / products / interested / countries / are / in ?
9 well / you / market / know / the / Polish / Do ?

>> For more exercises, go to **Practice file 4** on page 113.

6 You have a new employee in your department. He/She has a lot of questions for you. Make complete questions using the prompts.

Example: How many people work in the department?

1	Number of people in department?	6	Key or security pass?
2	Start/Finish work?	7	Restroom?
3	Lunch?	8	Car park?
4	Coffee or tea breaks?	9	Payment of salaries?
5	Photocopier?	10	Administrator

7 Work with a partner. Ask and answer the questions in **6**. Take it in turns to be the new employee.

Practically speaking | How to confirm information

1 Somebody wants to introduce you to their colleague. You think you know him but you want to be sure. How can you complete the questions to confirm the information?

1 _____ he work in International Sales?
2 He travels a lot to South America, _____?
3 He went to the trade fair in San Francisco, _____?

2 ▶4.3 Listen and compare your answers. What are the three different ways for confirming information used in **1**?

3 Use different ways of confirming the information in the sentences below.

Example: You work in IT, right? / Don't you work in IT? / You work in IT, don't you?

1 You work in IT.
2 She's in charge of Accounts.
3 He's coming to the meeting.
4 She lives in London.
5 You're from Hamburg.
6 I met you yesterday.

4 Think of five pieces of information that you think you know about your partner. Then ask questions to confirm the information.

Example: A Don't you work in Marketing?
B That's right. / No, not exactly. / No, I don't. I work in Sales.

Business communication | Welcoming a visitor

1 Someone is visiting your company for the first time. What questions can you ask to make your visitor feel welcome?

2 ▶ 4.4 Jim Berman is visiting a company to give a presentation. Listen to the conversations that Jim has and answer questions 1–3.
1 What does the receptionist ask Jim to do? What does she give him?
2 How was Jim's journey to the company? Where does Olivia take him?
3 What does Jim ask for? What does he want to do before he's ready to give his presentation?

3 Complete these sentences from the conversations in **2**. Who is speaking: the receptionist (R), the visitor (V) or the host (H)?
1 I have _____ Olivia Gonzalez.   _V_
2 Can I see some _____, please?   ___
3 So _____ passport, and this is your
_____.   ___
4 Did you have a _____?   ___
5 Thank you _____ me.   ___
6 So _____ my office. It's this way.   ___
7 Can _____ something to drink?   ___
8 Can I _____ my computer somewhere?   ___
9 _____ to milk and sugar.   ___
10 I _____ check my email, then I'll be ready.   ___

4 Match responses a–j to sentences 1–10 in **3**.
a Great, thanks. ___   f Thank you. ___
b Yes I did, thanks. ___   g No hurry. ___
c It's a pleasure. ___   h Yes, please. ___
d Sure. Here you are. ___   i After you. ___
e Yes, of course. ___   j OK. Can I have your name, please? _1_

5 ▶ 4.4 Listen and check your answers to **3** and **4**. Then practise the exchanges with a partner.

>> For more exercises, go to **Practice file 4** on page 112.

6 Work with a partner. Use the flowchart to have a similar conversation. Then change roles.
Student A   You are visiting Student B's company to give a presentation.
Student B   You are the receptionist and then the host.

IN RECEPTION	IN RECEPTION
Visitor: Say why you are there	**Receptionist**: Sign in the visitor and offer a seat

ON THE WAY TO MEETING ROOM	
Visitor: Ask questions about company (it's your first visit)	**Host**: Welcome visitor, ask about journey, go to meeting room

IN MEETING ROOM
Visitor/Host: Ask about or offer: • a glass of water/coffee/tea • Internet connection • restroom • photocopier/photocopies • phone call • anything else • video projector

TALKING POINT

The question game

Work with a partner. You are visiting a company or receiving a visitor. Take turns to be the visitor and the host. Have a conversation in each 'place' in the table below. The aim of the game is to ask more questions than your partner.

1 The host starts each conversation with the 'conversation opener'.

2 Use a question form in the 'Questions' column to continue each conversation.

3 Use the ideas in the 'Subjects' column to help you, or your own ideas.

4 Tick (✓) the 'Points' column every time you use one of the question forms.

5 The winner is the person who has the most points.

> *Example:* RECEPTION **Host**   Nice to see you again. **Did** you have a good trip? **(1 point)**
> **Visitor**   Yes, thanks. Sorry I'm late. **Is** the traffic always so bad? **(1 point)**

PLACE	CONVERSATION OPENER	QUESTIONS	SUBJECTS	POINTS (✓)
RECEPTION	*Nice to see you again.*	*Is(n't) …?* *Are(n't) …?* *Do(n't) …?*	• Visitor's journey, hotel, etc. • Programme for visit	
HOST'S OFFICE or DESK	*Here's my office.*	*Does(n't) …?* *Did(n't) …?* *Can I …?*	• Host's job and department • Visitor's job and department	
COLLEAGUE'S OFFICE or DESK	*My colleague isn't here today, but he/she …*	*Can you …?* *Where …?* *What …?*	• Colleague's job • Visitor's work colleagues	
ANOTHER DEPARTMENT	*Now we're in the (name) department.*	*Which …?* *Who …?* *Why …?*	• What it does • Relations with host's department	
MEETING ROOM	*This is the room for your presentation.*	*When …?* *How …?* *How many …?*	• What the visitor needs • People coming to presentation	
RESTAURANT	*I think you'll like this restaurant.*		• Town where company is located • Visitor's home town	
			TOTAL POINTS*	

* Give yourself 1 point for each tick. Deduct 2 points for each question form you haven't used.

5 Customer service

Starting point

1 Read the comments from people who phoned customer service numbers. Have you had similar experiences? Which one is the most annoying?

- 'They put you on hold and you can't turn off their awful music.'
- 'You wait ages to speak to somebody. Then if you call again, you have to repeat the information.'
- 'They try and sell you other products or services.'

2 What other problems can you have with customer service?

Working with words | Customer service

1 Look at the picture below. What channels does it show for customers to communicate with a company? Which ways do you prefer?

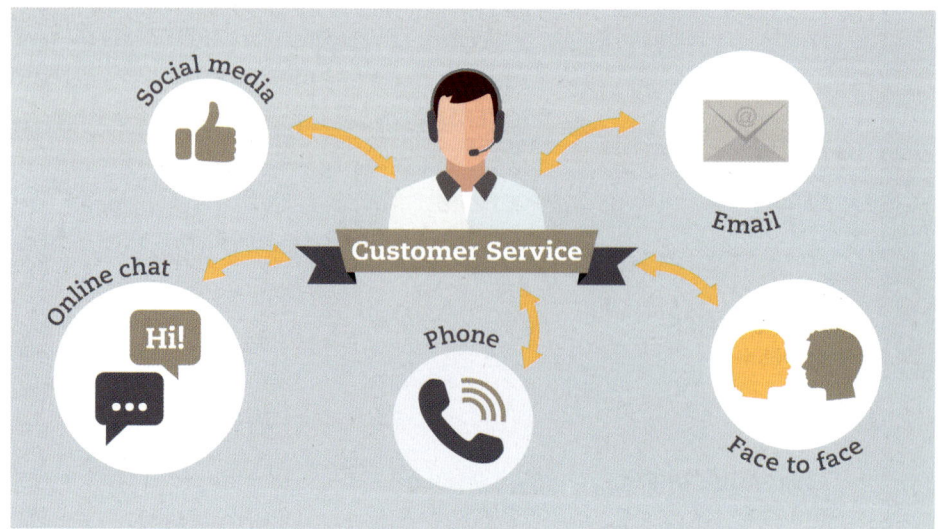

2 Read this text and answer questions 1–3.
1 What are the advantages of multi-channel customer service?
2 What problems can customers have?
3 What is the result of these problems for companies?

Multi-channel customer service

Most companies provide customers with many options for how they communicate with the company. Customers can contact companies by email, by online chat, through the company website or via social media such as Facebook or Twitter. Communication is now easier for customers who **have a query** about a product or order or want to **report a problem**. It also gives companies more opportunity to **get feedback** on the customer experience.

The problem is that there often isn't enough communication between the customer service channels. For example, a customer emails a company to **make a complaint** about a product that doesn't work. If there isn't a quick reply, he/she tries the online chat. They have no record of the email, so the customer has to **explain the issue** again. They can't **offer a solution**, and tell him/her to call **Customer Support**. The customer

spends 30 minutes on hold and then has to explain the problem again.

For multi-channel communication to be a success for a company, it needs to improve the customer experience. Customers today do not want to wait, so companies must improve their **response times**, and also make sure that the communication channels are connected. The prize for success is **customer loyalty**. The cost of failure is customers who don't come back.

3 Work with a partner. How do you think companies can improve communication with customers?

4 Match the phrases in **bold** in the text in **2** to definitions 1–9.
 1 Say you're not happy with something _____
 2 Inform (a company) that something is wrong _____
 3 Give detailed information about a problem _____
 4 The time it takes to answer a customer _____
 5 The idea that customers will always choose a company's products
    _____
 6 A department that answers customer questions _____
 7 Ask customers what they think about your company
    _____
 8 Suggest an answer to a problem _____
 9 Ask for more information about something that isn't clear
    _____

5 Work with a partner. Talk about customer service in your own company or a company you regularly buy from. Which of these things does it do well? Which does it do badly?
 • Different communication channels
 • Dealing with queries or complaints
 • Encouraging customer loyalty
 • Response times
 • Getting feedback

>> For more exercises, go to **Practice file 5** on page 114.

6 What solutions are these customer support assistants offering? Choose from the list.
 compensation   a replacement   a discount   a refund   a credit voucher
 1 We'll offer you 20% off if you buy it today. _____
 2 We can't repair it, but we will send you another one. _____
 3 If you return it to the shop, we'll give you your money back. _____
 4 It's valid for 12 months, and you can use it in any of our stores. _____
 5 Sorry, you can't have your money back for the holiday, but we will send you a cheque for €200. _____

7 ▶5.1 Listen to two people talking about customer service. Did they have a good or a bad experience?

8 ▶5.1 Listen again and answer the questions for each situation.

	Situation 1	Situation 2
What did the customer order?	A talking toy	A tablet computer
What was the problem?		
How did they contact the company?		
How did the company respond to the problem?		
What solution did the company offer?		

9 Work with a partner. Talk about a good and/or bad customer experience you have had. Use the questions in **8** to help you.

Language at work | Comparisons

1 Work with a partner. Why do people shop online? Make a list of reasons.

2 ▶ 5.2 Listen to an extract from a radio programme about why people shop online and note the reasons. Are they similar to yours?

3 ▶ 5.2 Listen again and <u>underline</u> the correct words in *italics* to complete sentences 1–5.

1 Online retailers offer the *cheapest / most expensive* products.
2 Online stores have the *most / least* flexible hours.
3 It's not as *difficult / easy* to compare products in physical stores.
4 Internet shopping offers a *more limited / wider* choice than in-store shopping.
5 Online retailers offer *better / less detailed* information about a product.

4 Read the explanations in the *Language point*. Then complete the examples with the adjectives in **3**.

> **LANGUAGE POINT**
>
> 1 Most comparative forms of one-syllable adjectives end in *-er* (or *-r* when the adjective ends in *e*). For the superlative form, add *the -est*.
> *cheap, cheaper, the _____   wide, _____, the widest*
> 2 Most two-syllable adjectives, and all adjectives of three or more syllables, use *more* and *the most* + adjective. You can also use *less* and *the least* + adjective.
> *expensive, more expensive, the _____*
> *detailed, _____, the least detailed*
> 3 *Good* and *bad* have irregular comparative and superlative forms.
> *good, _____, the best   bad, worse, the worst*
> 4 We use *not as* + adjective (+ *as*) to say something isn't similar to something else.
> *not _____ easy (as)*

❯❯ For more information, go to **Grammar reference** on page 115.

5 ▶ 5.3 Listen to some shoppers being interviewed in the street. What reasons do they give for shopping in a physical store?

6 ▶5.3 Complete the shoppers' answers with the correct form of the adjective in brackets. Then listen again and check your answers.

1 I get _more professional_ (professional) advice in a shop than online. The staff in a store have a _____ (good) knowledge of the products.

2 I know the prices aren't _____ (low) as online, but it's the _____ (quick) way to get the product I want.

3 The _____ (important) thing for me is to see and touch the products. It's _____ (easy) to make the right choice.

4 It's _____ (difficult) to return or exchange items than when you buy online. It's also the _____ (expensive) way because you don't pay for postage.

5 The postal service isn't _____ (reliable) now. Delivery times are _____ (long) and a lot of packages are lost.

>> For more exercises, go to **Practice file 5** on page 115.

7 Work with a partner. Talk about your preferences for 1–4 below. Give examples and explain your reasons, using comparative and superlative forms.

Example: I prefer looking for products online because it's quicker and easier to compare them.

1 Looking for and evaluating products.	Online, in physical stores or both?
2 Buying new products.	Online, in physical stores or both?
3 Buying second-hand products.	Directly from the seller or online?
4 Reporting a problem with a product bought online.	By phone, by email, by letter or on the website?

Practically speaking | How to 'soften' a message

1 In what situations do you need to choose your words carefully and 'soften' what you say?

2 ▶5.4 A manager is complaining to an employee. What's the problem and what's the solution?

3 ▶5.4 Listen again and tick (✓) the expressions each time you hear them. Who uses the expressions: the manager (*M*), the employee (*E*) or both (*B*)?

	✓	M / E / B
I'm afraid …		
Sorry, but …		
I'm sorry to say this, but …		
Sorry about that.		
Well, actually …		
… isn't very (+ positive adjective)		

4 Which of the expressions in **3** does the speaker use to …?
- complain   • respond to a complaint   • correct wrong information

5 Practise the conversation with a partner.

6 Work with a partner. Take turns to complain and reply in these situations. Use the expressions in **3**.

1 An IT technician came to install new software on your computer yesterday. Today your screen freezes every time you try to open it. Phone the technician.

2 Your colleague asked you to check a report he wrote. A lot of the information is unclear or wrong and it's full of spelling mistakes. Speak to your colleague.

Business communication | Making and dealing with complaints

1 Look at the advice below. Do you agree? Why/Why not?

> "When making a complaint, never get angry."

> "When dealing with a complaint, never say 'it's not our fault' or, even worse, 'it's your fault'."

2 ▶5.5 Listen to four different conversations. Note down the problem and solution in each.

	Conversation 1	Conversation 2	Conversation 3	Conversation 4
Problem				
Solution				

3 ▶5.5 Listen again. In which conversation do you hear these sentences?
1 I'd like a refund. ___
2 Oh dear. Can you give me more details? ___
3 Don't worry. I'll deal with it now. ___
4 I'm sorry to hear that. We'll send you the correct version today. ___
5 It's my fault. I'm sorry. ___
6 It still hasn't arrived. ___
7 It's not working again. I'm not very happy about it. ___
8 Customer Service. How can I help you? ___
9 We can offer you a replacement. ___
10 I'll look into it and get back to you right away. ___

4 Work with a partner. Take turns being the people in the situations in **2** and have similar conversations.

>> For more exercises, go to **Practice file 5** on page 114.

5 Work with a partner. Read these situations. What are the possible solutions?
1 You ordered sandwiches and drinks for a working lunch with a customer in your company. The catering company promised to deliver before 12.30 p.m. but it's now 1 p.m. and you're still waiting. Your customer doesn't look very happy. You phone the catering company.
2 You have received an order from a computer supplier but there's a mistake. You ordered 50 laptop computers with 15-inch screens but they've sent you mini-computers with 10-inch screens (and there are only 40!). You phone the supplier.
3 You asked a colleague to send you some PowerPoint slides for an important presentation you have this morning. When you open your email, you see that he/she has sent you slides for the wrong product. Your presentation is in half an hour. You phone your colleague.
4 You rented a car on a business trip from your usual rental company but the satnav stopped working after two hours. You then lost your way and were late for your meeting. This is the third time in six months you've had a problem with a rental car. You speak to the manager.

6 Have a conversation for each situation in **5**. Take turns to complain and deal with the complaint.

Key expressions

Asking about the problem
How can I help?
What can I do for you?
Can you give me more details?
What exactly is the problem?

Making the complaint
I'm sorry, but / I'm afraid …
(The machine) doesn't work
There's a problem with …
(It) still hasn't arrived.
I'm not very happy (about it).
I'd like (a refund/replacement).

Sympathizing/Apologizing
I'm very sorry about that.
I do apologize.
I'm sorry to hear that.
It's our/my fault. I'm sorry.
I'm afraid we can't …
We're sorry for the inconvenience.

Dealing with the complaint
I'll look into it / deal with it right away.
I'll get back to you.
Let me check.
We'll send you …
We can offer you …
I'll wait to hear from you.

The WOW! Awards

The WOW! Awards is an organization that recognizes the 'best of the best' in customer service. Companies and other organizations can choose to participate in the awards. Customers who have had excellent service can then nominate people working in those companies for an award. Customer stories are often about ordinary employees who did something very special to satisfy the customer: the hotel receptionist who lent her shoes to a female guest because she needed them for a business meeting, or the hospital cleaner who spent time after work every day talking to a patient who didn't have any other visitors. It's an opportunity for customers to give the names of employees who 'wowed' them, and to say a special thank you to them.

Discussion

1 What do you think of the idea of the WOW! Awards?

2 What are the possible benefits for a company that decides to participate in the awards?

3 How is it possible for your company to 'wow' customers? Is it possible in your job?

4 Here are some possible criteria for choosing a WOW! Award winner. Which ones do you think are more important? What other criteria would you use?
  • Finding original ways to satisfy customers
  • Turning unhappy customers into satisfied ones
  • Taking a real interest in the customer as a person
  • Putting customers' needs before your own
  • Understanding customers' real needs
  • Doing more than your job description demands

Task

1 Work in small groups. You are going to read about an employee nominated for a WOW! Award. Turn to **page 137** and each choose a different candidate. Then tell your group:
  • who this person is
  • why they are a good candidate for the award

2 Use the criteria you discussed in **4** to decide who will win the WOW! Award. Who will be in second and third place?

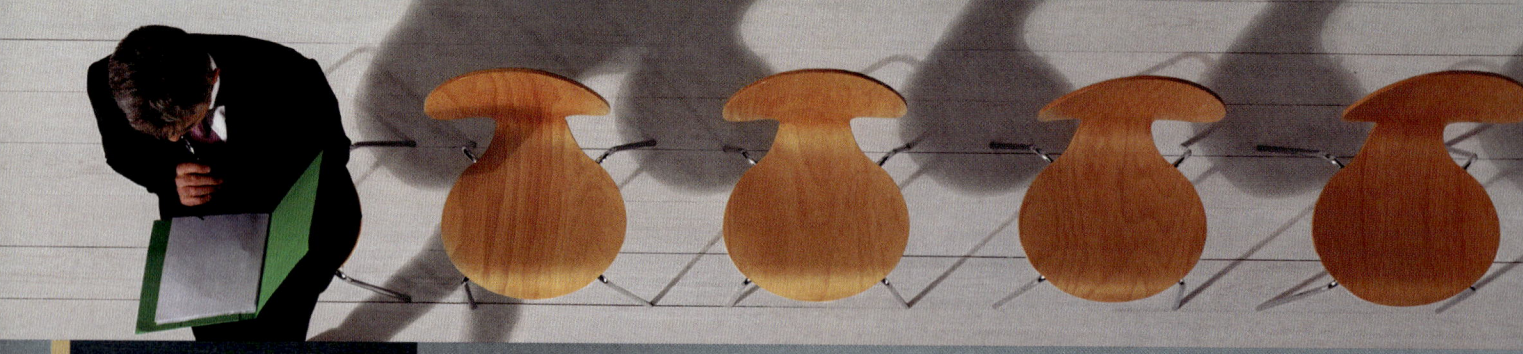

6 Employment

Starting point

1 What's the best way to find a new job?

2 Is it easier or more difficult than ten years ago? Why?

Working with words | Employment

1 Are you a member of any of these social networks? Why do/don't you use them?

2 Read the article and answer the questions.
1 How many people and companies use LinkedIn?
2 How does LinkedIn make it easier for …?
   • people to find jobs
   • employers to find new staff

LinkedIn – the world's largest professional network

Today the Internet is making it easier and quicker for employers and employees to find each other.

One of the most popular websites for both employers and employees is LinkedIn, a social network service for professionals. The company has more than 400 million users in over 200 countries. Many of the world's top companies use LinkedIn to help them **recruit** new employees.

If you are looking for a job, it's very easy to join LinkedIn. Just post your profile on the site, including your **qualifications** from school or university,

More than 3 million companies have pages on LinkedIn

your **experience** in different jobs and the **skills** that you have learned, like managing a team or using different computer programs.

Next, you begin to develop your contacts. On LinkedIn, you can search for people who you studied or worked with. Maybe an old university friend or ex-colleague is now with a company that you'd like to work for. That person can post a **reference** on the site, saying how good your work is.

More than three million companies have pages on LinkedIn, and many of them

advertise new positions on the site. With one or two clicks, you can **apply for** the job, and attach your CV and covering letter. You can also discover the number of people interested in the position and know if you are one of the better **candidates**. And if the company decides to put you on its **shortlist** of candidates, you can find a lot of advice on the site about what to say in a job **interview**.

Two new people or companies join LinkedIn every second. So if you're thinking about a new job and you aren't already a member, now's the time to do it.

3 Answer the questions with a partner.
1 Do you think sites like LinkedIn really make life easier for companies and people looking for jobs?
2 Can you think of any disadvantages compared with traditional forms of recruitment?

4 Complete the stages of getting a job with the words in **bold** from the text in **2**.

> When a company decides to ¹_____ a new employee, it usually ²_____s the job in the press or online.

> You decide to ³_____ the job. You send a CV, which includes information about:
> • the exams that you have taken (your ⁴_____)
> • the companies that you have worked for (your ⁵_____)
> • the things that you have learnt to do (your ⁶_____)
> • people who you have worked with who can give you a ⁷_____

> The company studies the CVs of all the ⁸_____, and makes a ⁹_____ of the best ones. It invites these people to the company for an ¹⁰_____.

5 Discuss with a partner. Which parts of the recruitment process do you find easier/more difficult?

6 ▶ **6.1** Listen to two people describing how they got their job. Take notes about how each person was lucky.

Speaker 1	
Speaker 2	

7 ▶ **6.1** Listen again and complete sentences 1–8.
1 I only saw the _____ for my job at the last minute.
2 I only had about four hours to prepare my _____.
3 I really wanted the job, but I wasn't really _____ for it.
4 So I didn't think I would be _____, but I was.
5 I could see that the person who _____ me didn't like me.
6 The company wanted a highly-_____ technician.
7 I had the qualifications, but I wasn't at all _____.
8 He was responsible for the _____ of service technicians.

8 Match each word in **7** with a different form of the same word from **4**. Are the words nouns, verbs or adjectives? Where is the main stress on each word?
   Example: application (noun), apply (verb)

   ❱❱ For more exercises, go to **Practice file 6** on page 116.

9 Work with a partner. Tell them about when you got your present job. Talk about:
   • how you heard about the job
   • how you applied for it
   • the interviews you had
   • why you accepted the job

Language at work | Present perfect (1)

1 What questions do interviewers often ask at job interviews? Which questions are the most difficult to answer?

2 ▶ 6.2 Naomi Hasselin has an interview for a job as a team leader with a large non-profit organization. Listen to the extract. What experience does she have?

3 ▶ 6.2 Listen again and <u>underline</u> the verb forms you hear.
1 When *did you start / have you started* working in this field?
2 I *left / have left* university in 2009.
3 *Did you ever work / Have you ever worked* for a big organization?
4 No, I *didn't have / 've never had* the chance.
5 *Did you go / Have you been* to Africa?
6 I *spent / 've spent* some time in Tanzania.
7 Oh really? What *did you do / have you done* there?

4 Look at the sentences in **3**. Decide if the verb forms are in the past simple or present perfect. Then complete the explanations in the *Language point*.

> **LANGUAGE POINT**
>
> 1 We use the _____ to ask/talk about general experience in the past.
> 2 We use the _____ to ask/talk about actions at specific times in the past.
> 3 We form the present perfect with _____/has(n't) + past participle.
> 4 We form questions in the present perfect with _____/has + subject + _____.

》 For more information, go to **Grammar reference** on page 117.

5 ▶ 6.3 The interviewer asks Naomi more questions. Complete questions 1–5 using the prompts. Then listen and check your answers.
   Example: When did you go to Tanzania?
1 When / go / Tanzania? _____
2 How long / stay there? _____
3 What other projects / work on? _____
4 Ever / manage a team? _____
5 Why / decide / work in this field? _____

Tip | *been* and *gone*

Been and *gone* are both used as past participles of the verb *go*. *Been* means that they went and came back:
*Have you ever **been** to the USA for a holiday?*

Gone means that they are still there:
*He's not here. He's **gone** to Paris for the weekend.*

6 ▶ 6.3 Listen again and note Naomi's answers to the questions in **5**. Then work with a partner and take turns playing the role of the interviewer and Naomi.

>> For more exercises, go to **Practice file 6** on page 117.

7 Work with a partner. Take turns to ask and answer questions about your experiences, using the prompts.

> *Example:* **A** *Have you ever interviewed someone for a job?*
> **B** *Yes, I have.*
> **A** *Who did you interview? What was the job? What did you ask?*

1 Interview someone for a job
2 Refuse a job offer
3 Give someone a reference
4 Apply for a job online

8 You are interviewing candidates for a similar job to yours. First, think of the skills and the experience that are necessary for your job. Then make a list of questions to ask the candidates.

Questions for candidates:

_____

_____

_____

_____

_____

_____

9 Work with a partner. Take turns to interview each other using your questions in **8**.

Practically speaking | How to avoid negative answers

1 Look at the question that a boss asks his/her employee. What's wrong with the employee's answer? Can you think of a better response?
A Have you finished that proposal?
B No, I haven't. I've been very busy.

2 ▶ 6.4 Listen to four short conversations. Which conversation is about …?
a a document that somebody has to write ____
b a document that somebody has to read ____
c somebody's language skills ____
d somebody's work experience ____

3 ▶ 6.4 Listen again and complete responses 1–4. What kind of information comes after *but* in each sentence?
1 I haven't, but _____ of the product last month.
2 No, but _____ to do.
3 No, but _____ before the end of the week.
4 No, but _____ on holiday.

4 Write two or three questions that (a) a boss (b) an interviewer could ask you.

5 Work with a partner. Take turns to ask and answer your questions from **4**. Your partner must say 'no' but change it into a positive answer.

Business communication | Evaluating options

1 A company is looking for a new project manager. What are possible reasons for …?

1 recruiting somebody externally (i.e. from outside the company)
2 promoting somebody internally (i.e. from inside the company)

2 ▶6.5 Listen to three managers discussing the questions in **1**. What are the arguments for and against each option? Can you think of a possible solution?

	Arguments for	Arguments against
external		
internal		

3 ▶6.5 Listen again and match 1–9 to a–i to make complete sentences.

1 I prefer ___
2 I like the idea ___
3 I'm not sure that ___
4 I'd go for ___
5 Another disadvantage is ___
6 One other issue is ___
7 A key advantage is ___
8 I really think ___
9 The internal option is attractive ___

a that we save money.
b the cost of finding someone.
c internal promotion is too risky.
d to recruit internally.
e because it's quicker and cheaper.
f somebody with more experience.
g our engineers have enough experience.
h that we don't have time to recruit.
i that we send them a positive message.

4 Work with a partner. Evaluate the following suggestions from a company's HR Department.

1 Recruit only people under 30 years old.
2 All employees to receive English and Chinese lessons.
3 Senior employees can work just four days a week in their last year. They then work one day a week for a year after they retire.

》 For more exercises, go to **Practice file 6** on page 116.

5 Work in small groups. Your company wants to provide training for its employees. For each of the training courses, evaluate which of the three types of training would be best.

TRAINING COURSES: 1 Oral English   2 Computer skills   3 Customer service

Type 1: Internal peer training.	Type 2: External training.	Type 3: Individual online training.
Training will be provided by current employees who have experience in each field. There will be one session of 2 hours per week during normal working hours, and in small groups of 3–4 people. No official qualification.	Training will be provided by an external training organization in a series of 3-day sessions outside the company. Groups of 10–15 people from different companies. All participants will receive an official qualification at the end of the course.	Training will be done online using an external organization. This will take place outside of working hours and employees can choose when to do it. Weekly online tutorial with a trainer to review progress. Online written exam at the end of the course.

6 Work with a partner. Have you ever had any of the types of training in **5**? What was it for? What were the strengths and/or weaknesses of the training?

Key expressions

Saying why an idea is good
One/Another key advantage is (that) …
I like the idea that …
X is (*attractive*) because …
X is a (*really*) good idea/option because …

Describing weak points
One/Another disadvantage is (that) …
One/Another issue is (that) …
I'm not sure that …
(I think) X is too …

Stating a preference
I prefer (to do) X because …
I think X is preferable because …
I'd go for / choose X because …
X is better / more suitable (than Y).

The best companies to work for?

At Brazilian company Semco, employees:

- choose their own working hours
- decide their own salaries
- decide their own budgets within their own business unit
- have to choose a different desk to work at every day
- can go to any meeting they want, or not go at all
- can have a nap in a hammock
- choose their own colleagues and managers (there is no HR Department)
- evaluate their managers twice a year

At Google's Mountain View headquarters in California, employees:

- get free breakfast, lunch and dinner in a choice of 18 cafés
- can exercise in four different gyms
- can bring their laundry to the company and take it home clean in the evening
- can bring their pets to work
- have free use of electric cars to go shopping at lunchtime
- can have a nap in specially designed sleeping pods
- can have free consultations with the in-company doctor
- get a free massage on their birthday

Discussion

1 Which benefits or ideas do you find most attractive in each company? Why?

2 Why do you think the two companies offer these conditions?

3 Which company would you prefer to work for? Why?

4 What might be the disadvantages of working for either company?

Task

Your company wants to find ways of attracting new employees and keeping them.

1 Work with a partner. Make a list of six benefits you would like to offer staff. You can include ideas from Google and Semco, but also add your own. Think about the following points:

- benefits to the employee
- benefits to the company
- cost of offering each benefit
- possible problems

2 Work with a new partner. Compare your lists from 1 and explain why you chose these benefits. Decide on the three best ideas.

Preview

In this video lesson, different people talk about choosing a hotel. You will also watch an interview with Dagmar Mühle, General Manager of the Hilton Hotel in Dusseldorf, Germany. She talks about the Hilton brand and how it survives in a very competitive market.

Focus

1 When you book a hotel for a work trip, what affects your choice? Put the things in the list below in order of importance from 1 (most important) to 8 (least important).

- Level of service (e.g. star rating)
- Appearance (e.g. modern)
- Brand loyalty
- Facilities (e.g. gym, sauna, pool, etc.)
- Transport links (e.g. to and from the airport)
- Price
- City and location
- Business facilities (e.g. meeting rooms)
- Other

2 ▶01 Watch three people talking about choosing hotels. What affects their choice? Make notes about their answers in the table.

Speaker 1	Speaker 2	Speaker 3

3 Compare your notes in 2 with a partner. Were the answers similar to yours in 1?

The Hilton Hotel chain

4 You are going to watch an interview with Dagmar Mühle about the Hilton Hotel Chain. Before you watch, match the phrases a–h from the interview to the correct definition 1–8.
a mid-market segment ___
b unique feature ___
c loyalty programme ___
d incentive ___
e customer journey ___
f brand standard ___
g mystery customer ___
h quality inspector ___

1 A level of service that a business guarantees.
2 The path that you go on as soon as you start using a product or service.
3 One thing that makes you different from your competitors.
4 A person who checks that the product or service is at the correct level.
5 The part of the market between the luxury end and the basic.
6 A system where customers get points and benefits from being a member.
7 Something that encourages you to do something.
8 A person who pretends to use the product or service in order to test the company's customer service.

5 ▶**02** Watch the first part of the interview with Dagmar Mühle. Listen for these numbers and phrases and make notes about them in the table. Then compare your notes with a partner.

3,600	
10	
destination or brand?	
facilities	
120	
loyalty programme	

6 Which hotel chains are famous in your country? Which segments of the market are they popular with? How different is the level of service?

The customer journey

7 ▶**03** Watch the second part of the interview with Dagmar, where she talks about the importance of the customer journey and staff training. As you watch, make notes in the table.

Stages of the customer journey at the Hilton Hotel	
Ways of training staff for each stage in the journey	

8 When was the last time you stayed in a hotel? What was your customer journey like?

Mapping the customer journey

9 Work with a partner. Think of a new situation (not a hotel) where you experience a customer journey. For example at a bank, buying a new car, as a patient at your local hospital or your own choice.
  • List the stages in the customer journey.
  • Make notes about the training that staff will need for each stage in the journey.

10 Work with another pair of students. Compare your stages and ideas for training staff.

11 Now consider the customer journey for your own company or organization.
  • List the key stages in the customer journey.
  • Make notes about staff training for each stage.
  • Do you think your company could improve its customer journey? How?

12 Present your customer journey to the rest of the class and explain your ideas.

7 Travel

Starting point

1 Do you often travel on business/holiday?

2 What places do you like travelling to, for work or for pleasure?

3 Which form of transport do you prefer?

Working with words | Air travel

1 Here are some of the things that air travellers complain about. Which ones do you hear most often?

- Additional costs
- Other passengers
- Long waits at the airport
- Uncomfortable seats

2 Read the text and complete the headings with the words in 1.

What do air travellers find most annoying?

A recent air travel survey shows that the experience of taking a plane is often not a pleasant one. Here are the top complaints.

1 _____

Often, there's very little room for your legs, and then the person in front of you decides to move his or her seat back. It's no surprise that 58% of passengers prefer the **aisle seat**, which offers a little more legroom, at least for one leg. Many passengers aren't prepared to pay more for a **seat upgrade** to a more comfortable part of the plane.

2 _____

Passengers are particularly annoyed about **airline charges**. Twenty years ago, you paid for your flight and everything was included. Today, **baggage allowance**s are lower, and some airlines make you pay even for the first suitcase. Passengers often try to put everything in one small bag to take on the plane with them. However, some airlines now have **weight restrictions** which limit **hand baggage** to 8 kg or less. And if you want to choose your seat, or have a drink and something to eat on the plane, you may have to pay again.

3 _____

Even though airline passengers know that **security scans** are necessary, they would like more machines and employees to check their luggage more quickly. They also know that it is often bad weather or technical problems that cause a **delayed flight.** But they still complain about **missed connection**s when their first flight arrives too late for the next one.

4 _____

The biggest complaint here is about noisy children. Maybe you can avoid waiting in line with a screaming baby if you use the airline's **self-service check-in** to get your boarding pass. But there's nothing you can do if you find that the same baby and its parents are occupying the seats next to you on the plane.

3 Discuss these questions with a partner.

1 Which aspects of air travel do you find annoying? What about other forms of travel?

2 Do you ever complain to airlines or other travel operators? Why/Why not?

3 Do you think airlines or other travel operators respond well to complaints? Why/Why not?

4 Match the words in **bold** in the text in **2** to definitions 1–10.
1 The reason it's not possible to take a heavy bag _____
2 A change to a more expensive seat _____
3 When your plane is late leaving _____
4 You might sit here to have a little more space _____
5 Bags that you put above or under your seat _____
6 When you get your flight document from a machine _____
7 The maximum number of suitcases you can take _____
8 When you pay more for services before or during your flight
_____
9 They do this at airports to protect passengers _____
10 When your second plane leaves before the first one arrives
_____

5 Work with a partner. What travel problems might these people have? What would the consequences be?
1 A business traveller flying to an important meeting
2 A family of four with two young children leaving for a 2-week holiday
3 A student flying abroad for a 9-month work placement

6 ▶ **7.1** Listen to conversations 1–3. Which passenger …?
a will have to pay more ___
b made a mistake at check-in ___
c will arrive late ___

7 Cross out the word in each group that can't combine with the word in **bold**. Then compare your answers with a partner.
1 middle / ~~hand~~ / window	**seat**
2 online / priority / passport	**check-in**
3 free / First Class / electronic	**upgrade**
4 excess / hold / seat	**baggage**
5 connecting / airport / cancelled	**flight**
6 additional / delayed / extra	**charges**

8 ▶ **7.1** Listen again. Which compound words from **7** do you hear? With a partner, use the word combinations to describe each situation.

≫ For more exercises, go to **Practice file 7** on page 118.

9 Work with a partner. Talk about a recent experience of taking a plane. It can be:
• your own experience or the story of someone you know
• a good or a bad experience
• a flight taken for business or for a holiday

Tip | Compound words

Compound words are words that go naturally together. We can combine noun + noun (e.g. *flight ticket*) or adjective + noun (e.g. *delayed flight*).

The first word always describes the second:

flight ticket = a ticket for a flight
middle seat = a seat that's in the middle

Language at work | *will/going to*/present continuous

1 What are your plans for this weekend and for next week?

2 ▶ 7.2 Fabrizio wants to see his friend Emily in Montreal. Today is Monday 11th June. Listen to the phone call and make notes on what will happen at these times.

1 The end of July _____

2 September _____

3 Sunday 17th June _____

4 Wednesday 20th June _____

5 Friday 15th June _____

3 Read these sentences from the conversation in **2**. Underline the verb that refers to the future in each sentence.

1 I'm going to leave the company soon.

2 I'm coming to Montreal for a conference next week.

3 I'll call you again on Friday.

4 Complete explanations 1–3 in the *Language point* with *will*, *going to* or *present continuous*. Then match the sentences in **3** to each explanation.

> **LANGUAGE POINT**
>
> 1 We use _____ to talk about a plan that's already decided.
>   *Example:* _____
> 2 We use _____ to make a decision at the moment of speaking.
>   *Example:* _____
> 3 We use _____ for an arrangement with a fixed time or place. (You can often use *going to* here instead.)
>   *Example:* _____

» For more information, go to **Grammar reference** on page 119.

5 Complete sentences a–f with the correct form of the verbs in brackets. Then match sentences 1–6 to responses a–f.

1 Do you have any plans for the weekend? ___

2 Can you take me to the airport this evening? ___

3 I'm afraid I'm not here to help you on Saturday. ___

4 Have they decided on a date for their visit? ___

5 Sorry, but I'm not free in the morning now. ___

6 Can you let me know when your train arrives? ___

a That's OK. I _____ (change) the appointment to the afternoon.

b Yes, my brother _____ (come). We _____ (show) him round the town.

c Yes, 5.30. I _____ (send) you a text message from the station.

d Don't worry. I _____ (ask) someone else.

e Yes, they _____ (come) on 3rd May. They _____ (stay) for two days.

f Sure, I _____ (do) that. You _____ (leave) at 8.30. Is that right?

6 Practise the exchanges in **5** with a partner.

7 Your boss Meghan is on a business trip this week. You receive this email from her. Choose the correct words in *italics*.

Arianna Boyle from TFF is going to ¹*visit / visiting* us next Wednesday. It's her first time here and she's a very important customer. Unfortunately, I'm only free to see her for part of the day. ²*She's / She will* arriving very early in the morning on a night flight, spending Wednesday night in a hotel near the company and she is ³*leave / leaving* on Thursday. Can you meet her at the airport and decide what you ⁴*are / will* do with her during the day: restaurant, local visits, etc.? There's a provisional schedule on my desk. Can you complete it? There's also an email from Arianna. ⁵*I'm calling / I'll call* you tomorrow morning to check that everything's OK.

Meghan

» For more exercises, go to **Practice file 7** on page 119.

8 Work with a partner to plan Arianna Boyle's visit. **Student A**, turn to **page 138**. **Student B**, turn to **page 142**.

Practically speaking | How to ask for directions

1 What different ways can you think of to ask for directions?
   Example: Can you tell me how to get to …?

2 ▶ 7.3 Listen to three short conversations and complete the sentences.
   1 _____ the way to the station, please?
   2 Excuse me. _____ the registrations office for the conference.
   3 Excuse me. _____ the motorway?
     Oh, _____ the nearest petrol station is?

3 ▶ 7.3 Listen again and number the directions in the order you hear them.
   you'll see signs ____
   on your right ____
   take the third exit ____
   take the first left ____
   turn right at ____
   in front of you ____
   go straight on ____
   go past the ____
   then go down the stairs ____

4 Practise the conversations in **2** and **3** with a partner.

5 Work with a partner. Take it in turns to ask for and give directions from:
   • the room you're in to another part of the building
   • your present location to another place in the town

Business communication | Arranging to meet

1 Look at Fabrizio's schedule. Today is Sunday 17th June. What is he doing in the next few days?

June	Day	Week	Month	Year

Sun 17	Arr Montreal airport 14.30
Mon 18	Mon – Wed IEFA conference
Tues 19	Conference ends 17.00
Wed 20	Return flight 21.45

2 ▶ 7.4 Fabrizio calls Emily in Montreal to arrange a time to meet during his visit. Listen and make notes on:
1 why Sunday and Tuesday aren't possible
2 what day, time and place they decide

3 ▶ 7.4 Listen again and complete sentences 1–10.
1 When can we meet? _____ that evening?
2 I have a meeting there on Monday. _____ a different time?
3 I'm staying in Montreal until Wednesday. When _____ you?
4 I'm coming back on Monday evening. _____ lunch on Tuesday?
5 What's _____ later in the day?
6 How about Tuesday evening _____?
7 I'm afraid I've _____ that evening.
8 In that case, does Wednesday lunchtime _____?
9 Great. _____ outside the conference centre.
10 The morning session finishes at one. _____ one fifteen?

» For more exercises, go to **Practice file 7** on page 118.

4 Work with a partner. Fabrizio now has another meeting at Wednesday lunchtime.
Student A
You are Fabrizio. Call Emily and arrange another time to meet.
Student B
You are Emily. You really want to meet Fabrizio. Change your schedule if necessary.

5 Work with a partner or in groups. You want to organize a lunch together. Look at your diary and find a time when everybody can meet.

Key expressions

Asking when a person is free
When would suit you?
What's your availability (on Monday)?
When can we meet?

Suggesting a time and date
Are you free (that evening)?
What about (Tuesday)?
Does (Friday) work for you?
How about (Saturday) instead?
Where shall we meet?
Shall we say (3 p.m.)?
Let's meet (at your office).

Accepting
That's fine for me.
That suits me.
So that's (Sunday) at (9.30).

Refusing
I'm afraid I've got something on.
Sorry, but I'm (meeting a client).
Can we find a different (day/time)?

TALKING POINT

The travel game

Work with a partner. You both have a meeting at Chris Stein's office in Prague. **Student A** takes one route and **Student B** takes another. Take turns to toss a coin. Heads – move one space forward and use the information to have a conversation with your partner. Tails – miss a turn and pass the coin to your partner. The winner is the first person to reach Chris's office.

Your plane is delayed. Ask why and what time it is leaving.	The self-service check-in machine doesn't work. Ask for help.	**AIRPORT** A B	At check-in, your hand baggage is too heavy. Check it in as hold luggage.	Someone is sitting in your seat on the plane.
There's no space for your hand baggage. Ask for help.				Have a conversation with a passenger about your plans.
Have a conversation with a passenger about airport security.				You miss your connection in Paris. Ask about the next flight.
The car rental company doesn't have your car. Ask for a different one.				Now you'll be late for your appointment! Phone Chris Stein's assistant.
A customer calls you to change his appointment next week.				Ask for directions to the airport wi-fi area.
You're lost. Ask for directions to the Hotel Troja.				A supplier calls and asks if she can come to your office today.
Check into the hotel and ask about breakfast times.				On your next plane, the seat is broken. Ask to move to a different seat.
You see a friend from home in the restaurant! Arrange to meet for a drink.				Have a conversation with a passenger about the stress of air travel.
Ask the hotel how to get to Chris Stein's office. (Possible on foot?)	Chris Stein is late. Tell his assistant what you want to do in Prague after your meeting.	**CHRIS STEIN'S OFFICE**	Check into the company reception. You're 15 minutes late!	At the airport, ask about the next bus or train to the city centre.

8 Orders

Starting point

1 What are the most popular products and services bought online?

2 What do you most often buy online? Why?

3 Are there any products you would never buy online? Why?

Working with words | Orders and deliveries

1 What do you know about these annual celebrations? Do you have them in your country? Which ones do you think offer the best business for retailers?

| Valentine's Day | Diwali | Mother's/Father's Day |
| New Year | Thanksgiving | Christmas |

2 Read this text and answer questions 1–3.
  1 What is Black Friday?
  2 What problems have retailers had on this day?
  3 What solutions are suggested?

E-Commerce: Lessons learnt from Black Friday

Black Friday is the name given to the last Friday in November, the day after Thanksgiving. Retailers offer reduced prices on many of their products. Since 2005, it has been the busiest shopping day of the year in the USA. In recent years, other countries have adopted Black Friday as a way to boost Christmas sales. Last year, in the UK, it was the highest spending day on record, up 37.5% from the year before.

For online retailers, Black Friday presents a particular challenge. Demand in the UK last year was 30% higher than predicted and Tesco stores' online order service could no longer **guarantee** next-day **delivery**. Retailer Marks & Spencer had the same problem, and **deliver**ed certain **orders** up to two weeks late.

So what can retailers learn from the experience? Firstly, they have to do better with their forecasts and **check** they have enough items **in stock** to be sure they have enough goods to **meet** customer **demand**. Secondly, they may need more staff. With so many customers **placing orders** on Black Friday, warehouses may need to operate over the weekend. This could mean more call centre employees for customers calling to **enquire** about products, and warehouse operators to **process the orders**. The carriers who **transport** the goods may also need extra drivers over that weekend.

Finally, retailers can reduce the number of orders leaving the warehouse on Black Friday. To do this, they can **quote** much lower **prices** for non-urgent delivery. This isn't like Christmas, where everything must arrive before 25th December, so many customers will agree to wait.

If they can **track** their shipment online, and this information is correct, they will be satisfied.

3 What do you think of the idea of Black Friday? Do you have it, or something similar, in your country?

4 Match words 1–10 from the text in **2** to definitions a–j.

1	demand ___	a	to ask for information
2	stock ___	b	products to buy or sell
3	goods ___	c	to transport to the customer's address
4	to process ___	d	a request for a product to be sent
5	an order ___	e	to promise you will do something
6	to quote ___	f	to deal with (e.g. an order)
7	a shipment ___	g	the need of customers for products they want to buy
8	to enquire ___	h	products being transported to a customer
9	to guarantee ___	i	to say the cost of something
10	to deliver ___	j	products in your warehouse or shop

5 Choose from the verbs in **bold** in the text in **2** to complete these phrases.

1 _____ a price
2 _____ a delivery date
3 _____ / _____ / _____ an order
4 _____ a product is in stock
5 _____ the goods
6 _____ the shipment
7 _____ about a product
8 _____ the demand

6 Work with a partner. Use the phrases in **5** to talk about the order process.
Example: First, the customer calls to enquire about a product. The supplier …

7 ▶ 8.1 Listen to two phone conversations. In which conversation …?
a does the customer place an order _____
b has the customer called before _____
c does the supplier quote a price _____
d can the supplier deliver in about two weeks _____

8 ▶ 8.1 Complete the missing words in sentences 1–8. They are all from the same word family as the words in **4**. Then listen again and check your answers.
1 I'm calling about your recent _____.
2 And we told you we don't _____ that product here.
3 But I said we could _____ them for you.
4 If you like, I can give you a _____.
5 On your website, it says the _____ is for three years.
6 Well, the order _____ is a little longer than usual.
7 But we can _____ the product to you in the next 48 hours.
8 Please call me back with a _____ date.

》 For more exercises, go to **Practice file 8** on page 120.

9 Work with a partner. Have two conversations where a customer is phoning a supplier to enquire about a product. Change roles for the second conversation. Ask/Talk about these subjects.

- Stock
- Order process
- Delivery date
- Price
- Shipping date
- Guarantee

Conversation 1: The customer is ordering an antique table from an online furniture supplier.
Conversation 2: The customer is ordering a tablet computer from an online electronics supplier.

Tip | *to ship, shipping* *and shipment*
The *shipping* (or *shipment*) date is the day when the products leave the shop, factory or warehouse. You *ship* the products to the customer.
The word *shipment* also describes the products themselves during transportation.

Language at work | The passive

1 What problems can occur in the order process, from initial enquiry to final delivery? Make a list.

Example: The product isn't in stock. The supplier sends the wrong product.

2 ▶ 8.2 Listen to two conversations. Match each conversation to one of the descriptions below.

a A shipment problem
b A problem with an invoice
c An explanation of the order process
d The system for returns and refunds

3 ▶ 8.2 Choose the correct verb form in *italics*. Then listen again and check.

1 And the order *transfers / is transferred* automatically to the warehouse.
2 The products *ship / are shipped* the same day.
3 When orders *place / are placed* before 4 p.m., we *guarantee / are guaranteed* next-day delivery.
4 But when I *tracked / was tracked* my order online, it said the goods *delivered / were delivered* yesterday.
5 Yes, delivery *confirmed / was confirmed* by the courier at 9.15.
6 So it *sent / was sent* to the wrong address.

4 Look at the verb forms in **3**. Choose the correct words in *italics* to complete the explanations in the *Language point*. Then match the examples in **3** to each explanation.

> **LANGUAGE POINT**
>
> 1 We use the *passive / active* when it is not important to say who does something. We are more interested in what the action is.
> *Examples:* _____
> 2 We use the *passive / active* when we say *who* does something.
> *Examples:* _____
> 3 For the present simple passive we use _____ or *are* + the past participle.
> *Examples:* _____
> 4 For the past simple passive we use *was* or _____ + the past participle.
> *Examples:* _____

>> For more information, go to **Grammar reference** on page 121.

5 Complete sentences 1–5 with the verbs in the list, using the correct passive form.

guarantee   send   place   confirm   make   sell   check

1 Our cars _____ in our German factory, and they _____ all over the world
2 You say the order _____ to us last week, but we haven't received it.
3 The goods _____ in Quality Control before shipment, but they arrived broken.
4 The product _____ for two years. Is that right?
5 The order _____ last Monday and the details _____ by email the same day.

6 Complete the text about the Click and Collect service using the verbs in brackets in the appropriate passive or active form.

Click and Collect delivery is growing in popularity. The idea is that when an order ¹_____ (place) online, it ²_____ (not deliver) to your home, but to a local shop or other delivery point.

This form of delivery ³_____ (offer) not only by online retailers, but also by traditional stores. More and more customers ⁴_____ (choose) Click and Collect for

orders placed online with department stores or supermarkets. The service ⁵_____ (introduce) for customers who ⁶_____ (want) to drive to the store and pick up their shopping directly.

Delivery points are also appearing in car parks, stations and even airports. When the John Lewis chain ⁷_____ (open) its first Click and Collect store at London's St Pancras station in 2014, only a limited selection of products ⁸_____ (offer) in the shop itself, but customers ⁹_____ (invite) to go there to collect orders placed online. And in the same year, refrigerated lockers ¹⁰_____ (install) at Gatwick airport so travellers can now order their groceries while on holiday, and when they ¹¹_____ (return) they ¹²_____ (pick) up their shopping on the way home.

>> For more exercises, go to **Practice file 8** on page 121.

7 Work with a partner. What are the benefits and possible disadvantages of Click and Collect for …?
- customers/shoppers
- traditional retailers
- online retailers
- local shops used as delivery points

Practically speaking | How to discuss payment terms

1 What do you need to know about payment terms before you place an order?

2 ▶ 8.3 Listen to a conversation discussing payment. How much, how and when will the customer pay?

3 ▶ 8.3 Complete questions 1–6 with the words in the list. Listen again and check.

accept   include   forms   charge   discount   total   monthly   advance

1 What's the _____ price?
2 Does that _____ VAT?
3 Do you _____ extra for delivery?
4 Do you offer a _____ for payment in _____?
5 What _____ of payment do you _____?
6 Is it possible to pay in _____ instalments?

4 Match 1–3 to a–c to make complete sentences.
1 You can pay by   a includes VAT/is before tax
2 That price   b included/extra
3 Delivery is   c bank transfer/cheque/credit card

5 Work with a partner. Have similar conversations about these orders.
- A new photocopier/printer for the office (price, VAT, delivery, payment)
- A car bought from a garage (price, registration documents, payment)

Business communication | Making requests

1 You need a colleague to help you carry a heavy box. How would you ask for help if you think the response …?
- will be positive (e.g. your colleague isn't busy / it'll only take 30 seconds)
- could possibly be negative (e.g. it's your boss / the box is very heavy)

2 ▶ 8.4 A man is collecting a package from a shop. Listen to all three parts of the conversation. What does the customer ask for? What does the shopkeeper ask the customer?

3 ▶ 8.4 Listen again and match requests 1–8 with responses a–h. Then practise the exchanges with a partner.

1 Do you mind if I see this gentleman first? ____
2 Would you mind giving me some small change? ____
3 Could I see your confirmation email, please? ____
4 Is it all right if I just show you my driving licence? ____
5 Could I ask you to wait a moment? ____
6 I need some identification, too, please. ____
7 Could you just sign here, please? ____
8 Do you think I could have a bag? ____

a I'm afraid not.
b I'm afraid I don't have one that size.
c I'm sorry, but I need the order reference.
d Sure.
e Yes, sure. Go ahead.
f Oh sorry, I didn't realize.
g Certainly. Here you are.
h No, not at all.

4 Which expressions in **3** are often used for …?
- simple requests, where we think the response will probably be positive
- less simple requests, where it's possible the response will be negative

5 With a partner, take turns to make and respond to requests. Ask your partner:
- for their phone number
- if you can leave work early
- for an order reference
- to drive you to the airport
- if you can open the window
- for the same order reference (you've lost it!)

» For more exercises, go to **Practice file 8** on page 120.

6 Work with a partner. A customer wants to place an order with a regular supplier. Look at the information in the table and have a conversation, using appropriate requests and responses.

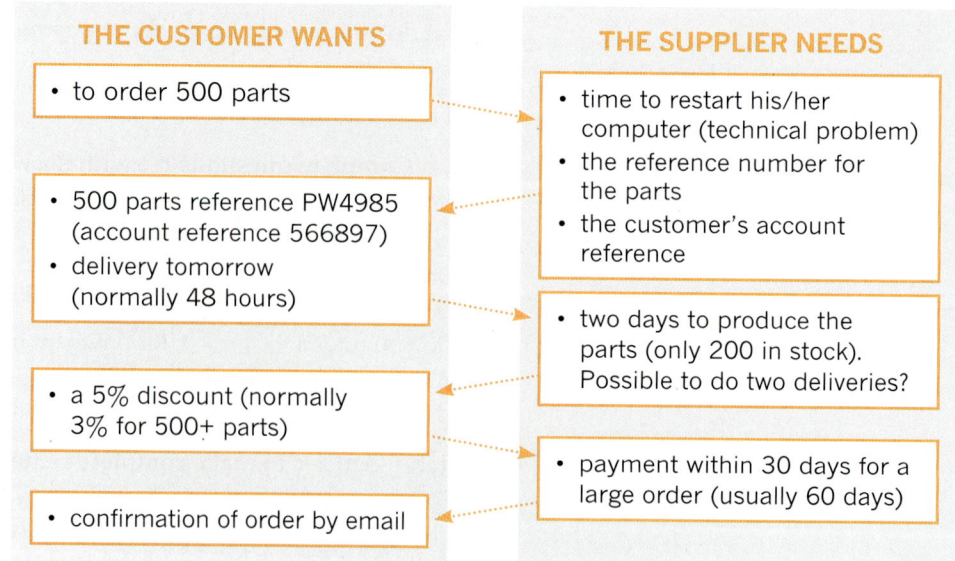

THE CUSTOMER WANTS	THE SUPPLIER NEEDS
• to order 500 parts	• time to restart his/her computer (technical problem) • the reference number for the parts • the customer's account reference
• 500 parts reference PW4985 (account reference 566897) • delivery tomorrow (normally 48 hours)	• two days to produce the parts (only 200 in stock). Possible to do two deliveries?
• a 5% discount (normally 3% for 500+ parts)	• payment within 30 days for a large order (usually 60 days)
• confirmation of order by email	

Comparing payment methods

Discussion

1 Look at the different payment methods above. Which ones do you use the most to buy goods or services? Which ones do you use less? Why?

2 ▶ 8.5 Listen to five retailers giving their opinions about each payment type. Which type of payment is each retailer describing and what advantages and disadvantages do they mention?

	Payment type	Advantages	Disadvantages
1			
2			
3			
4			
5			

3 Do you agree with the advantages/disadvantages mentioned?
Can you add more advantages/disadvantages for each payment type?

Task

1 Work with a partner or in small groups. You are going to open a new business. Discuss these questions.

1 What products are you going to sell?
2 Who will your customers be, and where will they be?
3 How are you going to sell your products: online, in store or a combination of the two? If you have a store, where will it be located?
4 What payment methods will you use to maximize orders and sales?
5 If it's possible to order products online, what delivery options will you offer?

2 Present your ideas to the class and give feedback on their ideas.

9 Selling

Starting point

1 What sorts of advertising do you notice most?

2 Which of these statements do you agree with?
- There is too much advertising on TV and the Internet.
- Advertising keeps the Internet free.
- There should be strict controls on what is advertised, and to whom.

Working with words | Advertising

1 What advice would you give to a new start-up company that wants to advertise its products for free?

2 Read the text and compare the advice it gives with your ideas in **1**.

SOCIAL MEDIA AND THE START-UP

Advertising doesn't have to be an expensive business for new companies. Social media offers the possibility to **get free publicity** by using tools such as Twitter, Facebook and YouTube. Both small start-ups and big firms use social media to **increase awareness** of their company or brand and **attract new business**.

However, it is vital that you select the right media for the customers you want. There is no point using a tool like Facebook to **reach a target audience** of professionals aged 40+, when statistics show that around 80% of UK Facebook users are under 40.

Always add value for your customer by thinking of how they will gain from your activity. For example, a Facebook page can **promote your latest range** and **offer discounts** to the first 3,000 customers. This will help to **boost sales**. It will also get people talking to friends and other users. **Word of mouth** can be the best form of publicity.

Finally, don't forget the power of a funny video when you **conduct an advertising campaign** on social media. US company Orabrush realized this when they offered a free product in exchange for YouTube views and 'likes' on Facebook. The result was more than 46 million video viewings and 2.3 million products sold. That's not bad for a company which sells tongue brushes for people with bad breath!

3 Work with a partner. Do you think it's easier to promote your business today than before the age of the Internet? Why/Why not?

4 Match definitions 1–9 to the phrases in **bold** in the text in **2**.
1 Find new customers or get new orders _____
2 Increase your revenue by selling more products _____
3 Advertise your company without paying _____
4 Do a series of advertisements using different media _____
5 The process of telling other people about a product or service

_____
6 Find the customers you want to sell to _____
7 Advertise your most recent products _____
8 Make your company or products better known _____
9 Sell products for lower prices _____

5 Choose the correct word or expression in *italics* to complete the questions. Then answer the questions with a partner.
1 Do you often hear about new products by *word of mouth / offer discounts*? Where from?
2 How can you *boost / promote* your *awareness / sales* when your competitors are cutting prices?
3 How do film producers *attract new business / get free publicity* for their films?
4 What is Apple's *latest range / target audience* and how does it *reach / conduct* those customers?

>> For more exercises, go to **Practice file 9** on page 122.

6 ▶ 9.1 Listen to three people talking about promoting their business. Match the speaker to the business they work in.
Office supplies ___   Health clubs ___   Internet service providers ___

7 ▶ 9.1 Listen again and answer the questions for each speaker.
1 What problems do they have?
2 What are they doing to attract new business?

8 Work with a partner. Discuss the six forms of advertising from the list. Which would you recommend for the companies in **6**?
*social media   click ads   targeted emails
advertising boards   search engines   promotional events*

9 ▶ 9.2 Listen to the speakers in **6** describing how they advertise and compare with your answers in **8**.

10 How does your company attract new customers? How does it advertise?

Tip | *ad, advert, advertisement, advertising*
Advertisement is a countable noun. We see an advertisement for a product in the newspaper, on TV, etc. The short forms of the word are *advert* and *ad*.
Advertising is an uncountable noun. It's the general word to describe the action of promoting companies, products or services:
*There's a lot of **advertising** on TV.*
*He works in **advertising**.*

Language at work | Modal verbs (1)

1 Has your town/city changed much over the last ten years? How?

2 Read the text. How is Grenoble different from before? What do you think of the mayor's idea?

GRENOBLE WHERE HAVE ALL THE BILLBOARDS GONE?

The residents of Grenoble in the east of France **don't have to** look at commercial advertising in the street any more. Companies **aren't allowed to** promote their products outdoors. In the year 2015, the city's 326 advertising signs disappeared.

The decision was made by Grenoble's Green Party mayor, Éric Piolle. Local cultural and social groups **can** still advertise their events and activities and they **don't need to** pay anything. However, their adverts **have to** be smaller in size, and more visible to pedestrians than car drivers. The mayor's idea is to promote 'areas for public expression'.

The new law has its critics: 'We now **need to** find €600,000 in lost advertising revenue,' said a local opposition politician. But the mayor's office said that advertising rates are falling every year, and that €150,000 was a more accurate figure.

3 Match the six verbs in **bold** in the text in **2** to the correct meaning in the *Language point*.

> **LANGUAGE POINT**
>
> 1 It's necessary
> _____   _____
>
> 2 It's not necessary
>   *don't have to*
> _____   _____
> 3 It's possible/permitted
> _____   _____
>
> 4 It's not possible/permitted
> _____   _____
>
> Which two verbs can you use to complete the remaining gaps above?

>> For more information, go to **Grammar reference** on page 123.

4 ▶9.3 Listen to four people talking about advertising. Which speaker thinks …?
a some advertising laws aren't good ___
b online advertising is important ___
c outdoor advertising isn't attractive ___
d advertising laws are necessary ___

5 ▶9.3 Work with a partner. Complete sentences 1–9 with verbs from **3**, then listen again and check. Do you agree with the different opinions expressed?
1 Companies _____ advertise to sell their products.
2 You _____ have big billboards everywhere.
3 I think you _____ have laws on advertising.
4 You _____ stop companies advertising products which are bad for you.
5 In some countries, you _____ advertise cigarettes.
6 You _____ advertise alcohol on TV, but you _____ do it before 8 p.m.
7 When we use the Internet, we usually _____ pay to get the information we need.
8 Many website owners make their profits from advertising, so we _____ use their websites for free.
9 There are a lot of ads online, but you _____ look at them.

6 Work with a partner. Look at these sales and advertising messages. Say what they mean, using the verbs in **3**.

> *Example:* You can buy now, but you don't have to pay before next year.

1
Buy now,
pay next year.

2
30% off everything
throughout the store.
Offer ends today.

3
Sorry, no cheques.
Card and cash payments only.

4
Free delivery
on orders over €100.

5
NB This ticket is
non-refundable. Protect
yourself with cancellation
insurance. Click here.

6
NO ADVERTISING
HERE PLEASE!

» For more exercises, go to **Practice file 9** on page 123.

7 Work with a partner. Ask and answer questions about advertising laws in your country, using the language from the list and the ideas below.

Can you …?   Are you allowed to …?   Do you have to …?
Do you need to …?   I'm not sure, but I think …

- Compare products with your competitors
- Advertise credit cards and loans
- Promote products directly to children
- Have a health warning on certain foods
- Advertise alcoholic drinks
- Advertise slimming products

Practically speaking | How to interrupt and avoid interruption

1 ▶9.4 Listen to the conversation and answer the questions.
  1 What are the two people talking about?
  2 Do they agree?

2 ▶9.4 Listen again and number phrases a–e in the order you hear them.
  a Can I just say something here? ___
  b Please let me finish. ___
  c Sorry, go ahead. ___
  d Can I just finish? ___
  e Sorry, but … ___

3 Which phrases in **2** are used when you want to …?
  1 interrupt someone who is speaking
  2 continue speaking
  3 tell the other person to continue speaking

4 Work with a partner. Choose a subject from the list and prepare a few ideas about it on your own. Then take turns to talk about it and interrupt each other.
  Online advertising   Outdoor advertising   Advertising to children

Business communication | Controlling the discussion in meetings

1 ▶9.5 Three managers of Fitstart, a sports-shoe manufacturer, are discussing a new sales campaign in Central Europe. Listen and complete the notes.

Advertising:

Money spent last year: _____

Budget this year: _____

Extra money to be used for:
_____

Sales:

This year: _____% increase

Next two years: _____%

Key markets: the Czech Republic,
_____, _____

Action:

Edward to prepare detailed
_____
_____ to provide details
of social media campaign

2 ▶9.5 The sentences in B are the follow-up sentences to A. Match 1–6 with a–f and then listen again and check your answers.

A	B
1 We're here today to talk about Central Europe. ___	a Can we sum up what we've agreed?
2 Sorry, I didn't catch that. ___	b Could you be more specific?
3 We're getting off the subject. ___	c What was the last figure?
4 OK, I think we've covered advertising. ___	d Can we move on to the next point?
5 Sorry, I'm not with you. ___	e Can we come back to that later?
6 I think that's everything. ___	f We need to discuss our new marketing campaign.

3 Work with a partner. You are in a meeting. Take turns to say the sentences and to think of different responses, using the phrases in **2**.

Example: Sorry, I didn't catch that. What do you want to discuss?

1 We need to discuss sales figures.
2 We need a few more people in the department.
3 Can we talk about the Christmas party now?
4 The figures were 17.9% for May, 19.3% for June and 18.8% for July.
5 Does anybody have anything else to say on recruitment?
6 It's 12.30 now. Any other business?

>> For more exercises, go to **Practice file 9** on page 122.

4 Work in small groups. A big oil company wants to boost sales in its petrol stations in towns and on motorways. Have a meeting to discuss the items on the agenda. You can choose more than one proposal or even suggest other ideas.

AGENDA

1 Proposals

• New loyalty card: customers get one free litre of petrol for every 200 litres bought
• Offer a half-price car wash when customers buy 40 litres of petrol
• Children eat free in petrol station cafés
• Employ temporary staff to operate the petrol pumps at busy times

2 Advertising campaign

• Billboards   • TV   • Social media   • Other

Key expressions

Introducing the subject
We're here today to talk about …
We need to discuss …

Saying you didn't hear
Sorry, I didn't catch that.
What was (that/the last number)?

Saying you didn't understand
Sorry, I'm not with you.
Could you be more specific?

Keeping to the right subject
We're getting off the subject.
Can we come back to that later?

Changing the subject
I think we've covered (this point).
Can we move on to (the next point)?

Concluding and summarizing
I think that's everything.
Can we sum up what we've agreed?

Going viral

What is a viral video? There is no official definition, but we could consider that a video which is viewed several million times over a period of a few days has 'gone viral'.

So what are the secrets of making a viral video for a company that wants to promote itself? Here are five tips you can use to improve your chances of viral success.

1

Be up-to-date. What news stories or aspects of popular culture are current? If your video relates to a popular subject, you will increase your views.

2

Use emotion. People share videos which produce strong emotions. And they share more with friends when that emotion is positive, rather than negative.

3

Get to the point. Your video needs to interest people straight away. Many people close the video after a few seconds and the majority don't last more than a minute!

4

Make people think. Tell a story that will make your audience think positively about the world. For example, stories of people who survived difficult situations or found success.

5

Give useful information. People are always searching for new information and better ways to do everyday tasks. If they learn something they didn't know, they will share it.

Discussion

1 How are the five tips similar or different to traditional TV advertising?

2 Which of the tips do you think are more/less important? Would you add any other ideas?

3 What sort of videos do you share with friends and family?

Task

1 Work in small groups. You are going to plan a 2–3 minute video to promote your company or a company you know well.

2 Decide on the subject of your video – your company, its products or a theme related to the activity of your company.

3 Discuss which of the five tips above will be important for you.

4 Plan your video, indicating the timing for each scene or section.

5 Present your plan to another group and give feedback on their plan.

Focus

1 Work with a partner. What famous logos can you think of? How important is a company logo? What does your company logo look like?

2 ▶01 Watch two people talking about company logos. Make notes about their answers in the table.

	Speaker 1	Speaker 2
What do you think makes a good logo?		
Can you tell us about your company logo?		
How important is colour in a logo?		

3 Look at the words in the list for talking about logos. Put the words into the four categories below.

small van   modern optimistic
website round excited bright
happy supermarket safe   packaging

small

How it looks **Where you see it** **How it makes you feel**

Colourful messages

4 Work with a partner. Look at the colours below. Which types of businesses do you think use each of the colours in their logos? Why do you think they use these colours?

Example: Fast food restaurants often use yellow and red in their logos.

YELLOW RED GREEN

BLUE GREY RAINBOW

5 ▶02 Watch a video about the colour of logos for different types of businesses. Complete the notes in the table.

Colour	Type of business	What message does the colour send?
Yellow	Fast food	Bright and optimistic, warm and 1 _____
2 _____	Fast food Medical emergency	Exciting Danger
Green	Drinks, energy and organic food	Healthy, clean and 3 _____ for you.
Blue	Pharmaceutical and 4 _____ businesses	Safety and reliability
Grey and silver	Technology and 5 _____	Strength and performance
Rainbow	6 _____	"We are many things to many different people!"

6 ▶02 Complete the expressions 1–7 from the video. Then watch the video again to check your answers.

1 Yellow is a bright and optimistic colour. **It m**_____ **us f**_____ warm and happy inside.

2 **It s**_____ **to customers**: 'Hey! We're a happy place to bring the kids and have fun.'

3 Red **can also m**_____ danger.

4 Green **s**_____ **the m**_____ **that** the product is clean and good for you.

5 Green **is also g**_____ if you're an energy company.

6 We **a**_____ blue **with** safety and reliability so blue **is p**_____ **with** the pharmaceutical industry

7 A classic timeless grey or silver logo is also the choice of many car companies because **it r**_____ strength and performance.

7 Work with a partner. Discuss these questions.

1 Look back at the colours in **5** and think about your examples of companies. What message does the company send to the customer with this colour?

2 What does your company logo say about your business? How does it make your customers feel?

Designing a logo

8 Work in small groups. You work for a consultancy company. Three businesses want you to design their logos. Discuss what each logo might look like and the colours you can use. Use the information in **6** to help you. Draw a sketch of each logo.

The businesses are:

1 A successful family-run restaurant which serves healthy international cuisine.

2 A local IT service which helps small businesses with their computer problems.

3 A company which supplies and fits solar panels on houses and offices.

9 Present your logos to the class. Explain how they look and how they will make the customer feel.

10 Environment

Starting point

1 Say why you agree or disagree with the following statements.
- We all need to do more to protect the environment.
- Progress on environmental problems is very slow.

2 What do you think are the most urgent environmental problems?

Working with words | Environmental protection

1 Large quantities of data are produced on computers and the Internet. Discuss these questions with a partner.
1 Where does this data come from?
2 Where do you think it is stored?
3 What environmental problems might be created by the storage of this data?

2 Read the text and compare with your answers in 1. How have they solved the problem in Helsinki and at Google?

GREEN DATA

So many products end their life in the bin, but one thing we rarely **throw away** is information. Large quantities of information are stored online in data centres. This data comes from governments, companies and every individual who stores personal files online. But these big servers consume lots of energy, often generated from **fossil fuels** like coal or oil, which produce high quantities of **carbon emissions**. More than 2% of the world's energy is used to power data centres, making them a significant factor in **global warming**.

However, 30 metres under Helsinki's Uspenski Cathedral, in an old bomb shelter, you will find one of the world's most **eco-friendly** data centres. The cooling of servers normally represents half of a data centre's **energy consumption**, but this system uses a natural cooling system – the freezing waters of the Baltic Sea. The water heated by the servers is then **recycled** to provide heating for up to 1,000 homes in a city

More than 2% of the world's energy is used to power data centres

where winter temperatures are often –20°C. After the heat is extracted, the same water is **reused** to cool the servers again.

Fuel and energy are expensive in Finland, so there was a need to find a cost-effective solution to power the new data centre. But even in countries where energy production is cheaper, operators of big data servers are trying to **reduce pollution** by using cleaner energy from **renewable sources**. For example, Google has bought the complete output of a nearby windfarm for its new €600 million data centre in Eemshaven, Netherlands.

3 Work with a partner. Do we need so many data centres? What do you think of the initiatives in Helsinki and at Google?

4 Complete the sentences with a word or phrase in **bold** from the text in **2**.

1 The quantity of electricity or gas that you use is your

_____.

2 A product or resource is _____ when it is made into a new product.

3 A product or resource is _____ when it is used again for the same purpose.

4 An _____ product or action helps to protect the environment.

5 The sun and the sea are _____ of energy that will always be present.

6 You _____ products that you don't want any more.

7 _____ are natural sources of energy like gas that are found underground.

8 People who cycle to work help to _____ in cities.

9 _____ are produced from the burning of coal, oil or wood.

10 _____ is the regular increase in world temperatures.

5 Work with a partner. Which noun in B does NOT go with the verb in A? Take turns to make example sentences with some of the other verb-noun combinations

Example: If more people take the bus, it will reduce our consumption of petrol.

	A	B
1	reduce	consumption / carbon emissions / ~~the environment~~ / waste
2	recycle	metal cans / fossil fuels / paper / bottles
3	reuse	bags / towels / glasses / petrol
4	consume	warming / energy / gas / electricity
5	pollute	the environment / emissions / the water / the air
6	throw away	food / packaging / photocopies / energy

6 ▶ 10.1 Listen to four people talking about green initiatives in their companies. Match the speakers to the pictures.

A ___ B ___ C ___ D ___

7 ▶ 10.1 Work with a partner. Listen again and note which of the verb-noun combinations in **5** are used.

» For more exercises, go to **Practice file 10** on page 124.

8 Discuss the four initiatives in **6** with a partner. What do you think of them? What are the advantages or possible disadvantages?

9 Work with a partner and answer questions 1–4.

1 What does your company do to help the environment?

2 What other initiatives could your company take?

3 What do you do at home to help the environment?

4 What more could you do?

Tip | green

We can use the word *green* to describe things that help protect the environment:

*My company hasn't got a very clear **green** policy.*

*Sales of **green** products have increased in recent years.*

Language at work | First conditional

1 You have to choose between a tram system and electric buses for your town or city. Which one would you prefer? Why?

2 ▶10.2 Listen to two city planners discussing the options in **1** and complete the information.

	Trams	Electric Buses
Start-up costs/km (€)		
No of passengers/hour		
Running costs/km (€)		

3 ▶10.2 Underline the correct option from the words in *italics*. Then listen again and check your answers.

1 If we *choose / will choose* the bus system, the start-up costs *are / will be* much lower.

2 It *costs / will cost* us a lot more if we *have to / will have to* create special bus lanes.

3 If we *don't / won't* have enough passengers, your system *will / won't* be cost-effective.

4 What *do / will* we do if the system *loses / will lose* money?

4 Read the explanations in the *Language point*. Then match the sentences in **3** to explanations 2–4.

LANGUAGE POINT

1 We use the first conditional to describe the probable future result of a present or future action.

2 We form the first conditional with *If* + present simple, *will/won't* + infinitive.
   Example: _____

3 We can also put the *if* structure in the second part of the sentence.
   Example: _____

4 To form a first conditional question, we usually put the *if* structure in the second part of the question.
   Example: _____

>> For more information, go to **Grammar reference** on page 125.

5 Work with a partner. You are considering three different measures to improve life in your city. Use the information to discuss the probable results.

Example: **A** *What will happen if we make parking more expensive?*
B *We'll reduce the number of cars. If we do that, there'll be less pollution.*

Measure	Result 1	Result 2
make parking more expensive	reduce number of cars	less noisy
improve public transport	increase running costs	maybe increase ticket prices
create more cycle lanes	earn more money from ticket sales	less pollution
	borrow money to pay for initial investment	maybe not increase ticket prices
	not have extra revenue	be popular with the public
	make the roads safer	increase local taxes

» For more exercises, go to **Practice file 10** on page 125.

6 Your company wants to introduce some green initiatives. With a partner, discuss the probable result of these measures and decide which one(s) it should choose.
1 Only allow employees who carpool to use the company car park
2 Use organic, local products in the staff restaurant
3 Restrict the printing of documents
4 Buy second-hand computers
5 Reduce the number of business trips
6 Limit the use of air-conditioning in the summer

Practically speaking | How to ask for clarification

1 If you are in a meeting and don't understand something, what can you say?

2 ▶ **10.3** Listen to two managers talking about carbon reduction measures. Underline the correct words in *italics*.
1 Guido is referring to *Teresa's department* / *the whole company*.
2 The company has to cut its carbon emissions by the end of *this year* / *next year*.
3 Guido wants to tell people they *can* / *can't* open the windows.
4 Teresa agrees to turn the heating off for *the whole day* / *part of the day*.

3 ▶ **10.3** Listen again and complete questions 1–4 for asking for clarification.
1 _____ in my department or in the whole company?
2 _____ by the end of this year?
3 _____ that we should tell people they can't open the windows?
4 _____ part of the day?

4 Work with a partner. Use the information to have short conversations. Take turns to ask for clarification, using the prompts in B and the expressions in **3**.

Example: **A** *We have to send the report on 21st October.*
B *Sorry, did you say the 21st or the 31st?*
A *I said the 21st.*

A	B
Send / report / 21st October	21st? / 31st?
Reduce / energy consumption / next year	The whole company? / Just the factory?
Improve / results / recycling	Recycling? / Paper? / Other materials too?
Need / 15% reduction / heating bills	15? / 50?
Company canteen / not eco-friendly	Not eco-friendly?

Business communication | Giving a formal presentation

1 Work with a partner. Discuss the advantages for a company of having green policies.

2 ▶10.4 Listen to the presentation and complete the notes. How many of the advantages did you talk about in **1**?

> ### Advantages of adopting green policies
>
> 1 Reduce _____ costs and increase company _____
>
> 2 Protect the _____ and attract more _____
>
> 3 Improve reputation as an _____
>
> 4 Be prepared for new _____

3 ▶10.4 Work with a partner. Match 1–8 to a–h to make complete sentences from the presentation. Then listen again and check.

1 I'm here to tell you about ___
2 I'll come to ___
3 First of all, I'll give you ___
4 Let's start with ___
5 My next point concerns ___
6 Finally, I want to talk about ___
7 So, to sum up, ___
8 That brings me to ___

a the subject of profits.
b your company image.
c the importance of taking action now.
d the end of my talk.
e the advantages of going green.
f a quick overview of my talk.
g the new regulations later.
h cutting carbon emissions is good for your profits.

4 Work with a partner. Your company has decided to switch to 100% e-billing. Take turns to present the idea, using the notes below and the expressions in **3**.

> **Subject**
> Switching completely to e-billing
>
> **Advantages**
> Customers can view bill at any time of day or night
> Faster and cheaper than post
> Helps environment – saves on paper + plastic bags for collecting waste paper
>
> **Disadvantages**
> Special secure software needed – not all customers have it
> Some customers still worried about security
>
> **Conclusion**

➤➤ For more exercises, go to **Practice file 10** on page 124.

5 Work in groups. You are going to prepare and give a short presentation. Group A, turn to **page 138**. Group B, turn to **page 142**.

Key expressions

Starting the talk
I'm here to tell you / talk about …
I'll give you a quick overview of …
First of all/Firstly, …
I'm/We're going to (look at) …
Then we'll …

Introducing each point
Let's start with …
My next point concerns …
Finally,/Lastly, (I want to talk about) …

Referring backwards and forwards
As I said before, …
I'll come to that later.

Closing
So, to sum up …
That brings me to the end of my talk.
Thanks very much for listening.
Are there any questions?

Nudging

The Golden Rules of Nudging

- Keep the message simple.
- Make it fun.
- Make it visual.
- Create a spirit of competition.
- Reward good results.
- Make people feel good about the results of their action.

How can you get motorists to respect the speed limit? The preferred method is often radars, but in 2010 Stockholm in Sweden tested a speed camera with a difference. It took photos not only of cars that drove too fast, but of every car that passed. Those who respected the limit then had the chance to win money in the 'Speed Camera Lottery'. During the three-day trial, average speeds went down from 32 to 25 km/h. The Speed Camera Lottery is an example of a 'nudge' – a way of changing people's behaviour without forcing them. People usually know what the right action to take is, but they sometimes need a little push. Nudging is often more successful than making rules or imposing punishments.

Discussion

1 Which of the 'Golden Rules' does the Speed Camera Lottery follow?

2 Can you think of any disadvantages of the Speed Camera Lottery?

3 What other examples of nudging have you seen in everyday life?

4 Do you think nudging works better than rules and punishments? Why/Why not?

Task

1 Work in pairs. Think of ways to nudge employees in the workplace to do the things in the list.
- Reduce running costs. (Electricity? Paper? Water?)
- Have a healthier lifestyle. (Eating habits? Exercise?)
- Make meetings more efficient. (Organization? Use of time?)
- Learn and use English.

2 Present your ideas to the group and vote for the best idea in each category.

11 Entertaining

Starting point

1 What forms of entertainment do you enjoy in your free time?

2 How do companies often entertain their clients or employees?

Working with words | Corporate hospitality

1 Work with a partner. Discuss the questions.
1 For what reasons do companies invite clients to corporate events?
2 Why are they ready to pay high prices for corporate entertainment?

2 Read the text and compare it with your ideas in **1**.

CORPORATE HOSPITALITY

Why is it impossible to get tickets for many major sports and cultural events? Because so many of the tickets are bought by firms to entertain their clients and other VIPs. It is called corporate hospitality, but why do companies do it?

Corporate hospitality is a marketing tool. Companies use it to improve relationships with their customers, suppliers or staff. 'I work for a law firm,' says Virginia Allen. 'Every year, I invite my best clients to a concert sponsored by the firm. The main purpose is to give them a good time. Invite them to a special **event** and you will ensure their loyalty for the coming year.'

The **venue** for corporate events is as varied as the activities offered. **Guests** might play a round of golf on a famous course with a professional player. It could be a riverboat for a wine-tasting cruise or a drive in a Formula 1 car. The more important the customer, the bigger the **budget** of the **host company** that is paying. A seat at a Champions League football final, for example, can cost as much as €10,000 per person for a **package** that includes dinner and drinks. Even at these prices, many companies consider it to be good value for money.

In the words of one CEO, who asked not to be named: 'It's a lot cheaper than offering a 2% discount on our whole product range!'

3 Work with a partner. What are the advantages or disadvantages of corporate hospitality for …?
- event organizers
- ordinary people going to the same events

4 Complete the 'Information' column in the table with the words in **bold** from the text in **2**.

Information	Details
	Banco de Santander
	Leading VIPs from banking world
	Premium seat + champagne + 4-course meal
	Camp Nou Stadium
	FC Barcelona vs Real Madrid
	€150,000

5 ▶ **11.1** Listen to two people talking about corporate events they have attended. Complete the table.

	Speaker 1	Speaker 2
Host company		
Guests		
Venue		
Package		
Events/Activities		

6 ▶ **11.1** Match verbs 1–6 to nouns a–f. Then listen again and check your answers.

1 hold ____
2 arrange ____
3 have ____
4 entertain ____
5 book ____
6 accept ____

a clients
b an invitation
c a venue
d a great time
e a trip
f an event

7 Work with a partner. Which phrases in **6** have a similar meaning to …?
1 enjoy an activity
2 say yes to an offer of hospitality
3 look after guests
4 organize a journey to a place and back
5 reserve a place for an event
6 organize something special for your clients

≫ For more exercises, go to **Practice file 11** on page 126.

8 Work with a partner. Have you ever been to a corporate event? Tell your partner about it. If not, what would be your dream corporate event?

9 Work in small groups. You work for a corporate hospitality company. Plan a corporate event for your company, using the ideas below.
- Budget
- Venue
- Transport
- Guests
- Activities
- Food and drink
- Time
- Accommodation
- Entertainment

Tip | *customer* and *client*

A *customer* buys a product from a company:
The shop gives loyalty cards to its regular **customers**.
A *client* receives a service from a company or professional person:
My lawyer has many important **clients**.

Language at work | Countable and uncountable nouns

1 Why do you think big sporting events are a popular choice for corporate entertainment?

2 ▶ **11.2** A supplier has invited some customers to a big tennis tournament. Listen and answer the questions for each conversation.
Conversation 1: Has everybody arrived? What drinks does the host order?
Conversation 2: What time is it now? What does the guest want to do?

3 ▶ **11.2** Listen again and complete these questions.
1 _____ _____ any other guests in your party?
2 _____ _____ bottles would you like?
3 _____ _____ any coffee?
4 _____ _____ time do we have before play starts?
5 _____ _____ a souvenir shop inside the stadium?

4 Complete the explanations in the *Language point* with *countable* or *uncountable*.

LANGUAGE POINT

1 _____ nouns have a plural form (e.g. *a guest* – (*some*) *guests*).
2 _____ nouns have no plural form (e.g. *information* – (*some*) *information*).
3 We use *How many?* with _____ nouns, and *How much?* with _____ nouns.
4 We use *Is there a …?* with singular _____ nouns and *Is there* (*any*) *…?* with _____ nouns.
5 We use *Are there* (*any*) *…?* with plural _____ nouns.

≫ For more information, go to **Grammar reference** on page 127.

5 Complete these questions about the Wimbledon tennis tournament with *Is there, Are there, How much* or *How many*.
1 _____ tea and coffee is drunk by visitors?
2 _____ champagne is served to visitors?
3 _____ portions of ice cream are eaten?
4 _____ bananas do the players eat during the two weeks?
5 _____ a pharmacy inside the grounds?
6 _____ any banks inside the grounds?
7 _____ a library?
8 _____ any facilities inside the grounds for leaving luggage?
9 _____ any hotel accommodation for visitors inside the grounds?
10 _____ prize money is paid to the players?

6 ▶ **11.3** Listen to a tour guide talking about Wimbledon and note the answers to the questions in **5**. Are you surprised by any of the information?

≫ For more exercises, go to **Practice file 11** on page 127.

Tip | countable or uncountable?

Most nouns to describe types of drinks are uncountable:
*We need to buy **some** coffee and orange juice for the party.*
But when we describe drinks served in a glass or cup, we often use a countable form of the word:
*Can I have **three** coffees and **an** orange juice, please?*

7 Work with a partner. You are opening a hotel which specializes in corporate hospitality. Decide what facilities and services you will provide and complete the 'Our hotel' column.

	Our hotel	Competitor's hotel
Number of rooms		
Meeting or function rooms		
Evening entertainment		
Organized trips		
Other services		
Other facilities		
Special events (outside hotel)		
Packages (room + meals, etc.)		

8 You have been asked to do an analysis of your competitors. Form new pairs, and phone your new partner for information about their hotel using the prompts below. Complete the final column in the table in **7**.

How much …?   How many …?   Is there …?   Are there …?

9 Return to your original partner. What did you learn about your competitors? Do you want to change any of the services or facilities of your hotel?

Practically speaking | How to ask about food on a menu

1 How do you choose what to eat in a restaurant? Do you sometimes find it difficult to decide what to order? Why?

2 ▶ 11.4 Listen to two colleagues discussing what to eat. Who knows the restaurant, the man or the woman? What do they choose from the menu below?

STARTERS	PARMA HAM	TOMATO AND MOZZARELLA SALAD	GARLIC MUSHROOMS
MAIN COURSES	SPAGHETTI CARBONARA	LASAGNE	PIZZA OF YOUR CHOICE
DESSERTS	ICE CREAM	RICH CHOCOLATE CAKE	FRUIT SALAD

3 ▶ 11.4 Work with a partner. Match questions 1–4 to responses a–d, then listen again and check.

1 What's good here? ____
2 What are the pizzas like? ____
3 What are you having? ____
4 What do you recommend? ____

a I think I'll have the lasagne.
b You must try the Parma ham.
c I think you'll like the ice cream.
d They're not bad, but I recommend the pasta.

4 Why do you think the man asks his colleague the questions in **3**?

5 Work with a partner. Use the language from **3** to have a similar conversation in a restaurant. You can use the menu in **2** or make your own.

Business communication | Inviting and offering

1 What invitations/offers could you make to these people?

Example: Would you like a coffee?

a a visitor to your company   b a new employee   c a colleague

2 ▶ **11.5** Listen and match Conversations 1–4 to places a–d.

a next to a drinks machine ___

b outside a hotel ___

c in a company reception ___

d in an office ___

3 ▶ **11.5** Listen again. Match and complete invitations/offers 1–5 and responses a–e from the conversations.

1 _____ join us?

2 _____ bring you a glass of water?

3 _____ a coffee?

4 _____ going again?

5 _____ get you a ticket?

a Thanks for _____, but I'm not here this weekend.

b Oh yes. That would be _____.

c No, thanks. But I'd _____ a tea.

d Yes, please. That's very _____ of you.

e Thank you for the _____, but I'm really tired.

4 In which conversation in **2** do the speakers know each other well? Which more informal expressions do they use for inviting and responding?

5 Work with a partner. Look at these situations and take turns to make and respond to invitations and offers, using the expressions in **3**.

Example: A Would you like to take a break now?
          B Yes, please. That would be nice.

1 Your visitor is looking tired.

2 Your visitor doesn't have enough copies of a document for her presentation.

3 It's the opening night of *Madame Butterfly*. You know your colleague loves opera.

4 The meeting is finished and your visitor's hotel is on the other side of town.

5 It's lunchtime and your colleague hasn't eaten since breakfast at 8.00.

6 Your colleague has a problem connecting a laptop to the video projector.

7 There's a Picasso exhibition at the art gallery and your visitor has a free afternoon.

» For more exercises, go to **Practice file 11** on page 126.

6 Work with a partner. Take turns to invite each other, using the ideas in the 'Invitations' column. If your partner accepts, make an offer from the 'Offers' column.

Example: A Would you like to go to the Arsenal game on Saturday?
          B Oh yes. That would be great.
          A Shall I buy two tickets then?
          B Yes, please. That's very good of you.

Invitations	Offers
a sports event	get information about dates/times/prices
a special exhibition	look online
a concert	make a reservation
a meal in an expensive restaurant	buy tickets
a play or musical at the theatre	invite other people
an unusual sports activity	see if there are places/seats/tables available

Key expressions

Inviting
Would you like ...?
Do you fancy ...?
Would you like to ...?
Do you fancy (*-ing*) ...?

Offering
Do you want me to ...?
Would you like me to ...?
Shall I ...?

Accepting
Yes, please.
Thanks. That's (very) good of you.
That would be nice.
That would be great.

Declining
Thank you for the invitation, but ...
Thanks for asking, but ...
No, thanks, but I'd love ...

Hospitality or bribery?

When a company makes a secret cash payment to a customer to be sure of getting their business, this is a clear case of bribery. However, sometimes the line between bribery and hospitality is not so clear. Some countries have introduced strict new regulations and many companies are worried about breaking the law. When deciding whether to accept or provide corporate hospitality or gifts, these questions may provide a useful starting point.

- What is the value of the gift or hospitality?
- Is this value proportional to the business provided by the customer?
- Is it just one person receiving it or people from different organizations?
- When is the gift or hospitality to be given? For example, is it near the time of signing a new contract or is it a regular event to promote the host company?
- How easy or difficult is it for the customer to refuse it?

Discussion

1 Look at the questions above and think of examples of what *would* or *wouldn't* be considered bribery.

2 Corporate hospitality is legal, but some people see it as a form of bribery. Do you agree?

3 Does your company have any similar guidelines for corporate hospitality?

Task

1 Work with a partner. Discuss the situations below and decide if they are examples of (a) bribery or (b) hospitality/gifts.

1 Every October, a company offers its five biggest customers a one-week holiday in an exotic island location. Prices for the next year are always negotiated in November and December.

2 A businessman donates $100,000 to his old university. Six months later, his son applies for a place at the same university.

3 A company invites 50 customers to a launch party for its new product range in the best hotel in town. They are offered dinner and a room in the hotel, and receive gifts of champagne, a computer bag and a pen, all with the company logo on them.

4 A customer tells a supplier that his/her products are no longer competitive. The supplier invites the customer to a top restaurant to discuss the situation, but nothing is decided. Two days later, the customer receives a designer watch from the supplier in the post to thank him/her for 'ten years of loyalty'.

5 Over a three-month period, an office manager gives his/her cleaner a box of chocolates, a bunch of flowers and a €10 tip to thank her for her work. Two days later, the office manager asks the cleaner to change the morning routine. The Office Manager now wants his/her office to be cleaned before the others in the building so that the cleaner finishes before the other employees arrive.

2 Turn to **page 138** to see an expert's view of the situations in **1**. Were you right? Do you disagree with any of the verdicts? Why?

12 Performance

Starting point

1 How do we usually measure the performance of …?
- a company
- a sportsperson
- a government

2 How do you measure your performance in your job?

Working with words | Evaluating performance

1 Work with a partner. Here are different ways of measuring company performance. Which do you think are more or less important?
- How much money it makes
- Who it employs
- How often employees leave
- How green it is
- How it treats its staff
- How safe it is to work there

2 Read the text. Which four of the categories in **1** are mentioned?

Company performance in a socially responsible world

Every investor loves companies that **achieve** their **sales targets**, **manage** their **costs** and **perform well** on the stock market and, therefore, make money.

However, a company nowadays also needs to think about its **reputation** with the public and its own staff. In other words, it has to be **socially responsible**. For example, it is expected to improve its **environmental performance**. In addition, it is often judged these days on **workplace diversity**: the number of women, people from ethnic minorities and disabled people in all positions, including senior management. This has become an important factor in recruitment. Finally, a company needs to have a good **safety record**, both in terms of its workers and the products which it produces.

In a recent survey, more than half (55%) of people worldwide said they are ready to pay more for products and services from companies that have positive social and environmental policies. This percentage is even higher in Asia-Pacific (64%), Latin America (63%) and the Middle East/Africa (63%). Without doubt, profits are no longer the only way to measure a company's success. Employees and customers expect a lot more.

3 What do you think of the survey results in the text? Are you willing to pay more to use products from socially responsible companies?

4 Complete the sentences with the words and phrases in **bold** from the text in **2**.

1 We're open to both sexes and all races. We believe in _____.
2 We protect people and nature. We are _____.
3 Our results are good, so our shares always _____.
4 People like us and respect us. We have a good _____.
5 We are careful not to spend too much. We _____ our _____.
6 We've had no accidents in two years, so we have a good

_____.

7 We always sell what we plan, so we _____ our _____.
8 We've reduced pollution by 30%. Our _____ is good.

5 Work with a partner. Which of the performance factors in **4** are important in your place of work? Why?

6 ▶ 12.1 Listen to five people talking about their employers. Which aspects of the company's performance is each person evaluating?

1 _____
2 _____
3 _____
4 _____
5 _____

7 ▶ 12.1 Listen again and complete sentences 1–5 with the adjectives from the list.

poor   excellent   satisfactory   encouraged   average   disappointing

1 It's very _____ – I really thought I had a big future here.
2 And we were _____ by the big fall in serious injuries last year.
3 We've had a really _____ year, much better than we expected.
4 It's been a very _____ performance – things can only get better!
5 I think we've had a _____ year, but our CEO says our performance has been very _____.

8 Which adjective in **7** means …?

1 good enough _____
2 not good, not bad _____
3 feeling positive for the future _____
4 not as good as we wanted _____
5 very good _____
6 bad _____

>> For more exercises, go to **Practice file 12** on page 128.

9 Choose three of the following topics and evaluate their performance last year. Then work with a partner and explain your answers.
- Your company
- Your department
- Your government
- Your country's economy
- The stock market
- A sportsperson or sports team that you like
- Another topic of your choice
  Example: My company's performance was disappointing. We didn't achieve our sales targets and we didn't manage our costs very well.

Tip | Adjectives with *-ed* and *-ing*

A thing is *disappointing* or *encouraging*, but a person is *disappointed* or *encouraged*:
The company's performance is *disappointing*.
The employees are *disappointed* by the company's performance.
The results were *encouraging*.
The CEO was *encouraged* by the results.

Language at work | Present perfect (2) – with *for* and *since*

1 ▶ **12.2** Listen to Raul and Lionel talking at a sales conference. Where do they work? When did they arrive there?

2 ▶ **12.2** Listen again. <u>Underline</u> the correct form in *italics*. Which verbs are in the past simple, and which are in the present perfect?

1 We *opened / have opened* our first sales office in 2012.
2 We *had / have had* disappointing results for the first two years.
3 Since 2014, our business *increased / has increased* by nearly 20%.
4 I *was / 've been* in Dubai for three years now.
5 My wife and children *moved / have moved* here last year.

3 Choose the correct option in *italics* to complete the explanations in the *Language point*. Then match a sentence in **2** to explanations 1–4.

> **LANGUAGE POINT**
>
> 1 We use the *past simple / present perfect* when the action starts and finishes in the past.
> *Example:* _____
> 2 We use the *past simple / present perfect* when the action starts in the past but includes the present.
> *Example:* _____
> 3 We use *for / since* with the present perfect to give the starting point of an action.
> *Example:* _____
> 4 We use *for / since* with the present perfect and past simple to describe the length of time of an action.
> *Example:* _____

>> For more information, go to **Grammar reference** on page 129.

4 Work with a partner. Make sentences in the present perfect and past simple about Lionel and Raul using the prompts in the table.
> *Example: Lionel's company has had a sales office in Dubai since 2012.*

Lionel's company	have	working in Dubai	for … years.
His business	live	in Dubai	since …
Lionel	start	a sales office in Dubai	in …
Raul	work	increasing	
Raul's family	arrive	more encouraging results	

5 Read about the history of Dubai's economy and answer the questions.
1 What is Dubai trying to do?   2 Has it been successful? How do you know?

In the 1970s	Dubai earns 64% of its GDP* from oil.
Early 1990s	The government decides to build the first non-oil economy in the Gulf. It begins to invest in services: tourism, trade, transport, finance.
1999	The government allows non-nationals to buy property for the first time.
2004	Construction starts on Burj Khalifa Tower – the world's tallest building.
2005	Mall of the Emirates shopping centre opens: 700 stores and a 22,500 m² indoor ski resort.
2006	First residents arrive on the artificial island of Palm Jumeirah.
2010	Burj Khalifa Tower opens.
2013	Dubai wins the right to hold Expo 2020 World Exhibition.
Today	Only 2% of GDP comes from oil.

*GDP (Gross Domestic Product) – the total value of all goods and services produced in a country

Tip | *How long ...?* and *When ...?*

We use *How long ...?* with the present perfect and the past simple.
We use *When ...?* with the past simple but not the present perfect.

6 Work with a partner. Use the prompts below to make questions in the past simple or present perfect. Then take turns to ask and answer the questions.
1 When / Dubai / earn / 64% / GDP / oil?
2 How long / Dubai / invest / services?
3 How long / government / allow / non-nationals / buy property?
4 When / Mall of the Emirates / open?
5 How long / Palm Jumeirah / have / residents?
6 How long / it / take / build / Burj Khalifa Tower?
7 When / Dubai / win / right to hold Expo 2020?
   Example: **A** *When did Dubai earn 64% of its GDP from oil?*
   　　　　　　B *In the early 1970s.*

>> For more exercises, go to **Practice file 12** on page 129.

7 Work with a partner. Take turns to ask and answer questions with *How long* and *When* using the ideas below. Do you have anything in common with your partner?
- Finish your studies
- Join your present company
- Be in your present job
- Work for your last company
- Live in your present home
- Have your car
- Travel abroad for the first time
- Need English for your job

Practically speaking | How to say complex numbers

1 ▶ **12.3** Work with a partner. How do you say these numbers? Listen and check your answers.
1.39%　　0.033　　102　　7,467　　906,570

2 Work with a partner. Look at the numbers in **1** and answer questions 1–4.
1 When do we use a point (.) and a comma (,)?
2 When do we say 'nought' and 'oh'?
3 When do we say 'and'?
4 How do we say numbers after the point?

3 ▶ **12.4** Listen to the stock market report and complete the table.

29th June, 5.55 p.m. GMT. World Stock Markets Summary			
Index	Value	Change	%
Nikkei	20,235.73	+ 126.57	+ _____ %
FTSE 100	6,561.21	– _____	– 0.89 %
DAX	10,968.05	– 18.95	– _____ %
Dow Jones	17,596.35	– _____	– 1.95 %
Nasdaq	_____	– 122.04	– 2.4 %

4 Work with a partner. Take turns to give all the stock market figures in **3**.
   Example: *The Nikkei was at 20,235.73. It was up by 126.57. That's 0.63%.*

Business communication | Describing trends

1 Which country in the world do you think produces (a) the most cars (b) the best cars?

2 ▶ **12.5** Listen to the presentation and label the graph with the names of the countries from the list.

Japan   USA   Germany   China

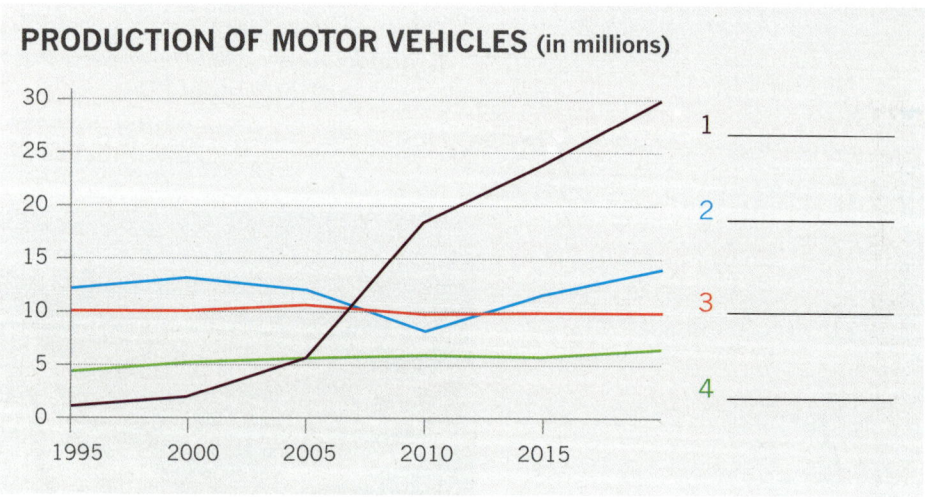

PRODUCTION OF MOTOR VEHICLES (in millions)

1 _____

2 _____

3 _____

4 _____

1995   2000   2005   2010   2015

3 ▶ **12.5** Decide if the verbs in the table describe an upward movement (↑), a downward movement (↓) or no change (↔). Then listen again and check.

	↑, ↓ or ↔		↑, ↓ or ↔
rise		grow	
decrease		fall	
remain stable		decline	
drop		increase	

4 Work with a partner. Take turns to ask and answer questions about the graph in **2**, using the verbs in **3**.

> *Example: Where did production fall at the beginning of the century? What has happened in China since 2010?*

5 What are the recent trends in the car market in your country? Think about small and big cars, electric and hybrid vehicles, petrol and diesel, etc.

6 Work with a partner. Decide which country these sentences are describing, using the graph in **2**. Then use the graph to make other sentences with *from*, *to*, *at* and *by*.

1 Production fell from 10.8 to 9.6 million between 2005 and 2010.
2 Production remained stable at about 10 million throughout the nineties.
3 Production rose by 1.2 million in the period 1995–2015.

>> For more exercises, go to **Practice file 12** on page 128.

7 Find or draw a graph describing the recent performance of your company or department, or your country (inflation, unemployment, car production, etc.). Then present it to your partner.

The performance game

1 Work in groups. You are starting a new company which manufactures plastic tables and benches from recycled plastic. Your furniture looks like wood, but is stronger and lasts longer. It's also more expensive. Your main customers will be local councils, who will buy your products for parks, schools and other public areas.

Your objective is to achieve the highest level of performance. This means excellent sales and profits, but also a good reputation for socially responsible action.

Discuss each of the questions below and agree on the best answer. Then turn to **page 139** to find out the score for each of your answers.

START HERE

Where are you going to locate your factory?
a In an old industrial town with high unemployment? **Go to 6**
b In a pleasant middle-class town with a reputation for green policies? **Go to 16**

What will your recruitment policy be?
a Equal numbers of men and women? **Go to 3**
b Just advertise and take the best? **Go to 10**

What will be your key advertising message to promote your products?
a Helps to preserve the environment? **Go to 7**
b High-quality and durable? **Go to 2**

Two people are injured when a bench collapses under them. You discover that this is due to a defect in the screws you bought from a supplier in Year 1. What will you do?
a Replace the 300 benches you sold in Year 1 with new ones? **Go to 14**
b Replace any damaged benches which are returned? **Go to 17**

Your results in Year 2 are more encouraging, but the price of recycled plastic is rising dramatically. What will you do?
a Increase the prices of your products? **Go to 8**
b Use cheaper recycled plastic from Asia? **Go to 15**

Sales have been very disappointing in Year 1, and you need to reduce your salary costs. What will you do?
a Lay off two of your five sales reps? **Go to 13**
b Ask your production workers to go part-time? **Go to 18**

In Year 3, your business has grown so quickly that your factory is now too small. What will you do?
a Extend your existing factory – this will give you 30% more capacity? **Go to 5**
b Outsource part of your production to a low-cost country? **Go to 11**

You want to promote your image to the public as a socially responsible company. What will you do?
a Include new pages on your website about your employment and environmental policies? **Go to 4**
b Visit schools in towns which have bought your products to teach children about recycling? **Go to 9**

It's Year 5, and you have two offers to buy shares in your company. Who will you sell them to?
a A company which manufactures and recycles plastic packaging? **Go to 1**
b A multinational oil company which wants to invest in eco-friendly companies? **Go to 12**

2 How did you score?

22–27 points	11–21 points	0–10 points
You have combined successful sales policies with a great sense of social responsibility. This will help you to achieve even better growth in the next few years.	You've made some good and bad decisions. To optimize your performance in the future, you should look back and learn from your mistakes.	Your sales performance has been disappointing and your public image is very poor. It's probably time to make some changes in your management team!

Focus

Preview

In this video lesson, different people talk about environmental issues at work. You will also watch an interview with Peter O'Hara, the Managing Director of the company Edible Oil Direct.

1 How environmentally-friendly is your workplace? Take this quiz to find out.

In the workplace, does your company ...?

1 use recycling bins for paper, bottles, etc.

☐ Yes   ☐ No   ☐ Don't know

2 replace old light bulbs with energy-efficient light bulbs

☐ Yes   ☐ No   ☐ Don't know

3 encourage employees to cycle to work, use public transport or car-share

☐ Yes   ☐ No   ☐ Don't know

4 check the energy rating of any new electrical equipment

☐ Yes   ☐ No   ☐ Don't know

5 buy paper and stationery made from recycled products

☐ Yes   ☐ No   ☐ Don't know

6 switch off all electrical equipment at the end of the working day

☐ Yes   ☐ No   ☐ Don't know

2 Work with a partner. Ask each other the questions from the quiz in **1**.

3 ▶01 Watch interviews with people talking about their company. How do they answer the six questions in **1**?

Edible Oil Direct

4 You are going to watch a video about Edible Oil Direct, a company which recycles cooking oil. Before you watch, match the words and phrases in **bold** in sentences 1–8 to definitions a–h.

1 Biofuel is **sustainable** for all types of applications. ___
2 That is the company **in a nutshell**. _a_
3 The company was based on a **closed loop philosophy**. ___
4 It lowers the **emissions level**, there's hardly any CO_2. ___
5 It's also a very good **lubricating factor** for engines. ___
6 It **helps the pocket** as well. ___
7 The government has allowed a **differential on duty** of 20p and therefore that 20p is passed on to the consumer. ___
8 We're able **to portray a better image** of our business. ___

a summarized in a few words
b the amount of carbon dioxide sent into the air because of a process
c use of natural products and energy that does not harm the environment
d a cycle where every part of a product is used again in different ways
e products that help machines run better (e.g. oils)
f make yourself look good to other people
g reduction in tax
h saves money

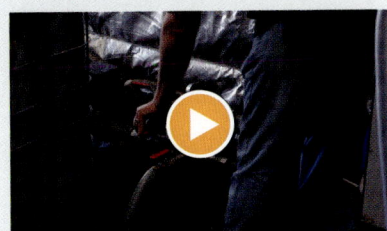

5 ▶02 Watch the video. The Managing Director, Peter O'Hara, answers six questions. Match Parts 1–6 of the video to questions a–f.

Part 1 ___   a   How do consumers benefit from using sustainable fuel?

Part 2 ___   b   Can you explain what makes Edible Oil Direct's product sustainable?

Part 3 ___   c   How do you see the future for the company?

Part 4 ___   d   What does your company do?

Part 5 ___   e   Why did you decide to set up Edible Oil Direct?

Part 6 ___   f   How has Edible Oil Direct developed since it began?

6 ▶02 Watch the video again. Then complete the summary.

Edible Oil Direct sells [1] _cooking oil_ to the food companies. Once it is used, they turn it into [2] _____. The company is based on a closed [3] _____ philosophy, meaning it has a starting point and [4] _____ point. Biodiesel is a [5] _____ fuel and has [6] _____ CO_2 emission levels. It is good for engines and it has low government tax, which means customers save [7] _____ pence per pound. Pete O'Hara started the company [8] _____ years ago, from a van. It now has a turnover of [9] £_____ and employs [10] _____ people. He thinks the future for the company looks bright and [11] _____.

Giving a short presentation

7 Work with a partner and practise a conversation between Peter O'Hara of Edible Oil Direct and the CEO of a large truck manufacturer.

Student A: You are Peter O'Hara. Prepare a short presentation for Student B. Explain:
- how your business works
- why biofuel is good for the environment
- the benefits to Student B's transportation company

Student B: You are the CEO of a truck manufacturer. Prepare some questions to ask Peter O'Hara about his company. Explain that:
- you are interested in manufacturing new trucks with biofuel engines
- you'd like to know more about biofuels and working with Edible Oil Direct

8 Make notes to prepare a short presentation about a green initiative in your company. Think about: how it works, why it is good for the environment and what benefits it provides.

9 Work with a partner. Take turns to give your presentation. Ask each other follow-up questions.

13 Future trends

Starting point

1 What global issues are most often in the news?
Example: global warming, ageing population

2 Which issues are you most worried about? Why?

Working with words | Global issues

1 Work with a partner. Discuss if you think these sentences are true or false.
  1 The amount of usable water in the world is decreasing.
  2 The world will need more and more water in the future.
  3 We consume more water than we think.
  4 Water is used to produce a lot of consumer products, such as clothing.
  5 The problem of water only exists in certain parts of the world.

2 Read the text and compare with your ideas in 1.

Crisis? What crisis?

The earth is getting hotter because of **climate change** and this is having a negative effect on water resources in many countries. At the same time, there is a **rising demand** for water, which comes from **population growth** and the **economic development** of countries like China and India. In years to come, it is likely that the world's **water supply** will no longer be able to meet the demand.

In countries with lots of water, it's easy to think that the **water shortage** isn't a problem. In the UK, for example, the price of water is quite low and the average person consumes 145 litres per day, considerably less than in many developed countries. However, large quantities of water are used to make the products we consume: 15,500 litres for a kilo of beef, 2,700 litres for a cotton T-shirt. If you include all this 'virtual water', the average

> In years to come, it is likely that the world's water supply will no longer be able to meet the demand.

daily consumption in the UK is around 4,500 litres per person, of which 3,000 litres are imported, according to the environmental charity WWF (World Wide Fund for Nature).

A recent study describes the water situation in the world as a **serious threat** to economic growth and our food supply. If we don't stop thinking about water as somebody else's problem, this situation could soon turn into a **global crisis**.

3 How do you think the water situation could have an effect on economic growth? What can we do to reduce water consumption?

4 Match the phrases in **bold** in the text in **2** to definitions 1–8.

1 A possible dangerous situation _____

2 An increase in the need for something _____

3 An improvement in the financial situation of a country _____

4 A very difficult situation in the world _____

5 An increase in the number of people _____

6 A situation where there is not enough water _____

7 Increases in temperature and their effects _____

8 The amount of water available in the world _____

5 Work with a partner. Discuss issues relating to the world's natural resources (e.g. oil, gas, coal) using words from **4**.

Example: *There is a rising demand for oil from countries like China.*

6 ▶ **13.1** Listen to a radio show about the future of oil and say what these numbers refer to.

5% 400% 60% 20 2.5% 200

7 ▶ **13.1** Listen again and complete sentences 1–6.

1 How will this growth _____ oil prices?

2 One report _____ that a 5% shortage could lead to a big price rise.

3 This crisis would really _____ the automobile industry.

4 Some analysts have _____ that the car will become a luxury item.

5 So you don't think the oil situation will _____ _____?

6 We're not going to _____ _____ _____ gas because we have enough reserves.

8 Work with a partner. Replace the words in *italics* with a verb or phrase from **7**.

1 Climate change *has an impact on* people in poor countries more than in the developed world.

2 We'll *have no more* natural resources if we don't stop buying things we don't need.

3 The standard of living of people in rich countries will continue to *go down* in the years to come.

4 We *predict* that air pollution will be the biggest risk to people's health in the future.

5 Social media and the Internet *are dangerous for* our private lives.

6 A recent study *calculates* that by 2050, 2.5 billion more people will live in cities and this could create many social and environmental problems.

≫ For more exercises, go to **Practice file 13** on page 130.

9 Work with a partner. Look at the sentences in **8** and answer questions 1–3.

1 Do you agree or disagree with the opinions and predictions? Why?

2 How can we resolve the different issues?

3 What action would you like to see from governments?

Tip | *get + adjective*

When used with an adjective, *get* means *become*. We often use it with the comparative form of the adjective:
The situation will **get worse***; it won't* **get better***.*
The population is **getting older***.*

Language at work | Future predictions

1 Work with a partner. Discuss what trends you think there will be in the workplace in the future. Then read the text and compare your answers.

ADAPTING TO FUTURE TRENDS IN THE WORKPLACE

Companies who adapt to changing trends in the workplace are more likely to survive than those who resist change. So what trends should companies be looking at and how can they adapt?

BUSINESS PRESSURES

Competition between businesses will be much stronger in the future and the winners will be the first to get their products on to the market. Managers may need to restructure their companies.

AGE OF EMPLOYEES

In the future, employees might not retire before the age of 75 because of a possible pensions crisis. Employers will have to adapt the workplace to meet the needs of an older workforce.

WORK–LIFE BALANCE

Male and female employees will want to spend more time with their families. This will affect working hours, and managers will have to be more flexible in order to keep their staff.

TECHNOLOGICAL CHANGES

Advances in technology will mean that employees won't need their own desk anymore. In the future, employers will redesign work areas to have more space for meetings, and also for leisure activities.

2 Choose the correct answer from the words in *italics*. Then read the text again and check your answers.
1 Managers *may / may not* need to restructure their companies.
2 In the future, employees *might / might not* retire before the age of 75.
3 Employees *will / won't* want to spend more time with their families.
4 Employees *will / won't* need their own desk any more.

3 Complete the explanations in the *Language point* about making future predictions. Then match the sentences in **2** to explanations 1–4.

LANGUAGE POINT

1 We use _____ + infinitive when we are sure something will happen.
   Example: _____
2 We use _____ or _____ + infinitive when we think that perhaps something will happen.
   Example: _____
3 We use _____ or _____ + infinitive when we think that perhaps something will not happen.
   Example: _____
4 We use _____ + infinitive when we are sure something will not happen.
   Example: _____

» For more information, go to **Grammar reference** on page 131.

Tip | Short forms of *will*
The short form of *will* is *'ll* and the short form of *will not* is *won't*. We usually use short forms in spoken English and informal writing:
I'm sure I'll enjoy working from home.
We won't have enough time to finish the report.

4 Work with a partner. Use the information to make predictions about the typical workplace in 2030, using *will, won't, may* (*not*) or *might* (*not*).

In 2030	will	may/ might	may/ might not	won't
Many jobs / be part-time				
Management positions / be easy to find				
More people / work from home				
Colleagues / see each other less often				
Office buildings / be used in the same way				
Employees / stay long with the same company				
Employers / offer better working conditions				
Companies / provide leisure facilities				
Many employees / decide to take career breaks				

5 ▶ **13.2** Listen to a talk on the same subject and tick (✓) the correct column in the table in **4**. Are the speaker's predictions the same as yours?

>> For more exercises, go to **Practice file 13** on page 131.

6 Work with a partner. Make predictions about your own jobs using the ideas below. Which of your ideas were similar?
- hours
- office
- salary
- pensions
- technology
- training
- benefits

Practically speaking | How to link ideas

1 Match 1–3 to a–c to make complete sentences.
1 More women will work *and* ___
2 Companies will still have offices *but* ___
3 More people will work from home *so* ___

a they will be smaller than today.
b colleagues may see each other less often.
c their numbers may exceed working men.

2 Which words in *italics* in **1** are used to …?
1 show a result _____
2 add more information _____
3 show a contrast _____

3 Read these sentences and add the linking words in *italics* to the categories in **2**.
1 *In addition*, working arrangements will be more flexible.
2 More employees will work together in self-managed teams. *Therefore*, management positions might not be easy to find.
3 Many employees may decide to take career breaks. *However*, they will be allowed to rejoin the company with the same job and salary as before.

4 Work with a partner. Use your own ideas to finish these predictions using the linkers from **2**.
- People will work fewer hours …
- Computers will be faster …
- Employees will travel less for work …
- Companies will offer more leisure facilities …

Business communication | Predicting and forecasting

1 Work with a partner. What is teleworking? What are the advantages and disadvantages of working from home for (a) the employee (b) the company?

2 ▶ 13.3 Listen to three people asking their manager about the company's new teleworking scheme. Compare your ideas from **1** with the manager's opinions.

3 ▶ 13.3 Listen again and complete sentences 1–8.
1 Just how much _____ we _____ to save?
2 We _____ the new scheme _____ save the company at least €20,000.
3 The office is _____ to close completely.
4 Do you _____ people _____ be happy to work alone?
5 Our employees _____ _____ feel more motivated.
6 It _____ _____ be easy for some people to start with.
7 Do you _____ to see an increase in productivity?
8 _____, our teleworkers _____ have similar results.

4 Work with a partner. Say each sentence in a different way, using the word in brackets.
1 Do you think you'll be more productive? (expect)
2 I'm sure we'll save money. (definitely)
3 I hope I won't work in the evenings. (Hopefully)
4 You'll probably find it difficult at first. (likely)
5 I'm unlikely to work from home. (probably)
   Example: Do you expect to be more productive?

5 Work with a partner. You have both agreed to try working from home. Take turns to ask for and make predictions. Use these ideas to help you.
• Get bored   • Have more free time
• Miss your colleagues   • Save money
• Get up earlier   • Enjoy working at home
• Work longer hours   • Go out more
   Example: Are you likely to get bored?

>> For more exercises go to **Practice file 13** on page 130.

6 Work with a partner. Your head office wants to stop all business trips and use video-conferencing instead. Have a meeting to predict the effects of this measure on your company, using the ideas below.
• Reduce costs
• Buy new equipment
• Where to put equipment
• Special training
• Technical problems
• Clients have video equipment
• Clients like idea

Key expressions

Asking for predictions
Is ... likely to ...?
Are ... likely to ...?
Do you think ... will ...?
Do you expect ...?

Making predictions
... will probably/definitely ...
... probably/definitely won't ...
... is likely/unlikely to ...

Expressing hope
I hope ... will/won't ...
Hopefully, ... will/won't ...

Cause marketing

As we learn about global issues that affect us and other people in the world, many of us want to make a difference. Cause marketing is a cooperative effort between for-profit companies and non-profit organizations to increase awareness of these issues and give consumers the opportunity to help. In the USA, around one in two consumers buys at least one product every month that supports a cause.

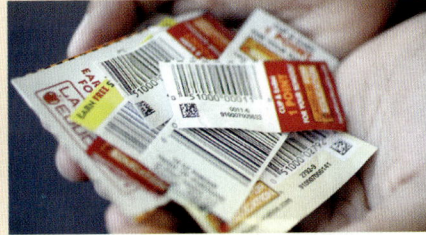

ONE FOR ONE

California company TOMS is best known for its 'one for one' slogan: when you buy a pair of TOMS shoes, the company donates another pair to a child in need. For a pair of glasses, part of the profit is used to save the eyesight of a person in a developing country. For a packet of TOMS coffee, one week of safe water will be provided to a person in the country the coffee beans come from.

CAMPAIGN FOR REAL BEAUTY

The Unilever company, producer of Dove beauty products and toiletries, uses advertising campaigns to challenge the stereotype of feminine beauty and to encourage public discussion on the subject through multimedia and various non-profit associations. The initiative started in 2004 after a study showed that only 2% of women in the world consider themselves beautiful.

BOX TOPS FOR EDUCATION

Started in 1992 by two sales executives at General Mills, the multinational food company, Box Tops for Education invites consumers to cut the tops from hundreds of different consumer products, and send them to a US school of their choice. Each box top has a value of 10 cents, and the school can use the money collected to buy whatever it needs. So far, US schools have earned over $600 million from the initiative.

Discussion

1 What are the benefits of cause marketing for (a) for-profit companies and (b) non-profit organizations?

2 Why do you think TOMS, Unilever and General Mills chose these particular causes?

3 How are the three examples similar, and how are they different?

4 Which of the three campaigns do you like best? Why?

Task

1 Work with a partner or in small groups. Plan a cause marketing campaign for your company. Think about these ideas.

• What cause do you want to promote? Why?

• How will this cause benefit your company?

• How will you use your company to promote it?

• What kind of non-profit organizations will you work with?

• What results do you want to achieve at the end of your campaign?

• What name will you give to the campaign?

2 Present your ideas from 1 to the class. Then discuss which of the campaigns are more/less likely to be successful. Why?

14 Time

Starting point

1 'There is never enough time in the day.' Do you agree with this?

2 Are these sentences always, sometimes or never true for you?
- I organize my working time well.
- I have a lot of interruptions at work.
- When I have important work to do, I finish it on time.

3 How do you feel about people who are always late or early?

Working with words | Managing time

1 Answer questions 1–3. Then discuss your answers with a partner.
1 What percentage of workers read email while speaking on the phone?
  a A third   b More than half   c More than three quarters
2 If you do two or more tasks at the same time, do you work more quickly?
  a Yes   b No   c Sometimes
3 What's the worst thing about people who multitask?
  a They don't really listen   b They make mistakes   c They think they're the best

2 Read the text and compare with your answers from 1.

Multitasking: time-saver or time-waster?

On the other end of the phone, you hear the sound of fingers on a keyboard. During a Monday morning department meeting, a colleague has their head down, **planning their schedule** for the week. At home, your husband or wife is answering emails while helping the children with their homework.

We have all learnt to multitask because we feel we don't **have enough time** to get everything done. According to a study by the Families and Work Institute, 45% of workers feel they are asked to work on too many tasks at once. Another survey by ComPsych, a provider of employee assistance programmes, reports that 54% of workers **spend time** reading email while on the phone and 11% make to-do lists during meetings.

We all have to **meet deadlines**, but is multitasking really the solution for finishing everything **on time**? Not really, if you believe the scientists. We think we **save time** by doing two tasks at once, but studies show that the brain is less efficient when performing similar tasks, such as reading and listening. And each time we switch to another task, we have to **allow time** for our brains to adapt to the new situation.

Perhaps the worst thing about people who multitask is the feeling that they are only giving you half an ear. So next time you ask a caller to repeat something because you are reading your emails and not listening to him or her, just remember one thing: you're **wasting time**, both yours and the caller's.

3 Discuss with a partner. Do you multitask like any of the people described in the text?

4 Choose the correct answer from the words in *italics*, using the words and phrases in **bold** in the text in **2** to help you.
1 If you *waste / spend* time doing something, you don't use your time well.
2 If you *plan your schedule / meet deadlines*, you'll know what work you have to do.
3 When preparing a presentation, you should *allow / save* time to practise it.
4 If there's *on / enough* time to do everything, you'll meet your *deadlines / task*.

5 Work with a partner. Make similar sentences with the phrases from the list.
meet deadlines   on time   save time   spend time

6 Work with a partner. Discuss what problems you have with time management. Use the ideas below to help you.
a Phone interruptions
b Administrative tasks
c Meetings
d Difficult deadlines

7 ▶ **14.1** Listen and match the four speakers to situations a–d in **6**.
Speaker 1 ___
Speaker 2 ___
Speaker 3 ___
Speaker 4 ___

8 ▶ **14.1** Listen again and complete sentences 1–8.
1 There's always one person who arrives _____.
2 To _____ time, we've tried introducing a one-hour limit.
3 We always _____ _____ of time.
4 I know reports _____ a long time to do, but I never _____ time for them.
5 I always leave paperwork until the _____ minute.
6 We even thought we could deliver _____ of time.
7 It was really difficult to get the job done _____ time.
8 I _____ so much time answering calls. It really _____ you down.

9 Work with a partner. Find phrases in **4** and **8** that indicate good or bad time management and complete the table.

Good	Bad
meet deadlines	arrive late

>> For more exercises, go to **Practice file 14** on page 132.

10 Work with a partner. Discuss how you could manage your time more effectively. Think about these points.
• Your own use of time (planning, time-saving activities, leaving certain tasks until later, etc.)
• Other people's use of your time (is there anything you can do about interruptions like phone calls, meetings, etc.?)

Tip | *on time* and *in time*

On time means 'exactly at the right time'. *In time* means 'before it's too late':
Our meeting was from 11–12, and we finished on time at midday.
We delivered the product in time, two days before the deadline.

Language at work | Second conditional

1 Work with a partner. Discuss the questions.
  1 Have you ever worked abroad?
   • Where did you work?
   • Did you enjoy it?
   • How long did you stay?
  2 If you haven't worked abroad:
   • Would you like to? Why/Why not?

2 ▶ 14.2 Silvia has just returned to Argentina after three months working on a project in New York. Listen and answer the questions.
  1 Did she enjoy her time in the USA?
  2 Would she like to work there?

3 ▶ 14.2 Listen again and <u>underline</u> the words in *italics* you hear.
  1 *I'll / I'd* go crazy if I *lived / live* in the USA.
  2 What *would / will* you do if they *offer / offered* you a job there?
  3 If it *is / was* only for a year or two, I *would / might* say yes.
  4 If they *want / wanted* me for longer, I *wouldn't / won't* accept it.

4 Look at the second conditional sentences in **3** and choose the correct words in *italics* to complete the explanations in the *Language point*.

> **LANGUAGE POINT**
>
> 1 We use the second conditional to talk about *real / imaginary* events in the *past / future*.
> 2 We form the second conditional with *If* + *present / past* tense, *would* (or *might*) + *past tense / infinitive*.
> 3 You *can / can't* put the *if* structure in the second part of the sentence.

>> For more information, go to **Grammar reference** on page 133.

5 Complete questions 1–6 in the second conditional with the correct form of the verbs in brackets.
  1 If you _____ (have) the chance to work in another country, which country _____ (you / choose)?
  2 What _____ (you / say) if your boss _____ (ask) you to work longer hours?
  3 If you _____ (can) study full-time for a year, what subject _____ (interest) you most?
  4 If there _____ (be) an extra hour in your working day, how _____ (you / spend) it?
  5 _____ (you / be) happier if mobile phones _____ (not / exist)?
  6 If you _____ (not / have) deadlines to meet, _____ (you / be) more or less efficient?

6 Work with a partner. Ask and answer the questions in **5**.
  Example: A If you had the chance to work in another country, which country would you choose?
  B I don't know, but I might choose China. What about you?
  A I think I'd go to Vietnam.

>> For more exercises, go to **Practice file 14** on page 133.

Tip | *might* and *could*

In second conditional sentences, we can use *might* to mean 'would perhaps' or *could* to mean 'would be able to':
*If they offered me the same salary, I **might** accept it.*
*If they increased the travel budget, we **could** go to the conference.*

7 Read the text. Then answer the questions with a partner.
1 Do you think people in your country live on 'event time' or 'clock time'?
2 Would you like to live in a country with a different time culture to yours? Why?

Different ideas of time

The social psychologist Robert Levine says that certain cultures live on 'event time', where events determine people's schedules, and others on 'clock time', where people's schedules determine events. People who live on 'clock time' are more punctual, and their countries tend to be more successful economically – but perhaps less fun at night!

8 Work with a partner. Do you live on 'event time' or 'clock time'? **Student A**, turn to **page 139**. **Student B**, turn to **page 142**.

Practically speaking | How to use time expressions

1 ▶ 14.3 Listen to two conversations about deadlines. In each conversation, what work do they have to do?

2 ▶ 14.3 Listen again and match 1–7 to a–g.

1 by ___	a away
2 within ___	b as possible
3 before ___	c have time
4 as soon ___	d Monday
5 right ___	e the end of next week
6 on ___	f a week
7 when you ___	g Friday

3 Which two phrases in **2** do not give a specific deadline? Today is Wednesday. Put the other phrases in the right order, from the most to the least urgent.

4 Work with a partner. Take turns to ask for the things in 1–6, using the words in brackets. Student B responds using a different time expression.
> *Example: A Can you give me an answer within two days?*
> *B Sorry, that's difficult, but I'll do it as soon as possible.*
1 Today is 13th April. You want an answer by 15th April. (within)
2 It's 9 a.m. You want to receive the report before 6 p.m. (end)
3 It's Tuesday. You want confirmation of the meeting before the weekend. (by)
4 It's 3rd December. You want the budget figures within four weeks. (before)
5 It's Friday. You want to see the new product now! (right)
6 Today is Tuesday. You want to have a meeting the day after tomorrow. (on)

Business communication | Negotiating conditions

1 What kind of problems can companies have with suppliers?

2 ▶ 14.4 Hans-Peter Berg receives a phone call from one of his foreign suppliers, Luca Peretti. Listen and complete the information.
Problem: _____
First solution: _____
Disadvantage of first solution: _____
Second solution: _____
Who will pay? _____

3 ▶ 14.4 Match 1–10 to a–j to make complete sentences. Then listen again and check.

1	We have an issue ___		a	be possible.
2	Basically, ___		b	pay the extra cost?
3	Would it be OK ___		c	with delivery.
4	Yes, that might ___		d	we've got a lorry drivers' strike.
5	What if ___		e	get the parts to the factory in time.
6	Could you ___		f	be acceptable.
7	I think we ___		g	we transported them by train to the border?
8	That would allow us to ___		h	send a lorry to pick them up?
9	Would you agree to ___		i	if we sent them by train?
10	Sorry, that wouldn't ___		j	could do that.

4 Which phrases in **3** are used to …?
1 introduce the problem ___ ___
2 propose solutions ___ ___
3 describe the advantages of a solution ___
4 ask if someone can do something for you ___ ___
5 agree to a solution ___ ___
6 reject a solution ___

5 Work with a partner. **Student A** is a supplier of computer processors. **Student B** is a computer manufacturer. Have a phone conversation, using the notes below.

> **A** Describe problem: processor ordered (Version 2.1) not in stock. Propose solution: send Version 2.2. Describe advantage: Version 2.2 is 50% faster.

> **B** Accept solution. Ask if A can send it by end of this week.

> **A** Reject proposal. Give reason: final tests on Version 2.2. No stock until next week.

> **B** Propose solution: delivery by Friday of next week if same price as Version 2.1 (€30).

> **A** Reject proposal. Propose unit price of €40 for Version 2.2 (normally €50).

> **B** Accept or reject proposal.

» For more exercises, go to **Practice file 14** on page 132.

6 Work with a partner. Have a phone conversation to negotiate new conditions for an order which has been placed. **Student A**, turn to **page 140**. **Student B**, turn to **page 143**.

Key expressions

Describing the problem
There's a problem with …
We have an issue with …
Basically, …
I can't guarantee …

Negotiating conditions
What if we did X?
Would you agree to do Y?
Could you do Y?
Would it be OK if …?

Responding
Yes, that would be possible.
I think we could do that.
Sorry, that wouldn't be acceptable.

Describing advantages
That would allow us/you to …

What happened to our free time?

Work-life balance *in the* USA

61% Number of employees who are willing **to work** during **their holidays**

Over 50% of employees say that each year is busier than the previous year. They **sacrifice family and friends** for success

16% of employees and **60%** of HR Directors **feel satisfied** with the **work-life benefits** their company provides

20% Number of Americans who have **regular sit-down meals** with their families compared to 20 years ago which was **60%**

Discussion

1 What do the statistics tell you about working life in America?

2 How is the situation similar or different in your country? What do you think the statistics would be?

3 Are our lives today really busier than before? If so, what are the reasons?

Task

1 Work with a partner or in small groups. You want to improve the work–life balance for employees in your place of work. Look at the list of suggestions below and answer the questions.

1 Which ideas would have the most positive effect on work–life balance?

2 How would they work in practice? (What specific measures, rules or activities would you introduce?)

You can also add any other ideas of your own.

- Introduce more flexible hours
- Encourage part-time work and job-sharing
- Close the offices earlier in the evening
- Restrict access to work documents and email outside the company
- Limit the hours of work phone calls
- Organize more social activities for employees and their families
- Allow extra days off for family or personal projects
- Offer 'activity weeks' for employees' children during school holidays
- Allow time in the day for personal Internet use (shopping, social media, etc.)

2 Present your favourite ideas to the class and explain your reasons for choosing them.

15 Training

Starting point

1 What skills do you need for your present job? Did your company offer you any special training?

2 What new skills would you like to learn for your professional and/or personal development?

Working with words | Personal development and training

1 What does a sports coach do? What about a business coach?

2 Read the text and compare with your answers from **1**.

THE BENEFITS OF BUSINESS COACHING

In recent years, business coaching has grown dramatically. Since 1999, the number of business coaches has risen from 2,000 to around 50,000 worldwide. The results are so impressive that some companies hire coaches for all their managers to **improve** their **performance**.

What do business coaches do? Basically, they let you talk about the problems you are having in your professional life and help you **set** new **goals**. They then meet or speak with you regularly to see if you are making progress to **achieve** your **objectives**. For example, they can find ways for you to get better sales results, to **motivate** your team to work better or to **improve** your promotion prospects in your company. Coaches do not actually make decisions for you, but use their own experience to **give** you **feedback** on your ideas. They can also help you identify what training you might need to **develop** your **skills**. Coaching can be an ideal opportunity to **take a step back** and evaluate your lifestyle. The result is often a better work–life balance.

Coaching is not cheap, but in a recent study 99% of companies or individuals said they were satisfied with the coaching experience, and a fifth of companies estimated that the value to them was fifty times the money they had spent on the training.

3 Work with a partner and discuss the following questions.
  1 Would you like to have a business coach? If you've already used one, how did it help you?
  2 Why do you think business coaching has become so popular? What does it give you that other forms of training do not?

4 Match the words and phrases in **bold** in the text in **2** to definitions 1–8.
1 Think about your life in a calm way _____
2 Give somebody the desire to do something _____
3 Learn how to do things better _____
4 Do your job better in general _____
5 Decide what direction you want to take in your life _____
6 Obtain the specific results that you want _____
7 Increase the possibilities of a better job in your company
_____
8 Tell someone what you think of their performance _____

5 Complete sentences 1–7 with words and phrases from **4**. Then take turns to ask and answer the questions with a partner.
1 What things _____ you to do your job well?
2 When was your last annual appraisal? Did you _____ any _____ for this year? What are you doing to try and _____ them?
3 How often does your boss _____ you _____ on your performance?
4 Do you think training is the best way to _____ your _____ _____? What other ways are there to move up in the company?
5 When is the best time to _____ a _____ _____ from your job?
6 What new _____ would you like to _____ in your personal or professional life?
7 Have you done any training courses recently to _____ your _____ at work? How have these courses helped you?

6 Match a company training course from the list to 1–5 below.
Project management   Managing stress   Motivating employees
Communication skills   Time management

Personal development at work
Five training courses to help you achieve your personal and professional goals

1 _____ Take a step back and achieve a better work–life balance.
2 _____ Be a better listener and express yourself more clearly.
3 _____ Learn to speed read and deal with emails more quickly.
4 _____ Set your team clear goals and give them better feedback.
5 _____ Improve your organizational skills and meet your deadlines every time.

>> For more exercises, go to **Practice file 15** on page 134.

7 ▶ **15.1** Listen to Scott Wesley, a sales director, speaking with different colleagues. Match extracts 1–3 to situations a–c.
a At the coffee machine ___
b At an annual appraisal ___
c At a meeting ___

8 ▶ **15.1** Work with a partner. Listen again and answer the questions.
1 Why aren't Scott's colleagues happy with what he says?
2 What courses in **6** would you recommend for him?

9 Work with a partner. Look again at the list of courses in **6** and answer the questions.
1 Have you been on any similar courses recently? What did you think of the training?
2 What other courses in the list would you like to do, and why?

Language at work | Modal verbs (2) – giving advice

1 Work with a partner. Read the advice on how to conduct an appraisal with an employee. Ignore the gaps in the sentences for now. Do you agree or disagree with the different points?

ANNUAL APPRAISALS

Advice for managers

1 You _____ use your own office.

2 You _____ do most of the talking.

3 You _____ start with one or two questions about the employee's personal life.

4 You _____ give positive feedback first.

5 You _____ discuss if the employee achieved last year's objectives.

6 You _____ offer constructive help when the goals haven't been achieved.

---

2 ▶ 15.2 Listen to a human resources manager giving a presentation on appraisals and compare the speaker's advice with your opinions in **1**.

3 ▶ 15.2 Listen again. Complete the advice in **1** with the modal verbs from the list.
must   mustn't   should   shouldn't   could

4 Complete the sentences in the *Language point* with the modal verbs in **3**.

LANGUAGE POINT

1 If it's really important to do something, you _____ do it.
2 If it's a good idea to do it, you _____ do it.
3 If it's possible, you _____ do it.
4 If it's not a good idea, you _____ do it.
5 If it's a very bad idea, you _____ do it.

>> For more information, go to **Grammar reference** on page 135.

5 Look at the advice for improving your promotion prospects. Are the points …?
a really important   c possible   e a very bad idea
b a good idea   d not a good idea

1 Leave work later than your colleagues ___
2 Apply for every management position advertised in the company ___
3 Express your opinion more often in meetings ___
4 Get to know your boss personally ___
5 Tell your boss you are thinking of leaving ___
6 Help work colleagues with their problems as much as possible ___
7 Ask for training courses at least once a year ___
8 Always send copies of your work to your boss ___
9 Speak to people in higher positions about the skills needed to do their job ___

6 Work with a partner. Discuss your answers to **5**, using modal verbs from **3**.
Example: You shouldn't work longer hours than your colleagues because …

Tip | *have to* and *must*

Have to describes things that our employers, the government, etc., ask us to do:
I **have to** work 39 hours a week.
We **have to** pay tax three times a year.

Must describes things that are urgent or personally important to us:
You **must** pay your tax bill this week.
I **must** try to work harder.

7 Work with a partner. Read about the problems Marek and Klaudia have at work and decide what advice you would give them.

MAREK KAMINSKI: 45-year-old Project Manager for a software company. Works 60–70 hours a week and is very stressed. Has too many projects to manage at the same time, all with difficult deadlines. His team refuse to work extra hours and his boss refuses to recruit another team member. His wife complains that she and the children never see him.

KLAUDIA WOJCIK: 28-year-old Sales Rep for an insurance company. In the job for five years. Excellent sales results. CEO promised her quick promotion when she arrived, but her boss says she's too young to be a manager. Applied three months ago for the position of Sales Manager, but didn't get the job. Her boss was on the interview panel, but the CEO wasn't.

8 ▶ **15.3** Listen to two experts talking about the problems in **7** and compare their ideas with yours.

≫ For more exercises, go to **Practice file 15** on page 135.

9 Work with a partner. Choose two of the subjects and discuss what advice you would give.
- How to get the most from your annual appraisal
- How to write a good CV
- When and how to say 'no' at work
- How to use your time when you're not very busy at work
- How to develop your skills

Practically speaking | How to give positive feedback

1 What positive things could you say to the different people in these situations?
a You want to thank the speaker for a very interesting talk ___
b Somebody has written a report for you but it still needs some work ___
c Somebody has done some very good work for you ___

2 ▶ **15.4** Listen and match Conversations 1–3 to situations a–c in **1**.

3 ▶ **15.4** Listen again and complete the feedback in A and the responses in B. Then repeat the conversations with a partner.

A	B
I really _____ your talk. It was very _____.	Thanks for the feedback. I'm glad you _____ it.
You did a really good _____. Well _____!	That's good to _____.
I can see you worked really _____ on this. You're on the right _____. It _____ needs a few changes.	Not so _____, then. What do you think needs to be changed?

4 Work with a partner. Give and respond to feedback in these situations.
1 You're the Sales Manager. A new customer has just called you to place a big order following a visit from one of your sales reps. Tell your sales rep.
2 A colleague has just practised his/her presentation in front of you and wants feedback. You think it was much too long and that he/she used too many slides.
3 You've had your first annual appraisal. Your boss wants feedback on what you thought of it.
4 Someone in IT has shown you a new application and wants some feedback. It's not very user-friendly.

Business communication | Making and responding to suggestions

1 Which of these ideas motivate you most to do your job well? What other things motivate you?

a Getting positive feedback for work you have done ___

b Having new challenges ___

c Understanding how your job helps the company to achieve its objectives ___

2 ▶ 15.5 A quality manager is talking with a business coach about a problem of motivation in his team. Listen and number points a–c in **1** in the order they are mentioned.

3 ▶ 15.5 Listen again and match suggestions 1–6 with responses a–f.

1 Why don't we start with motivation? ___   a Well, I'm not sure about that.

2 You could explain the value of their work. ___   b Yes. Let's do that.

3 You should always give feedback. ___   c Good idea.

4 I suggest you send each person an email. ___   d Yes, that might work.

5 What about introducing a team project? ___   e I don't think that would work.

6 Shall we talk about how to put them into practice? ___   f Yes, that's not a bad idea.

4 Which of the responses in **3** are …?

- very positive
- quite positive
- a little negative
- very negative

5 Work with a partner. Look at situations 1–6 and take turns to make a suggestion and respond, using the ideas in the table.

Example: ***A*** *Why don't we pay the team overtime when they have to work late?*
          B *I'm not sure about that. It'll be expensive. But we could …*

Situation	Suggestion
Your team refuse to work late during busy times.	Pay them overtime.
Important information isn't always shared.	Introduce a weekly meeting.
Your boss never shows appreciation of your work.	Look for another job.
Meetings in your department are always too long.	Set a time limit for meetings.
Employees are nervous about the annual appraisal.	Do mini-appraisals every month.
Your boss says you must take your work mobile phone with you on holiday.	Refuse.

>> For more exercises, go to **Practice file 15** on page 134.

6 Work with a partner. Each of you is going to suggest four ideas for improving motivation in your company. Respond to each suggestion, and decide on the three best ideas.

Student A, turn to **page 140**.
Student B, turn to **page 143**.

Key expressions

Making suggestions

Why don't we/you (+ verb) …?
Maybe we/you should (+ verb) …
We/You could (+ verb) …
How/What about (+ -ing) …?
Shall we (+ verb) …?
I suggest we/you (+ verb) …
One possibility would be to (+ verb) …

Accepting suggestions

That's not a bad idea.
That might work.
Good idea.
That's a great idea.
Yes/OK. Let's do that.

Rejecting suggestions

I'm not sure about that.
I don't think that will work.
That's out of the question.

TALKING POINT

Ambition!

1 Work with a partner. The object of the game is to be the first to reach the final square and get a promotion.

2 Start on the FIRST DAY square. Take turns to toss a coin. Heads, move one square. Tails, move two squares. Follow the instructions written on the square.

3 Each square refers you to the section of the Student's Book where you will find the language you need, if necessary.

Say how you think your company's market will be different 20 years from now. **20** (Unit 13 Business communication)	Your boss says you need to manage your time better. Suggest ways of doing this, then **MISS A TURN 21** (Unit 14 Working with words)	You'd like to work at home on certain days to improve your productivity. Negotiate the conditions with your boss. **22** (Unit 14 Business communication)	Suggest to your boss ways for your company to improve the quality of its products or services. **23** (Unit 15 Business communication)	**WELL DONE! YOU'VE GOT YOUR PROMOTION. 24**
Talk about your company's recent performance and trends in the market. **19** (Unit 12 Business communication)	You meet someone at a conference. Ask four questions beginning with 'How long …?' **18** (Unit 12 Language at work)	A colleague from a sister company is staying for the weekend. Invite him/her to do three things in your town. **17** (Unit 11 Business communication)	Describe five things your company does or could do to protect the environment. **16** (Unit 10 Working with words)	Tell a new colleague about the rules and regulations for employees in your company. **15** (Unit 9 Language at work)
A customer calls to complain about a mistake you made. Deal with the complaint, then **MISS A TURN 10** (Unit 5 Business communication)	Talk about the disadvantages of air travel or describe a bad flying experience you have had. **11** (Unit 7 Working with words)	Arrange to meet a customer for dinner one evening next week. **12** (Unit 7 Business communication)	Phone a supplier of printer paper to enquire about prices and delivery, and place an order. **13** (Unit 8 Working with words)	A friend is opening a new restaurant. Give him/her ideas for advertising his/her business. **14** (Unit 9 Working with words)
Tell a customer why your company is better than your competitors. **9** (Unit 6 Language at work)	Talk about the advantages and disadvantages of looking for a job online. **8** (Unit 6 Business communication)	You have a visitor today. Welcome him/her in reception. **7** (Unit 4 Business communication)	You are visiting another company. Ask your host five questions about his/her department. **6** (Unit 4 Language at work)	Recommend a product you like to a colleague and say why it's good. **5** (Unit 3 Working with words)
IT'S THE FIRST DAY OF YOUR NEW JOB!	Introduce yourself to a partner and tell them something about yourself. **1** (Unit 1 Business communication)	Tell a friend about your company's present projects. **2** (Unit 2 Language at work)	Call a client to confirm a delivery. He/She isn't in their office. **3** (Unit 2 Business communication)	Tell a colleague about your education and previous jobs. **4** (Unit 3 Language at work)

Focus

1 Match the types of companies 1–4 to definitions a–d.
   1 A sole trader
   2 A partnership
   3 A private limited company
   4 A public company

   a Two or more people own the business
   b A very large company with shares on the stock market
   c One person owns the business
   d Often a small business such as a shop with shares (but not on the stock market)

2 Work with a partner. Think of an example of each type of company.
   Example: Apple is a public company on the stock market.

3 ▶01 Watch three people talking about the types of company they work in. Make notes about their answers in the table.

	Speaker 1	Speaker 2	Speaker 3
Type of company			
Advantages			
Disadvantages			

4 What type of company do you work for? Which advantages or disadvantages in 3 are true for your company? Why?

The John Lewis Partnership

5 You are going to watch a video of an interview with Colin Goepfert from the John Lewis Partnership. Before you watch, match the words and phrases in bold in sentences 1–7 to definitions a–g.
   1 They are all partners in the **true sense** of the word. _____
   2 Whether you're **a Saturday-only partner** or the Chairman, you would all receive the same per cent. _____
   3 The turnover **feeds directly** into the bonus. _____
   4 We also look at feedback from **external bodies**. _____
   5 The market rate is **the going rate** for a particular job. _____
   6 We're trying to find new ways of making the life of a partner **fuller**. _____
   7 We hopefully have a pack that's **second to none**. _____

   a more complete
   b better than any other
   c has an instant effect
   d real meaning
   e someone who only works on one day
   f independent organizations
   g the current or typical amount

6 ▶02 Watch the interview and number slides A–D in the order you see them.

A ___

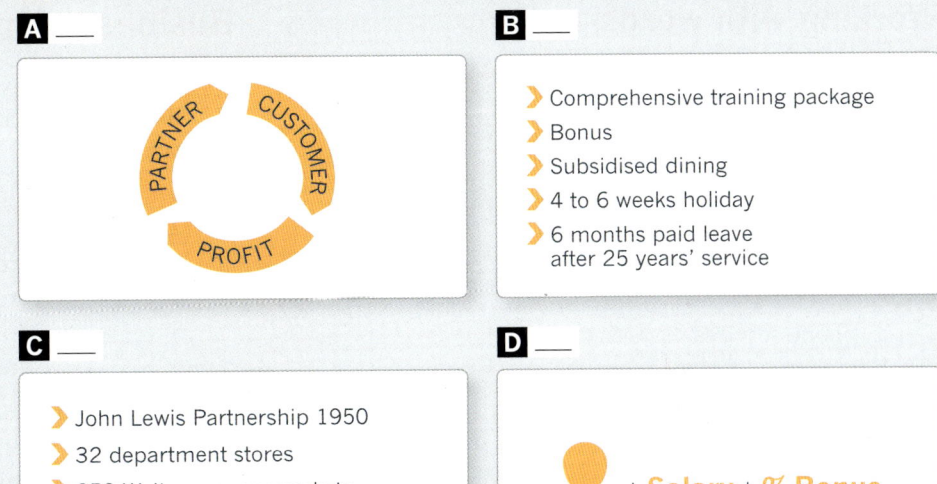

B ___

> Comprehensive training package
> Bonus
> Subsidised dining
> 4 to 6 weeks holiday
> 6 months paid leave
  after 25 years' service

C ___

> John Lewis Partnership 1950
> 32 department stores
> 250 Waitrose supermarkets
> 1 production unit
> 4,000-acre farm

D ___

👤 + **Salary** + **% Bonus**

7 Match titles 1–4 to the slides in **6**.
1 Company background ___
2 Sharing in the profits ___
3 The Partner/Customer/Profit Cycle ___
4 Partner benefits ___

8 ▶02 Watch the video again. Answer the questions with *Yes, No* or *Don't know* (if the information isn't in the video).
1 Does the John Lewis Partnership only sell food? ___*No*___
2 Are all John Lewis employees the partners of the company? _____
3 Is a bonus calculated as a percentage of employees' pay? _____
4 Does the company have external shareholders? _____
5 Is the partnership's annual profit very high? _____
6 Does the Horizon's training take a long time? _____
7 Do benefits increase the longer you are a partner? _____
8 Is pay the most important part of a partner's development? _____

9 What do you think about the John Lewis Partnership? Tick the opinon below which you agree with. Then compare your opinion with a partner and give your reasons.
☐ There are lots of advantages with this type of partnership. It could work at my company.
☐ This type of partnership is a good idea but I don't think it would work at my company.
☐ I'm not sure about it. I think there are some disadvantages with this type of partnership.

A new partnership scheme

10 Work with a partner. Imagine you would like to introduce a similar partnership scheme at your company. Discuss the three points and prepare a short presentation for your boss. Include:
- how a partnership scheme with employees will work (giving examples from John Lewis)
- what benefits the employees will receive
- how you will measure success and calculate the employees' bonuses

11 Present your ideas to the rest of the class and try to convince them to choose your scheme. After all the presentations, vote for the best partnership scheme.

1 | Practice file

Working with words

1 Match 1–6 to a–f.

1 Our annual revenue is *d*
2 We're based ___
3 We operate ___
4 We produce ___
5 We specialize ___
6 We provide ___

a phone services.
b in many different countries.
c in phones for children under 12.
d €300 million.
e mobile phones.
f in the north of Italy.

2 Choose the correct words in *italics* to complete the text.

My company [1]*produces / products* specialized software for the film industry. We are [2]*made / based* in San Francisco, but we also [3]*specialize / operate* in Europe and the Far East where we have two [4]*services / subsidiaries*. There are 450 [5]*revenues / employees* in the company. We sell our [6]*products / exporters* to companies like Dreamworks, which [7]*provide / produce* animated movies. Our technology is very new, so we don't have many [8]*competitors / companies*.

3 Complete the sentences using a suitable word from **2** in the correct form.

1 We have an annual _____ *revenue* _____ of $25 million.
2 France is a big _____ of wine to other countries.
3 Totalgaz is one of the _____ of Total Group.
4 We only sell these _____ in Europe and North America.
5 Where exactly is your company _____?
6 H&M _____ in good-quality clothes at low prices.
7 A lot of pizza restaurants _____ home delivery services.
8 The TATA Group _____ on all six continents.
9 We offer a wide range of consulting _____.
10 What exactly does your company _____?

Business communication

1 Complete questions 1–6 with the words from the list. Then match the questions to responses a–f.

Who   What   Why   What   Where   ~~Can~~

1 ___*Can*___ I introduce myself? *e*
2 _____'s your name? ___
3 _____ are you from? ___
4 _____ do you work for? ___
5 _____ do you do? ___
6 _____ are you here in Tokyo? ___

a I'm in the food business.
b I have a meeting with a customer.
c A German car maker.
d Caroline Hook.
e Yes, of course.
f New York.

2 Complete the conversation with sentences a–i.

a Nice to meet you too, Gideon.
b Can I introduce you to her?
c And what do you do?
d Sorry, what's your name again?
e What about you?
f This is Rachel.
g So why are you at an international car show?
h ~~Can I introduce myself?~~
i Nice to meet you.

Rachel Excuse me. Can I sit here?
Gideon Yes, of course.
Rachel Thanks very much. [1] *h* I'm Rachel Steadman.
Gideon [2]___ I'm Gideon Lack.
Rachel [3]___ Where are you from?
Gideon I'm from Switzerland originally. But I live in the Czech Republic now. [4]___ Where are you based?
Rachel In Toronto.
Gideon And who do you work for?
Rachel Bos. It's an advertising agency. I'm here with Honda. It's one of our clients. [5]___
Gideon I'm a teacher of Greek literature.
Rachel That's unusual. [6]___
Gideon I'm here with my wife. She works for BMW. Ah, there she is now. [7]___
Rachel Yes, of course. That would be nice.
Gideon [8]___
Rachel Rachel. Rachel Steadman.
Gideon Ursula. [9]___ She works for an advertising agency in Canada.

Language at work

GRAMMAR REFERENCE

Present simple

Form
Positive: Add -s or -es after the verb with *he/she/it*.
I/you/we/they **specialize** *in Latin American music.*
He/She/It **specializes** *in high-tech products.*

Negative: Use the auxiliary *do/does + not + verb.*
It **doesn't produce** *software.*
We **don't produce** *mobile phones.*

Questions
1 Use *do* and *does*, but don't change the form of the main verb (no -*s*).
   Does *it* **have** *a subsidiary in China?*
   Do *you* **have** *many competitors?*
2 With question words (*who, what, where, how,* etc.), use *do* and *does* after the question word.
   Where **do** *you* **work?**
   What **does** *he* **do?**
3 To give a short answer to questions in the present simple, use the subject + *does/do* or *doesn't/don't*.
   Do you work for a multinational company?
   Yes, I **do.** */ No, I* **don't.**
   Does your company operate in South America?
   Yes, it **does.** */ No, it* **doesn't.**

Exceptions
1 The verb *be* is irregular.
   I **am**
   You/We/They **are**
   He/She/It **is**
2 In questions with *be*, do not use *do* and *does*.
   Is *he Spanish?*
   Where **are** *the subsidiaries?*
3 In negative sentences with *be*, add *not* or *n't*.
   I'm **not** *from China.*
   They **aren't** *in the company today.*

Use
1 To talk about facts or things which are generally true.
   The company **provides** *insurance services.*
2 To talk about regular actions.
   We **have** *sales meetings every month.*
3 Do not use the present simple to talk about actions in progress at this moment. Use the present continuous for this (see page 109).

1 Complete sentences 1–10 with the verbs from the list.

start   starts   work   works   is   are   specialize   specializes   have   ~~has~~

1 Our company ___*has*___ shops in Europe and Asia.
2 She _____ in Manchester today.
3 We _____ in electronic toys for children.
4 The meeting always _____ at 2.30 p.m.
5 She _____ for an engineering company.
6 I usually _____ work at about 7 a.m.
7 We _____ one office in Paris.
8 He's a lawyer. He _____ in company law.
9 Most of our competitors _____ based in Europe.
10 I _____ in advertising.

2 Choose the correct words or phrases in *italics* to complete questions a–j. Then match the questions to answers 1–10 in **1**.
   a What *do / ~~does~~* you specialize in? __3__
   b Who *do / does* your wife work for? ___
   c *Have you / Do you have* an office in France? ___
   d Where *be / is* she? ___
   e What *do / does* you do? ___
   f Where *be / are* your competitors? ___
   g Where *has / does* your company operate? ___
   h When do you *arrive / arrives* at the office? ___
   i What time *do / does* the meeting start? ___
   j What *is / does* he do? ___

3 Complete the missing words. The last letter of each word is given.
   1 A __*I*_s your head office in London?
      B No, our company ___*isn*___'t British, it's American.
   2 I'm sorry, but we _____'t have a sales office in the Middle East.
   3 What sort of products _____s your company sell?
   4 A He _____'t work in Munich any more.
      B Really? So why _____s he have a flat there?
   5 They _____'t in the company today. They're on a business trip.
   6 I _____'t know how many employees they have.

Working with words

1 Complete sentences 1–7 with the words from the list.

customers   supplier   staff   consultant
colleague   employment agency   client

1 If I have a lot of work, my _colleague_ often helps me.

2 We always use the same _____ when we need new computers or printers.

3 The _____ say they have two people who are interested in the new sales job.

4 Our _____ buy from us because our prices are very good.

5 Over 200 members of _____ work in our New York office.

6 We use a Brazilian _____ to give us advice about the South American market.

7 I'm self-employed and am currently working for a _____ based in Paris.

2 Choose the correct words in *italics* to complete sentences 1–7.

1 My company *employs / employees* 300 people.

2 In my job, I *train / training* people to use new software.

3 We sell our *production / products* to customers all over the world.

4 We have the price per unit. Now we can *calculate / calculation* the total price.

5 That's Yann Pichon over there. He's the *organization / organizer* of this conference.

6 Yes, we can *supply / supplier* the tools that you have requested.

7 A half-day *consultant / consultation* costs between $200 and $250.

3 Match 1–5 to a–f to make complete sentences.

1 I work for _d_

2 I deal with ___

3 I work in ___

4 I work on ___

5 I work with ___

a the public relations department.

b some very interesting projects.

c colleagues in London and Paris.

d an IT services company.

e a lot of customer problems.

Business communication

1 Seth Guterson wants to speak to Elena Cascarino, but she isn't there. Complete his phone conversation with the receptionist using the words from the list.

help   speak   calling   afraid   give   take   back
Does   ask   This

Seth Could I [1] _speak_ to Elena Cascarino, please?

Receptionist Who's [2]_____, please?

Seth [3]_____ is Seth Guterson.

Receptionist I'm [4]_____ Elena's in a meeting at the moment. Can I [5]_____ a message?

Seth Yes, sure. Can you [6]_____ her to call me [7]_____?

Receptionist OK. So that's Seth Guterson. [8]_____ she have your number?

Seth Yes, she does.

Receptionist OK, Seth. I'll [9]_____ her the message.

Seth Thanks for your [10]_____. Goodbye.

2 A few hours later Seth is still waiting for Elena to call. He phones her again. Choose the correct words in *italics* to complete the conversation.

Seth Is Elena [1]*calling / there*, please?

Elena Yes, [2]*welcome / speaking*. Is that Seth?

Seth Yes, it is. Hi, Elena.

Elena Hi, Seth. Did you call earlier and [3]*take / leave* me a message?

Seth Yes, this morning.

Elena I'm sorry I didn't manage to call you back. What can I [4]*do / offer* for you?

Seth It's [5]*on / about* that Japanese customer. I'm [6]*phoning / asking* to give you his email address. It's f.hayashi@yahoo.jp.

Elena OK, I've got that. That's great, Seth. Thanks very much for [7]*help / calling*.

Seth [8]*Of course / You're welcome*.

Elena I'll phone you again on Monday to give you more news.

Seth OK. [9]*Listen / Speak* to you next week. Bye.

Elena Bye.

Language at work

GRAMMAR REFERENCE

Present continuous

Form

Positive: Use *am/is/are + -ing* form.
*He's **preparing** his presentation.*
Negative: Use *am/is/are + not + -ing* form.
*They're **not going** to the meeting.*
Questions
1 Put *am/is/are* before the subject.
***Are** you **staying** in this hotel?*
*Where **is she working**?*
2 To give a short answer to *yes/no* questions, use the subject + *am/is/are*.
***Are** you **working** on this now?*
*Yes, I **am**. / No, I'm **not**.*

Use

1 To describe actions happening at the moment of speaking.
*Hi. **I'm calling** you from my car.*
2 To describe actions in progress around the present time, but not always at the moment of speaking.
***He's doing** a very interesting course this month.*
3 We don't use the present continuous to talk about regular or repeated actions. Instead, we use the present simple (see page 107).
Do say: *She **calls** me every week.*
Don't say: *She's calling me every week.*

1 Complete sentences 1–6 with the present continuous form of the verbs in brackets.

1 (we / develop) _____ *We are developing* _____ a new range of products for South America.

2 (he / stay) _____ at the Intercontinental Hotel?

3 (you / not / listen) _____ to me. What did I say?

4 (I / leave) _____ now. See you tomorrow.

5 Why (those German engineers / visit) _____ the company?

6 (she / not / work) _____ this week. She's on holiday.

2 Match questions 1–6 to answers a–e.

1 What is she doing? _c_
2 What does she do? ___
3 Are you working this week? ___
4 Do you work at weekends? ___
5 Why do you leave the office so late? ___
6 Why are you leaving the office so late? ___

a She's a teacher.
b Yes, but only four days.
c ~~A Masters in Business Studies.~~
d I always have a meeting with my boss from 6.30 to 7 p.m.
e We had a very long meeting.
f No, never.

3 Read this email and choose the correct form of the verbs in *italics*.

Hello,

I [1] *write /* (*am writing*) to ask if you [2] *have / are having* a sales office or sales rep in Argentina. I [3] *work / am working* for a small computer producer here and we [4] *look / are looking* for a new supplier of sound cards. We usually [5] *buy / are buying* from a supplier in the USA, but their products [6] *become / are becoming* too expensive for us.

We have over 30 shops in Argentina and we [7] *open / are opening* another five this year.

We also regularly [8] *get / are getting* business by mail order via our website.

We [9] *try / are trying* to find a new supplier before the end of this month, so please contact me as soon as possible.

Best regards,

Elena Suarez

Working with words

1 Complete sentences 1–10 with the words from the list.

quality   high   pretty   helpful   original

reliable   extremely   value   user   popular

1 They have good prices on computers and other ___high___-tech products.

2 She gave me a lot of useful ideas about what product to buy. She was very _____.

3 I can't understand my new phone. It's not very _____-friendly.

4 Italian shoes are usually made of high-_____ leather.

5 It's not a _____ company. They often deliver the wrong products.

6 If you buy two, you get the third one free. That's good _____ for money.

7 It was a _____ good holiday but I don't think I'll go there again.

8 The video game is very _____ with teenagers.

9 This advertising agency has some very _____ ideas.

10 Her car is _____ quiet. You can't hear the engine at all at low speeds.

2 Cross out the word that doesn't go with the word in **bold**.

1 **high**	quality / tech / ~~customer~~
2 **helpful**	advice / staff / phone
3 **reliable**	value / car / staff
4 **good**	quality / value / reliable
5 **popular**	product / money / film
6 **really**	quality / original / expensive

Business communication

1 A catering company wants to find a new supplier of office products. Put the sentences of the research report in the correct order.

_1_ The purpose of our research was to find a new supplier of office products.

___ Finally, we asked our staff to compare the products from the three suppliers.

___ We also found that Office Plus were very quick and their staff were very helpful.

___ Then, we chose three companies and asked each of them to deliver the same 50 products.

___ Our conclusion is that Office Plus offers the best value with good products and a reliable service.

___ 85% of our employees thought the products from Office Plus were really high-quality.

___ We started by comparing the catalogues of ten different companies.

_9_ We recommend using them for all our office needs.

___ We wanted to find just one supplier who could deliver all the products we need in less than three days.

2 A restaurant is researching new uniforms for its staff. Complete the report with the phrases below.

Finally	*we recommend*	*We wanted*
First	*We did this by*	*showed*
~~*The purpose*~~	*Then we asked*	*the majority*

1 _____*The purpose*_____ of our research was to find a company that creates original designs at a reasonable price. 2 _____ to find a new uniform that was modern and attractive. 3 _____ testing three different designs and then getting feedback from our customers and staff.

4 _____, we asked three different designers to produce a new uniform. 5 _____ three of our staff to wear the uniforms for a week, and we asked customers what they thought of the designs. 6 _____, we asked the staff for their opinions.

Our research 7 _____ that the most popular uniform with customers and staff was from Fatima Fashion. However, 8 _____ of customers found that the colours weren't right for our image.

For this reason, 9 _____ asking Fatima Fashion to provide two different colour designs.

Language at work

GRAMMAR REFERENCE

Past simple

Form

Positive: Add *-ed* to the infinitive of **regular verbs**.

We started work at 7.00 yesterday.

Add *-d* to the infinitive of **regular verbs** ending in *-e*.

She lived in Switzerland.

Change the *-y* to *-i* and add *-ed* to **regular verbs** ending in consonant + *-y*.

He tried to find a new job.

Double the final consonant of short **regular verbs** ending in vowel + consonant.

I stopped the car.

Many verbs are irregular. Irregular verb forms do not end in *-ed*. For example:

become ➞ became	meet ➞ met
build ➞ built	say ➞ said
do ➞ did	speak ➞ spoke
go ➞ went	spend ➞ spent
get ➞ got	tell ➞ told
have ➞ had	write ➞ wrote

For a list of **irregular verbs**, see page 159.

Negative: Put *didn't* before the infinitive of both regular and irregular verbs.

*I **didn't** want to be late for the meeting.*

*They **didn't** see the manager.*

Questions

1 Put *did* before the subject and the infinitive of both **regular** and **irregular verbs**.

*When **did** they arrive?*

*Where **did** you go?*

2 To give a short answer to *yes/no* questions in the past simple, use the subject + *did/didn't*.

*Did he email you yesterday? Yes, **he did**. / No, **he didn't**.*

Exceptions: The verb *be* does not use the auxiliary verb *did* to form the negative or questions.

*The manager **wasn't** in the office yesterday.*

__Were__ the products user-friendly?

Use

Use the past simple to describe a finished action in the past.

*They **sent** the parcel on Monday, but it **didn't arrive** until Friday.*

Words and phrases we often use with the past simple are: *yesterday, last week, last year, in 2015, five years ago.*

1 Complete the text using the correct past simple form of the verbs in brackets.

The man behind the World Wide Web

Tim Berners-Lee [1]___was___ (be) born in London, England, on June 8th 1955. He [2]_____ (study) physics at Oxford University, where he [3]_____ (build) his first computer. He [4]_____ (have) several jobs before he [5]_____ (become) an independent consultant. During this time he [6]_____ (spend) six months in Geneva, Switzerland, where he [7]_____ (write) his first program for storing information. He [8]_____ (call) the program 'Enquire', but he [9]_____ _____ (not publish) it. In 1990, he [10]_____ (start) work on the World Wide Web, which [11]_____ (make) its first appearance on the Internet in 1991.

In 1994, Tim [12]_____ (create) the World Wide Web Consortium at the Massachusetts Institute of Technology. Today, this consortium coordinates web development worldwide.

2 Complete questions 1–8.

1 What time _____ *did they arrive* _____?
They arrived at nine o'clock.

2 Where _____?
We had lunch in the staff canteen.

3 Who _____ at the conference?
I saw our colleagues from the Buenos Aires office.

4 Why _____ the meeting?
Raul left the meeting because he had an urgent phone call.

5 Which hotel _____ at?
They stayed at the Hilton.

6 When _____ the company?
She joined the company last year.

7 How long _____ with the visitors?
I spent all day with them.

8 How many emails _____?
We sent about a hundred.

3 Choose the correct verb forms in *italics* to complete sentences 1–6.

1 I usually *arrive* / ~~arrived~~ at 8 a.m., but yesterday my train *is* / *was* late.

2 He *works* / *worked* at home most of the time but he *comes* / *came* to the office last week.

3 She *isn't* / *wasn't* there yesterday evening. Maybe she *doesn't* / *didn't* know there was a meeting.

4 In general, they *don't* / *didn't* go on holiday, but last summer they *decide* / *decided* to go to Costa Rica

5 I *don't* / *didn't* like his presentation yesterday. He usually *speaks* / *spoke* much better.

6 She *doesn't* / *didn't* come here very often, so I *am* / *was* surprised to see her last week.

Working with words

1 Match speakers 1–10 to departments a–j that they work in.

1 'When we checked, we found that several products were in the wrong boxes.' _d_

2 'We invoiced you in June but we never received your payment.' ___

3 'The CEO is asking us to recruit a new Assistant Manager.' ___

4 'We manufacture over 50 different products in this factory.' ___

5 'I'm sorry, but we don't have the money to increase your department's budget.' ___

6 'If we offer them a 5% discount, I think they'll sign the contract.' ___

7 'Can you phone three or four suppliers and see who offers the best price?' ___

8 'They say they're unhappy with their order. I'll call them and try to resolve the problem.' ___

9 'We need to dispatch the order before Friday.' ___

10 'Your computer doesn't work? I'll come and have a look.' ___

a Customer Service
b Logistics
c Accounts
d Quality Control
e Production
f Finance
g Human Resources
h Sales
i IT
j Purchasing

2 Choose the correct word in *italics* to complete sentences 1–5.

1 We have a lot of contact ~~to~~ / ~~on~~ / *with* the Finance Department.

2 She's in charge *to* / *of* / *for* the Logistics department.

3 The Sales Manager reports *with* / *to* / *at* the Sales and Marketing Director.

4 The IT Manager is responsible *for* / *of* / *to* developing new software solutions.

5 I work closely *by* / *from* / *with* the Human Resources Department.

Business communication

1 Match sentences 1–8 to responses a–h.

1 Can you sign here, please? _d_
2 Please take a seat. ___
3 Did you have a good trip? ___
4 Thank you for coming today. ___
5 Can I get you a glass of water? ___
6 I just need to make a quick phone call. ___
7 Can I use your pen for a second? ___
8 Sorry I didn't visit last month. ___

a Yes, please.
b Yes, it was fine, thanks.
c Of course. Here you are.
d Yes, sure.
e No hurry. Take your time.
f No problem. You're here now.
g Thanks.
h It's a pleasure.

2 Complete the sentences and use the answers to complete the crossword.

Across

1 I just called Mr Dyson to tell him you've arrived. He'll be ___right___ there.

3 Did you _____ any trouble finding your way here?

6 I have an _____ with Mrs Adams at 9 a.m.

8 I'm sorry I'm _____. I couldn't find a parking place.

Down

2 Thank you for _____ me here today.

3 There's more coffee if you want. Just _____ yourself.

4 Do you need anything _____ before we start?

5 Let's go to my office. It's this _____.

7 _____ to see you again after all this time.

Language at work

> **GRAMMAR REFERENCE**
>
> ### Questions
>
> **Form**
> 1 The normal order of words in a question is:
>   question word or phrase + auxiliary + subject + verb.
>   *Where do you work?*
>   *How many days is he staying?*
> 2 The order of words is the same even when the subject consists of several words.
>   *What time are the CEO and the Production Manager arriving?*
> 3 In questions with a *yes/no* answer, the order of words is auxiliary + subject + verb.
>   *Does he work in production?*
>   *Are you opening a new office?*
> 4 The auxiliary and verb form are different for each tense:
>   **Present simple:** *do/does* + verb
>   *Where does he live?*
>   **Present continuous:** *am/is/are* + *-ing*
>   *Why are you calling?*
>   **Past simple:** *did* + verb
>   *What time did you arrive?*
>
> **Exceptions**
> 1 When the verb *be* is the main verb, there is no auxiliary. The order of words in a question is:
>   question word(s) + verb + subject
>   *When is the meeting?*
>   *Where was he yesterday?*
> 2 When the question word (or words) is the subject of the sentence, there is no auxiliary. The order of words is:
>   question word(s) + verb
>   *Who works here?*
>   *How many people are coming?*

1 Choose the correct question from a or b.
  1 a Where does your boss work?
    b ~~Where works your boss?~~
  2 a What do you make products here?
    b What products do you make here?
  3 a Why is changing your logo?
    b Why is your logo changing?
  4 a Do you have a canteen here?
    b Do you a canteen here?
  5 a When the company did move here?
    b When did the company move here?
  6 a Who does the Sales Manager report to?
    b Who the Sales Manager reports to?
  7 a Does the company opening any new factories?
    b Is the company opening any new factories?
  8 a Where did you work before?
    b Where you worked before?
  9 a When do your offices are open?
    b When are your offices open?
 10 a How many people do work in this department?
    b How many people work in this department?

2 The manager of a chewing gum manufacturer is answering questions about his company. Look at his answers (A) and put the journalist's questions (Q) in the correct order.
  1 your / Where / sell / do / your / products / you
    Q *Where do you sell your products*_____?
    A In more than 150 countries.
  2 did / the company / When / start
    Q _____?
    A In 1891.
  3 people / does / employ / many / the company / How
    Q _____?
    A About 15,000.
  4 competitors / have / in the USA / Do / a lot of / you
    Q _____?
    A Yes, we do. There are about 14 chewing gum producers in the States.
  5 chewing gum / much / Americans / How / eat / do
    Q _____?
    A The average American eats 180 servings of gum per year.
  6 are / main customers / your / Who
    Q _____?
    A Young people in the 12–24 age group.

113

Working with words

1 Match 1–6 to a–f to make phrases.

1 get __e__   a a solution
2 make ___   b a problem
3 offer ___   c loyalty
4 customer ___   d a complaint
5 response ___   ~~e feedback~~
6 report ___   f times

2 A customer service manager is training new employees. Complete her words with a phrase from **1**.

We lost a lot of business to our competitors last year, so this year we are working hard to encourage [1]____*customer loyalty*____. Here are some important things you need to know.

When customers want to [2]_____ with a product they bought, it's important to answer them quickly. They know that mistakes happen, so if you can [3]_____ to the problem immediately, customers are usually satisfied. Customers generally only [4]_____ if they think you don't understand their problem or don't want to help.

If you can't answer immediately, call the customer back as soon as possible. We're trying to improve our [5]_____, so if you can't find a solution in less than 15 minutes, ask your Team Leader for help.

After each customer service call, we send out online questionnaires. Only about 30% of people respond, but it's still a useful way for you to [6]_____ on the work your team is doing.

3 Choose the correct words in *italics* to complete sentences 1–6.

1 I'm sorry, but I can't offer you ~~*an issue*~~ / *a solution* right now.
2 I have a *complaint* / *query* about the price. Is it €25.99 or €29.99?
3 We can offer you a 15% *refund* / *discount* if you pay today.
4 Bring the computer back, and we'll give you a *replacement* / *compensation* to take home today.
5 Can you explain the *feedback* / *issue* with your order in more detail?
6 I'm afraid we don't give refunds, but we can give you a *compensation* / *credit voucher* to use in the shop at a later date.

Business communication

1 Put this conversation in the right order.

___ Oh dear. I do apologize. Can you give me your order number?
___ Yes, it's SR235L. That was the reference on my order and on the photos I received.
___ Yes, that's right.
___ Well, I sent you pictures of my factory, but I received photos of somebody's birthday party.
_1_ Photo World. Good morning. How can I help you?
_10_ Yes, sure. I'll wait to hear from you.
___ Oh I'm sorry to hear that. Can you give me more details?
___ Let me check. So you're Mr Haddadi?
___ OK. I'll deal with it right away, Mr Haddadi. Can I call you back in five or ten minutes?
___ Hello. I'm calling because there's a problem with some photos you sent me.

2 Complete the conversation between the shop assistant (SA) and the customer (C) with the words and expressions from the list.

I'll deal with   I'm afraid   check   I'm sorry   ~~can I do~~
sorry for   we can offer you   I'm not very happy

SA Good afternoon, sir. What [1]_____*can I do*_____ for you?
C   I bought this item yesterday but it doesn't work. [2]_____ about it.
SA Oh dear. [3]_____ about that.
C   I'd like a refund, please.
SA [4]_____ we can't give you a refund, but [5]_____ a credit voucher.
C   Well, can't you replace it?
SA I'm not sure if we have any more in the shop. Let me [6]_____. One moment, please.
C   OK.
SA No, I'm afraid you bought the last one, but we can have one here for you tomorrow. I'm [7]_____ the inconvenience.
A   OK, no problem. What time tomorrow?
B   Well, [8]_____ it right now and then I can give you a time. Do you have two minutes?

Language at work

GRAMMAR REFERENCE

Comparative and superlative forms

Form

1 Add *-er* or *-est* to one-syllable and some two-syllable adjectives.

cheap   cheap**er**   the cheap**est**

quiet   quiet**er**   the quiet**est**

If an adjective ends in *-y*, change the *-y* to an *-i* and add *-er* or *-est*.

easy   eas**ier**   the eas**iest**

2 Double a consonant after a vowel at the end of short adjectives.

hot   ho**tter**   the ho**ttest**

big   bi**gger**   the bi**ggest**

3 Some adjectives are irregular.

good   **better**   the **best**

bad   **worse**   the **worst**

4 Add *more/less* and *most/least* to adjectives of two or more syllables.

expensive   **more** expensive   the **most** expensive

difficult   **less** difficult   the **least** difficult

5 Add *than* after the comparative to compare two things/people.

*The Sales Manager is more popular **than** the Financial Manager.*

Note: In the superlative form, you can also use *my, our, their*, etc. instead of *the*.

*It was **our** most successful year.*

Use

1 Use the comparative to compare two things.

*Fridays are **better than** Mondays.*

2 Use the superlative to compare one thing to many other things.

*Saturday is **the best** day of the week.*

3 To say something is the same, use *as* + adjective + *as*.

*My office is **as big as** yours.*

4 To say something is different use *not* + *as* + adjective + *as*.

*This machine **isn't as complicated as** the old one.*

---

1 Complete sentences 1–9 using the comparative or superlative form of the adjectives in brackets.

1 Let's go to the meeting room. It's
_____*quieter*_____ (quiet) than in my office.

2 Our company was _____
(profitable) last year than this year.

3 We have seven factories: the
_____ (new) one is in Mexico.

4 My hotel was _____ (near) to the company than the last hotel I stayed in.

5 Our _____ (popular) product is the VS52.0.

6 I think our new brochure looks
_____ (professional) than the last one.

7 Last year was the _____ (bad) in our company's history.

8 Germany is the _____ (big) country in the EU.

9 Our new Sales Manager is
_____ (good) than the one we had before.

2 This table shows the results of a customer survey for three different online shopping sites. Read the information and decide if sentences 1–8 are true (*T*) or false (*F*). Then correct the false sentences.

	PHOENIX	ARRIBA	TESLO
Easy to use website	85%	72%	43%
Good customer service	65%	75%	82%
Low prices	92%	84%	63%
Quick delivery	86%	95%	45%

1 Phoenix has better customer service than Teslo.
_____*F. Phoenix has worse customer service.*_____

2 Teslo has higher prices than the other companies.
_____

3 Phoenix's website is the most difficult to use.
_____

4 Phoenix has the lowest prices.
_____

5 Teslo offers quicker delivery than Arriba.
_____

6 Arriba's products are cheaper than Teslo's.
_____

7 Phoenix is the most popular for customer service.
_____

8 Arriba's website isn't as easy to use as Teslo's.
_____

Working with words

1 Choose eight words from the list to complete the letter of application.

interview   qualification   reference   candidate
recruit   experience   ~~apply~~   skills   advertised
shortlist

Dear Sir/Madam,

I am writing to ¹ ___apply___ for the position of Quality Manager ²_____ on your website.

As you can see from my attached CV, I have six years of ³_____ working as a quality technician in the automotive industry.

Last year, I obtained a new ⁴_____ when I completed a degree from the Bentham School of Engineering.

In the last six years, I have learnt many new ⁵_____ relating to Japanese production methods and I use them in my everyday work.

I believe that I am a very strong ⁶_____ for this post, and I hope you will give me the opportunity to speak to you at an ⁷_____.

My present employer will be very happy to provide you with a ⁸_____.

I look forward to hearing from you.

Yours sincerely,

Patrick Todd

---

2 Complete sentences 1–8. Choose from the list of words in **1**, but change the form where necessary.
1 I've received three new *applications* for the job.
2 He's not very _____ for the job because he doesn't have a university degree.
3 The HR Manager is responsible for the _____ of new employees.
4 I applied for the job, but they didn't _____ me for an interview.
5 The machines we use are very complex. We need _____ workers with technical knowledge to operate them.
6 Philips are recruiting at the moment. I saw an _____ on their website.
7 She's very _____ – she's worked for 20 years in the industry.
8 The person who _____ me asked some very difficult questions.

Business communication

1 Choose the correct answer from the words in *italics*.
1 I *prefer / ~~preferable~~* to wait another month.
2 One *advantage / issue* is that we don't have enough staff to do the job.
3 I think the second option is too *attractive / expensive*.
4 I'd *go / choose* for the first candidate because he has lots of experience.
5 One disadvantage is the time it takes. *Other / Another* is the salary cost.
6 Which of the products do you think is more *suitable / better* for our customers?
7 I like the idea, but I'm not *think / sure* it will work in practice.

2 Three managers are discussing different ways to do job interviews. Complete the conversation with phrases from the list.

I'd go for   another issue is   I like the idea that
are more suitable   I'm not sure   ~~I prefer~~
it's preferable   One key advantage

A Personally, ¹ _____I prefer_____ a video interview. ²_____ is that we can arrange to meet candidates very quickly and it's not necessary to make all those travel arrangements. And personally, ³_____ they do the interview in their own home because I think they are more relaxed than when they come to the company.

B ⁴_____ that they are more relaxed because it can be difficult talking in front of a camera, especially in a situation like this. And ⁵_____ that the audio and video quality is often bad. If we want an easier option, ⁶_____ the telephone interview. The audio quality is usually better and the candidate is less stressed because you can't see them.

C I think ⁷_____ to give the candidates the choice – some people feel good in front of a camera and others prefer the phone. But I also think that video or phone conversations ⁸_____ for first interviews. For final interviews, I think we need to see candidates face-to-face.

Language at work

GRAMMAR REFERENCE

Present perfect (1)

Form

Positive: *have / has* + past participle form

*I **have** (I've) **finished** my work.*

*He **has** (He's) **written** three letters today.*

Negative: *have / has* + *not* + past participle

*They **haven't done** the work this week.*

*The post **hasn't arrived** yet.*

Questions: Put *have / has* before the subject.

***Have you** met the new Production Manager?*

*Where **has she** been today?*

Use

1 To talk about past actions where the time includes the present.

*I've made three presentations **today / this week / this month**.*

2 To ask someone about general experiences in their life, we can use *ever*.

*Have you **ever** seen the Taj Mahal?*

No, never.

3 We also use the present perfect to talk about actions which started in the past and are continuing now. For more information, see page 129.

*I've **worked** here for three years (and I still work here now).*

4 For past actions where the time doesn't include the present, use the past simple.

*I **haven't seen** him **today**, but I **saw** him **yesterday**.*

5 For regular verbs, the past participle form is **always** the same as the past simple: verb + *-(e)d*

6 For irregular verbs, the past participle and past simple forms are **sometimes** the same. Common irregular verbs include:

Verb	Past simple	Past participle
become	became	become
do	did	done
find	found	found
go	went	gone
have	had	had
know	knew	known
make	made	made
see	saw	seen
speak	spoke	spoken
take	took	taken

For a list of **irregular verbs**, see page 159.

1 A manager is talking about his department. Complete the text with the present perfect form of the verbs in brackets.

This month [1](not / be) _____ *hasn't been* _____ a very good one for me. Three more members of my team [2](tell) _____ me that they are leaving the company. Two of them [3](not / find) _____ another job, but they say that the pressure of work [4](become) _____ too much for them. It's true that there [5](be) _____ a big increase in their work this year because two other customer service assistants [6](leave) _____ the department and we [7](not / recruit) _____ anybody to replace them.

I [8](ask) _____ my boss several times if we can employ some new people for the team, but each time he [9](say) _____ that we need to reduce our salary costs. But I know we [10](lose) _____ some business because we [11](not / have) _____ enough people to deal with customer calls.

The situation can't continue like this. I [12](not / made) _____ a final decision on this, but I'm thinking of leaving the company myself.

2 Choose the correct answer from the words in *italics* to complete questions 1–8. Then match them with responses a–h.

1 *Did you read* / ~~*Have you read*~~ that article about e-recruitment last week? *f*

2 *Did you* / *Have you* seen the new Dali exhibition? ___

3 *Have you ever* / *Did you* applied for a job online? ___

4 *Have you had* / *Did you have* any work experience before you joined this company? ___

5 *Has* / *Have* she made any more calls today? ___

6 *Have* / *Did* all the candidates come for their interviews yesterday? ___

7 Have you *been* / *went* to the USA? ___

8 When *have you sent* / *did you send* that letter? ___

a No, never. But I'd really like to go.

b Yes, once. But I didn't get the job!

c Just one or two this afternoon.

d Yes, I did. I had several jobs when I was a student.

e Two or three days ago.

f ~~Yes, it was very well-written.~~

g There was just one who wasn't there.

h No, I haven't had time.

Working with words

1 Complete sentences 1–10 using a word from A and another from B.

A seat ~~aisle~~ airline baggage weight security delayed missed self-service hand

B allowances charges restrictions flights scan upgrade ~~seat~~ baggage check-in connection

1 I don't want to sit by the window. Do you have an _____ *aisle seat* _____?

2 I don't have any suitcases to check in. I only have _____.

3 Bad weather is one of the biggest causes of _____.

4 It's quicker to get your boarding card at the _____.

5 A What are the _____ on this flight?
   B You can take up to 22 kg.

6 They saw something strange in my suitcase at the _____, so they asked me to open it.

7 I paid €20 more to choose my own seat. These _____ get higher and higher every year!

8 This airline's _____ are very good. You can check in two bags without paying extra.

9 I was in Economy, but they offered me a _____ to Business Class.

10 He didn't come to the meeting because he had a _____ in Paris and couldn't get to London in time.

2 Two travellers are describing flights they took. Complete the missing words. The first two or three letters are given.

I used the ¹on*line*_____ check-in at home, but I forgot to register my suitcase. So when I arrived at the airport, I had to pay an ²ext_____ charge to check it in. Then I discovered my seat was broken and I had to go in a ³mi_____ seat between two very large people!

At the airport, they told me my flight was ⁴can_____. But luckily, there was another flight two hours later. They even gave me a ⁵fr_____ upgrade to First Class, and they didn't ask me to pay for ⁶exc_____ baggage, even though my suitcase was more than 2 kg overweight.

Business communication

1 Match 1–10 to a–j to make complete sentences.

1 When would __*g*__
2 Are you ___
3 Does the 13th work ___
4 Let's meet ___
5 I'm afraid I've ___
6 Shall we ___
7 How about ___
8 So that's ___
9 Can we find ___
10 Sorry, but ___

a for you?
b say 6.30?
c free tomorrow evening?
d got something on.
e 2 p.m. in the café. See you later then.
f Tuesday instead?
~~g suit you?~~
h in front of the theatre.
i I'm busy at that time.
j a different time?

2 Choose the correct words in *italics* to complete the conversation.

A We need to prepare the presentation this week. When ¹*can / ~~are~~* we meet?

B ²*Is / Would* Friday afternoon suit you?

A ³*Afraid / Sorry*, but I'm finishing at lunchtime that day. Are you ⁴*say / free* on Friday morning?

B Yes, that ⁵*works / suits* me. But I prefer first thing in the morning. ⁶*Does / Is* 8.30 work for you?

A I'm ⁷*afraid / sorry* I can't meet as early as that.

B Well, ⁸*when / what* about 9 a.m. instead?

A Yes, that's ⁹*fine / suits*. Where ¹⁰*are / shall* we meet?

B Well, it's probably easier for you if I come to your office.

A OK, so ¹¹*let's / that's* my office at nine o'clock on Friday.

B Great. See you on Friday, then.

A Yes, see you on Friday.

Language at work

> ### GRAMMAR REFERENCE
>
> ### *will*
> **Form**
> **Positive:** *will* + verb
>   *I'll **meet** you at the reception desk in your hotel.*
> **Negative:** *won't (will not)* + verb
>   *I **won't disturb** you.*
> **Questions:** *will* + subject + verb
>   ***Will you call** me later?*
>
> **Use**
> To make decisions at the moment of speaking.
>   A *Can you give me a contact number?*
>   B *Just a moment. **I'll give** you my business card.*
>
> ### *going to*
> **Form**
> **Positive:** *am/is/are* + *going to* + verb
>   *I'**m going to look** for a new job after the holidays.*
> **Negative:** *am/is/are* + *not* + *going to* + verb
>   *He **isn't going to work** late tonight.*
> **Questions:** *am/is/are* + subject + *going to* + verb
>   ***Are they going to look** for a new head of department?*
>
> **Use**
> To talk about a plan that we have already decided on.
>   *We'**re going to move** to the new office in the spring.*
>
> ### Present continuous
> **Form**
> See page 109.
> **Use**
> 1 To talk about a future arrangement someone has made. The arrangement usually has a fixed time or place.
>   A *What **are you doing** tomorrow after work?*
>   B *I'**m taking** my daughter to the dentist.*
> 2 We can also use *going to* for a future arrangement.
>   *The CEO'**s going to visit** the office tomorrow.*

1 Choose the correct words in *italics* to complete sentences 1–10.

1 There's no real message. Just tell her ~~*I'm calling*~~ / *I'll call* back later this afternoon.

2 It's her 50th birthday so *she's going to* / *she'll* have a party.

3 You can call at any time because we *aren't going* / *won't go* out.

4 I'll be back in half an hour. *I'm going to* / *I'll* wash my car. It's really dirty.

5 He can't meet us tomorrow because *he'll visit* / *he's visiting* a client.

6 *I'll be* / *I'm being* there at 11 a.m. at the latest.

7 I hate my job, so *I'm going to* / *I'll* look for a new one.

8 *She's playing* / *She'll play* in a concert tonight so she can't go to the dinner.

9 We can start at 9 a.m. I *won't be* / *'m not being* late.

10 Sorry I can't make it. *I'm meeting* / *I will meet* a client then.

2 Complete conversations 1–10. Use *will*, *going to* or the present continuous form of the verbs in brackets.

1 A I can't hear you very well.
  B I'm sorry. I *'ll speak* _____ (speak) up a little.

2 A Will she be here tomorrow?
  B No, she _____ (visit) two suppliers near London.

3 A Do we have a date for that meeting?
  B We _____ (not have) it this week. It's now next Tuesday at 10 o'clock.

4 A Did you arrange a time to talk to your boss?
  B Yes, I _____ (meet) her today at two in her office.

5 A When do we have to pay?
  B I'm not sure. I _____ (ask) one of my colleagues and let you know.

6 A A lot of our deliveries were late yesterday.
  B I know. I _____ (call) our customers today and apologize.

7 A Can you tell me when my order will arrive?
  B Just a moment. I _____ (check) with the driver.

8 A Did they offer him the job?
  B Yes, but he _____ (not accept) it because the salary is too low.

9 A Keith isn't here yet. Shall we start anyway?
  B No, hang on. I _____ (give) him a call.

10 A So when are you moving office?
  B Next week. They _____ (start) to relocate us on Monday.

Working with words

1 Choose two possible correct answers from the words in *italics*.

1 I asked the company to give me *a quotation / a delivery date / ~~a demand~~*.

2 The supplier said they needed more time to *process / enquire / ship* the order.

3 Can you *quote / check / guarantee* that the product will be in stock next week?

4 You can look on our website to track the *shipment / order / stock*.

5 We can *ship / guarantee / deliver* the product to you in the next 24 hours.

6 We need to *transport / enquire about / check* the availability of goods for the busy Christmas period.

7 We had an IT problem, but now all the *orders / goods / processes* are ready for delivery.

2 Complete the sentences and use the answers to complete the crossword. The first letter of each word is given.

Across

2 We don't have enough stock to ___*meet*___ the demand.

4 We'd like to p_____ an order for 100 phones.

8 We o_____ three last week and we need two more.

9 Can you g_____ that we will receive it by Monday?

10 I'm trying to t_____ the shipment on their website.

Down

1 Can you tell me when you will d_____ our order?

3 How long will it take you to p_____ our order?

5 I wanted to c_____ that your prices are still the same.

6 I'm phoning to e_____ about my recent order.

7 The price you q_____ us is too high.

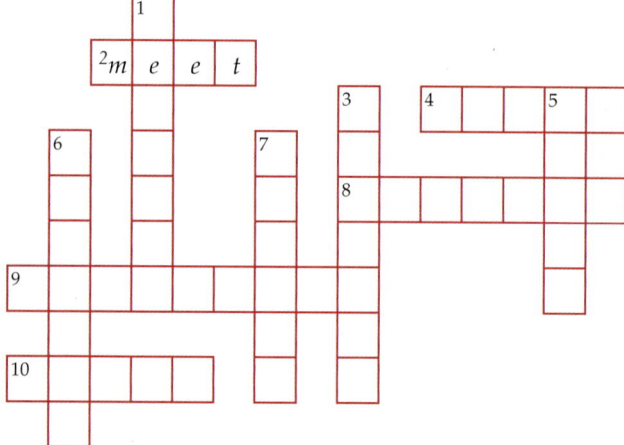

Business communication

1 Match requests 1–8 to responses a–h.

1 Could I send you the email tomorrow? _e_

2 Do you mind if I take this box? ___

3 Could you just sign here, please? ___

4 Would you mind waiting a few minutes? ___

5 Do you think I could leave early? ___

6 I need a quotation as soon as possible. ___

7 Is it all right if I phone back later? ___

8 Could I ask you to deliver on Saturday? ___

a No problem. How many do you need?

b No, not at all. Go ahead.

c Yes, sure, if you've finished everything.

d Yes, of course. I'll be here until 7 p.m.

e ~~I'm sorry, but I need it before the end of the day.~~

f I'm afraid not. Our drivers don't work that day..

g No, that's fine. I'm not in a hurry.

h Certainly. Could I use your pen?

2 Complete the conversation in a store with the words from the list.

of course   just   sorry   show   ask   go ahead
could   ~~afraid~~   would   mind

A Are you here to pick up a parcel?

B Yes, I am. But I'm [1] ___*afraid*___ I don't have the confirmation email.

A Don't worry, but [2] _____ I have your name, please?

B Yes, it's Mrs Denton. Marina Denton.

A And could you [3] _____ me some ID, please?

B Yes, [4] _____. Here's my driving licence.

A OK, that's fine. Could I [5] _____ you to wait just a moment – your package is in the back office.

B Yes, of course. Do you [6] _____ if I look at this catalogue while I'm waiting?

A No, [7] _____. You can take it with you if you like.

B Thanks.

(Two minutes later)

A So here's your parcel. Can you [8] _____ sign here, please?

B Sure. I'm [9] _____, but it looks a little heavy and I have a bad back. [10] _____ you mind taking it to my car for me?

A No problem.

Language at work

GRAMMAR REFERENCE

Passive forms

Form
Verbs in sentences can either be active or passive.

The passive is formed with the verb *be* + past participle of the main verb.

Present simple

*The photocopier **is serviced** once a year.*

*Our offices **are cleaned** in the evening.*

Past simple

*The meeting **was held** yesterday.*

*The new computers **were installed** last week.*

For a list of **irregular verbs**, see page 159.

Use

1 When the person who does the action is unknown.

*The flowers **are changed** daily.*

(I don't know who changes them.)

2 When the person who does the action is unimportant.

*The hotel **was built** in the 19th century.*

(It isn't important who built it – we're only interested in the hotel.)

3 When the person who does the action is too obvious to mention.

*The books **were delivered** this morning.*

(It's obvious a delivery company brought the books.)

4 When we want to say who does something in a passive sentence but we don't want to make them the focus of the sentence, we use the preposition *by*.

*The party **was organized by** the social committee.*

5 We use passive forms in formal written English more than in spoken English.

*Candidates **are required** to speak fluent English.*

1 Correct sentences 1–6.

1 Deliveries are make three times a week.

<u>   *Deliveries are made three times a week*   </u>.

2 The invoice sent yesterday.

                                          .

3 Over a thousand guests was invited to the event.

                                          .

4 The post collects at 10 a.m. every day.

                                          .

5 The software is wrote by our engineers.

                                          .

6 The meeting was cancel because of the strike.

                                          .

2 Complete sentences 1–8 with the correct passive form of the verbs from the list.

ask   process   deliver   give   hold   install
publish   ~~repair~~

1 When there is a problem, the machinery <u> *is repaired* </u> by our own technicians.

2 The training course _____ by an online sales expert.

3 The staff _____ to work overtime last week.

4 Orders _____ in the call centre.

5 Interviews _____ every year in January and September.

6 The new software _____ by our IT team yesterday.

7 The shipment _____ last Tuesday.

8 The magazine _____ weekly.

3 Rewrite sentences 1–6 in the passive form, starting with the words given.

1 They serve hot meals in the staff canteen.

Hot meals <u> *are served in the staff canteen* </u>.

2 The HR department sent an email to all employees.

An email _____.

3 Someone stole the money.

The money _____.

4 The heads of department informed the staff about the decision.

The staff _____.

5 We discuss salaries with employees individually.

Salaries _____.

6 He keeps the key to the safe in his desk.

The key to the safe _____.

Working with words

1 Complete the text using a word from A and another from B.

A free   target   word   ~~latest~~   advertising   new

B campaign   business   of mouth   audience
publicity   ~~range~~

So you've launched your ¹_____ latest range _____
of products and you want to be sure they
sell well. We can help you to reach your
²_____ in the most
effective way.

We will work with you to plan an exciting and
original ³_____ using a
wide range of social media.

And it doesn't have to be expensive.
80% of ⁴_____
attracted by companies comes through
⁵_____. Yes, that means from
people who already love your products. We will
show you how to use your existing customers to get
⁶_____ and maximize your
sales.

2 Choose the correct words in *italics* to complete sentences 1–6.

1 We use a lot of social media to *promote* / ~~attract~~ our products.

2 We *get* / *offer* discounts to customers who spend more than €150.

3 We didn't *conduct* / *reach* a very good campaign and sales were disappointing.

4 They've added an 'Employment' page to their website to *increase* / *advertise* awareness of their recruitment policies.

5 If you want to *reach* / *boost* sales, try reducing prices.

6 We need to rethink our advertising if we want to *promote* / *reach* a younger audience.

3 Match descriptions 1–5 to the types of advertising in the list.

~~click ads~~   targeted emails   search engines
advertising boards   promotional events

1 You see them on most commercial websites.
_____ click ads _____

2 For your company to appear on the first page of results, you usually have to pay.
_____

3 You see them in the street.
_____

4 You start receiving them from companies after you buy something from them.
_____

5 You are invited to them when a company has a new product to sell. _____

Business communication

1 Match 1–10 with a–j to make complete sentences that you can use in a meeting.

1 We're here today _d_   a catch that.
2 I'm not ___   b time of the meeting?
3 I didn't ___   c with you.
4 What was the ___   ~~d to discuss ...~~
5 Could you be ___   e to the next point?
6 We're getting off ___   f more specific?
7 We've covered ___   g what we've agreed?
8 We can come back ___   h the subject.
9 Can we move on ___   i everything.
10 Can we sum up ___   j to that later.

2 Complete the conversation with the sentences from **1**.

Mike OK, can we start? ¹ _We're here today to discuss_ how to make our meetings more effective. John, can you tell us about what you're doing in your department?

John Well, we've introduced the concept of the five-minute meeting. And it's working very well.

Pilar I'm sorry, ²_____. Did you say a five-minute meeting?

John Yes, but it sometimes goes on for half an hour.

Hachirou Sorry, but ³_____. How can it be a five-minute meeting if it's half an hour long?

John Well, the important thing is that it's short.

Mike ⁴_____, John? How does the meeting work exactly?

John We meet every day after lunch and you inform everyone of where you are on your work and ...

Pilar Sorry, ⁵_____?

John After lunch. Usually about two o' clock.

Sabine Why after lunch? Everyone's falling asleep then.

Mike I think ⁶_____. Let's just talk about the idea itself. The time of day isn't important. If we have time, ⁷_____.

(15 minutes later)

Mike OK, I think ⁸_____ on the subject of the five-minute meeting. ⁹_____ on the agenda: how to inform staff of decisions made in meetings?

(20 minutes later)

Mike So, very quickly, ¹⁰_____ today? Sabine and Pilar are going to ...

Language at work

GRAMMAR REFERENCE

Modal verbs (1) – obligation, necessity, permission

Use

1 To describe an action which is necessary, or a legal obligation, we use *have to* or *need to*.
   You **have to** wear a seat belt when you are driving.
   We **need to** complete our tax form before 5th April.

2 To describe an action which isn't necessary, we use *don't/doesn't have to* or *don't/doesn't need to*.
   We **don't have to** work at weekends in our company.
   The report **doesn't have to** be finished today.

3 For an action which is possible or permitted by law, we use *can* or *allowed to*.
   You **can** leave early today because we're not very busy.
   Companies **are allowed to** advertise alcohol after 10 p.m.

4 If the action isn't permitted, we use *can't* or *am not/isn't/aren't allowed to*.
   Sorry, but you **can't** smoke here.
   Cyclists **aren't allowed to** use motorways.

Form

1 To ask a question with *have to* or *need to*, we use *do* or *does*.
   Do I have to write this report now?
   Does the company **need to** have quality certification?

2 To ask a question with *allowed to*, use *am/is/are*.
   Are cigarette companies **allowed to** advertise?
   Am I allowed to park here?

3 Questions with *can* begin with the word *can*.
   Can foreigners vote in national elections?
   Can I use my phone for personal calls?

1 Are sentences 1–10 true or false for your country? Correct them where necessary.

1 You're not allowed to drive a car if you don't have a licence.
2 Car drivers have to wear a seatbelt.
3 Car passengers don't need to wear a seatbelt.
4 You can't smoke in restaurants and pubs.
5 You're allowed to vote when you are 16-years-old.
6 Products with lots of sugar need to carry a health warning.
7 Schoolchildren don't have to wear a uniform to school.
8 You can retire when you are 55-years-old.
9 Advertisers aren't allowed to compare their products with their competitors.
10 Shops can open seven days a week.

2 Complete the missing words in the guide for new employees, using a suitable form of *have to, need to, can* or *allowed to*.

WORKING AT FTC

Frequently Asked Questions (FAQs)

1 Q Where ___*can I / am I allowed to*___ park my car?

A In the car park behind the main building.

2 Q _____ I _____ to wear formal clothes to work?

A No, you don't. Jeans and a shirt are fine.

3 Q What hours do I have to work?

A Everyone _____ _____ be in the company between 10 a.m. and 4 p.m. But you _____ _____ to choose when you start and finish work, e.g. 8–4, 10–6.

4 Q _____ I _____ to take my paid holiday when I want?

A Yes, but you have to take at least two weeks in the summer.

5 Q Who do I see if I have a problem with my contract?

A You _____ _____ speak to the HR Manager.

6 Q Can I use the Internet for personal research?

A You _____ use it during your lunch break, but you _____ _____ to use it during office hours.

7 Q Am I allowed to use my office phone for private calls?

A You can make local calls to landlines and you _____ _____ to pay for these. You _____ use the office phone for long-distance calls or calls to mobiles.

Working with words

1 Match 1–8 to a–h.

1	renewable _d_	a	emissions
2	throw ___	b	consumption
3	fossil ___	c	pollution
4	global ___	d~~sources~~
5	carbon ___	e	fuels
6	energy ___	f	friendly
7	reduce ___	g	away
8	eco-___	h	warming

2 Complete sentences 1–8 with the phrases in **1**.

1 It's important to develop _renewable_ _sources_ of energy like wind or water.
2 I try not to fly because planes produce a lot of _____ _____ that go into the atmosphere.
3 _____ _____ is a big problem: temperatures are continuing to rise and our weather is changing.
4 We need to stop using _____ _____ like coal and oil.
5 Our _____ _____ is much higher in the winter because we have to heat the house.
6 If we don't _____ _____ in the sea, hundreds of species of fish will disappear.
7 I try to buy _____ _____ products that are made without polluting the environment.
8 Don't _____ _____ all that paper – it should be recycled.

3 Match the words in the list to verbs 1–4.

less water   _glass_   _petrol_   _cities_   _newspapers_
~~emissions~~   _plastic_   _electricity_   _the environment_
pollution   _rivers_   _consumption_

1 reduce   _emissions_
            _____
            _____

2 recycle   _____
            _____
            _____

3 consume   _____
            _____
            _____

4 pollute   _____
            _____
            _____

Business communication

1 Complete the presentation using the phrases from the list.

As I said before   _that brings me_   _Thanks very much_
My next point   _I'm here today_   ~~Hello and welcome~~
lastly   _to sum up_   _let's start with_   _I'll come_

> [1] _Hello and welcome_ . I'm Georgio Belatoni from Green Sheen. [2] _____ to tell you about the advantages of using our cleaning service. We provide a professional and effective service at a reasonable price. [3] _____ to the question of prices at the end of this presentation.
>
> But [4] _____ the benefits of employing Green Sheen to clean your offices. Well, the most important advantage is the clean and healthy working atmosphere we create by using only eco-friendly products.
>
> [5] _____ concerns our cleaning professionals. We choose our staff carefully, and every one of them has to pass a strict training course. You'll find our cleaners are polite and friendly, and are a pleasure to have in the building.
>
> And [6] _____, I want to talk about your company image. By employing a green cleaning service, you will show your commitment to the environment, attract more customers and boost your sales.
>
> So, [7] _____, we offer a clean, healthy environment, well-trained cleaners and an opportunity to show your eco-friendly image to all your customers.
>
> So [8] _____ to the end of my talk. [9] _____ for listening. [10] _____, I'm going to finish by giving you a few details about our prices. But before that, do you have any questions?

2 Complete the introduction to a presentation. The first letter of each word is given.

Hello everybody, and [1]_thanks_ for coming today. I'll [2]s_____ with a quick [3]o_____ of my presentation. First, we're going to [4]l_____ at the reasons we've decided to install solar panels on the factory roof. [5]T_____, I'll talk briefly about the company that's going to do the work for us. And [6]f_____, we'll compare the investment costs with the money we will save. So first of [7]a_____, let me [8]t_____ you why we have made this important decision.

Language at work

GRAMMAR REFERENCE

First conditional

Form

There are two parts to a sentence in the first conditional, the condition and the result.

Positive and negative

Use *if* + present simple for the condition and *will/won't* + verb for the result.

> *If we **turn off** the heating, **we'll reduce** our energy bills.*
>
> *If we **don't invest** in renewable energy now, we **won't have** the money later.*

We don't use *will/won't* straight after *if*.

> ✗ *If ~~I'll see~~ her tomorrow, I'll tell her.*
>
> ✓ *If **I see** her tomorrow, I'll tell her.*

The sentence may begin with the condition or the result. Put a comma to separate the two parts only when the condition comes first.

> *If we **reduce** emissions, it'll be good for our image.*
>
> *It'll be good for our image if we **reduce** emissions.*

Questions

The result often comes first in first conditional questions. Put *will* before the subject and the verb after the subject.

> *How **will you increase** revenue if you reduce prices?*
>
> ***Will people use** their bikes more if we create cycle lanes?*

Use

To talk about the probable future result of an action in the present or future.

> *If temperatures **continue** to rise, many people **will lose** their homes.*
>
> *If we **finish** the installation by Friday, we **won't have** to work at the weekend.*

1 Choose the correct words in *italics* to complete sentences 1–10.

1 If they *~~won't reduce~~ / don't reduce* their running costs, they *~~lose~~ / 'll lose* money.

2 If more employees *agree / will agree* to use public transport, we *'ll have / won't have* more space in the car park.

3 What *does he say / will he say* if the company *asks / will ask* for another quotation?

4 If we *don't improve / won't improve* our product range, we *lose / 'll lose* some of our customers.

5 My boss *don't accept / won't accept* the idea if she *won't know / doesn't know* all the details.

6 If we *don't print / won't print* so many emails, we *'ll use / won't use* less paper.

7 They *'ll use / use* a lot more energy if they *leave / don't leave* their windows open in the winter.

8 He *doesn't pay / won't pay* the lower price if he *'ll wait / waits* any longer.

9 How long *does it take / will it take* if we *go / will go* by train?

10 If we *don't decrease / won't decrease* carbon emissions, global temperatures *will continue / won't continue* to increase.

2 Two managers are talking about buying hybrid electric cars for their sales reps. Complete the conversation with an appropriate form of the verbs in brackets.

A If we [1] _replace_ (replace) our old company cars with hybrid electrics, we [2] _'ll reduce_ (reduce) our carbon emissions significantly.

B Yes, but how much [3] _____ (it / cost) us if we [4] _____ (decide) to buy hybrids? They're a lot more expensive than normal cars.

A Yes, but the difference in price is less than a few years ago. And if we [5] _____ (not / sell) the cars for at least three years, we [6] _____ (save) money because hybrids consume less petrol.

B I think our sales reps [7] _____ (consume) less fuel if they [8] _____ (do) most of their driving in cities. But I think it [9] _____ (not / be) cheaper if they [10] _____ (drive) a lot on motorways. Most of our sales reps have to drive long distances.

A Well, if you [11] _____ (look) at the figures I have here, you [12] _____ (see) that fuel costs are a lot lower for all drivers, even when they do more than 25,000 km a year. And this saving [13] _____ (increase) even more if the price of petrol [14] _____ (rise) again.

Working with words

1 Put the letters in CAPITALS in the right order to form a word.

1 We held our last corporate ___event___ at the America's Cup. VETEN
2 The _____ for the dinner was the top-class restaurant Triton in Prague. ENEUV
3 Over 500 _____ were invited to attend. TUSEGS
4 We had a _____ of €5,000. UTDEBG
5 The _____ _____ didn't provide transport, so we had to take a taxi. TOSH OYPCAMN
6 The _____ included dinner and one night in a hotel. GACAKEP

2 Complete sentences 1–6 with a suitable form of the verbs in the list.

entertain   book   have   arrange   accept   ~~hold~~

1 My company ___held___ its last corporate event in June.
2 We _____ a great time at the Hard Rock Café.
3 The host company _____ a trip to the Taj Mahal.
4 Our bank always _____ its clients at Roland Garros.
5 The venue we _____ last year was too small.
6 I couldn't _____ the invitation because the dinner was the same day as my daughter's graduation.

3 Complete the description of a corporate event with a suitable form of the words from **1** and **2**.

> The last corporate [1] ___event___ I attended was a day at a Champions League Final. The [2]_____ was a well-known publicity agency that wanted to [3]_____ their VIP clients.
>
> The event was [4]_____ in the hospitality area of the San Siro Stadium in Milan, which was a [5]_____ I had always wanted to visit. Of course, I [6]_____ my invitation as soon as it arrived!
>
> Fortunately the company had a big [7]_____, because the tickets were very expensive and they had invited more than 100 [8]_____. They had to [9]_____ the seats months in advance to make sure there was room for all of us. The football match was in the evening, so they [10]_____ a trip to the Duomo cathedral in the afternoon and then we had dinner before leaving for the stadium. Everyone [11]_____ a fantastic day, and the event was a complete success for the publicity agency.

Business communication

1 Put these words in the correct order to make complete sentences.

1 very / you / good / that's / of
   ___That's very good of you___ .
2 to / you / lunch / like / would / join / for / us
   _____?
3 the / I / concert / ticket / a / shall / you / for / get
   _____?
4 but / for / I'm / asking / thanks / free / not
   _____.
5 you / book / like / table / me / would / to / a
   _____?
6 water / you / of / would / a / like / glass
   _____?
7 going / do / cinema / fancy / you / the / to
   _____?

2 Rewrite sentences 1–6 with the words in brackets.

1 Do you want something to eat? (like)
   _____ ___Would you like something to eat___ ?
2 Shall we take a break? (like)
   _____?
3 Do you want to see a football game? (fancy)
   _____?
4 Would you like me to reserve a table? (shall)
   _____?
5 Shall we visit the new factory now? (like)
   _____?
6 Shall I meet you at the airport? (like)
   _____?

3 Complete conversations 1–6. The first letter of each word is given.

1 A ___Would___ ___you___ ___like___ some water?
   B Yes, please. That would be nice.
2 A Would you like to join us for a drink?
   B T_____ f_____ t_____ invitation, but I have to call my boss.
3 A Shall I find out if there's a concert this evening?
   B Yes, please. That's v_____ g_____ o_____ you.
4 A Would you l_____ m_____ t_____ email you the agenda?
   B Yes, please.
5 A Would you like me to order a taxi for you?
   B Thanks for a_____, b_____ I'd prefer to walk.
6 A Do you fancy visiting the new sports facilities?
   B Yes, please. That would b_____ g_____.

Language at work

GRAMMAR REFERENCE

Countable and uncountable nouns

Form

1 Nouns are either countable or uncountable. Countable nouns have a single and plural form. Uncountable nouns have one form.
   Countable nouns: *room (rooms), bus (buses), city (cities)*
   Uncountable nouns: *money, information, accommodation*
2 Most plural countable nouns end in *-s* but some are irregular.
   person → people   woman → women   child → children
3 Use *a* or *an* with singular countable nouns.
   *I have **a reservation / an appointment**.*
   Use *some* with plural countable nouns and uncountable nouns.
   *We have **some guests / some information**.*
4 Single countable nouns use a singular verb form.
   *Your **ticket is** in the post.*
   Plural countable nouns use a plural verb form.
   *The **tickets are** very expensive.*
   Uncountable nouns use a singular verb form.
   *Your **advice is** very good.*
5 Some nouns can be either countable or uncountable.
   *Would you like **tea** or **coffee**?*
   (Uncountable to refer to the drinks in general.)
   *I'd like **a coffee** please.*
   (Countable to refer to a cup of coffee, which can be counted.)
6 Some nouns that are countable in a lot of other languages are uncountable in English.
   I need (some) information/advice/accommodation.

many/much

Use

1 Use *many* with plural countable nouns.
   ***How many events** did we organize last year?*
2 Use *much* with uncountable nouns.
   ***How much money** did you spend?*
3 *Much* and *many* are mostly used in questions or negative statements.
   ***How many** guests / **How much** time do we have?*
   *We didn't drink **many bottles / much champagne**.*

Is/Are there ...?

Use

1 With countable nouns, use *Is there a(n) ...?* in the singular form and *Are there (any) ...?* in the plural.
   ***Is there a** match today? **Are there any** banks open?*
2 With uncountable nouns, use *Is there (any) ...?*
   ***Is there** time to buy souvenirs before the game?*
   ***Is there any** information about opening hours?*

---

1 Complete the table with the words in the list.

person   entertainment   event   accommodation   hotel information   shop̶   reservation   luggage   money

Countable	Uncountable
shop	

2 Choose the correct words in *italics* to complete sentences 1–9.
   1 I can't drink *much / many̶* wine because I'm driving.
   2 My suitcases *is / are* still at the hotel.
   3 *Is / Are* there many cars on the road today?
   4 How *many / much* people are waiting for the bus?
   5 We've organized *an / some* accommodation for our guests.
   6 *Is / Are* there any money in the budget for a drinks party?
   7 How *much / many* time do we have before the match starts?
   8 The information that the hotel receptionist gave us *was / were* wrong.
   9 We don't have *much / many* events in the first half of the year.

3 Two managers are discussing a product launch event. Complete their conversation with the words in the list.

many̶   an   some   any   is   a   much   are

A So how ¹ ___many___ people are coming to the event?
B We sent ² _____ invitation to 300 people and about 120 have accepted.
A ³ _____ there ⁴ _____ customers from Germany in that list?
B Yes, our three biggest contracts.
A That's good. ⁵ _____ the accommodation near the venue?
B Yes, we booked ⁶ _____ hotel next to the venue. But we still need to organize ⁷ _____ entertainment for the evening – maybe a jazz band. How ⁸ _____ money do we have in the budget?
A Only about €600.

Working with words

1 Match 1–8 to a–g.

1 achieve _e_   a responsible
2 manage ___   b reputation
3 perform ___   c diversity
4 socially ___   d performance
5 safety ___   e your targets
6 workplace ___   f costs
7 good ___   g record
8 environmental ___   h well

2 Complete conversations 1–8 with the phrases from **1** and choose the correct answer from the words in *italics*.

1 A Why were you *disappointed / satisfactory* by my sales results?
   B Because you didn't ____*achieve your targets*____ once last year.

2 A Did your _____ improve last year?
   B Yes, our results were *excellent / poor*. We only had three accidents all year, and none of them were serious.

3 A Did your team _____ at the competition?
   B Well, we didn't win, but we did better than last year.
   A Well, that was *encouraging / disappointing*.

4 A It's not *satisfactory / average* for a company just to make profits.
   B No, it must also be _____ and look after its staff.

5 A Why were your profits so *encouraging / poor* this year?
   B It's very difficult to _____ because our suppliers keep increasing their prices.

6 A When you evaluated our _____, were the pollution levels acceptable?
   B Well, the results were only *average / disappointing*. We could still do a lot better.

7 A This article here says that we have a _____ for reliable service and quick response times.
   B Well, that's *poor / excellent*. The press often prefer to talk about our bad environmental record.

8 A Have you improved your record on _____?
   B Not really. Our performance here has been *disappointing / disappointed*. Only 5% of our employees are from ethnic minorities.

Business communication

Soft drinks sales in Europe

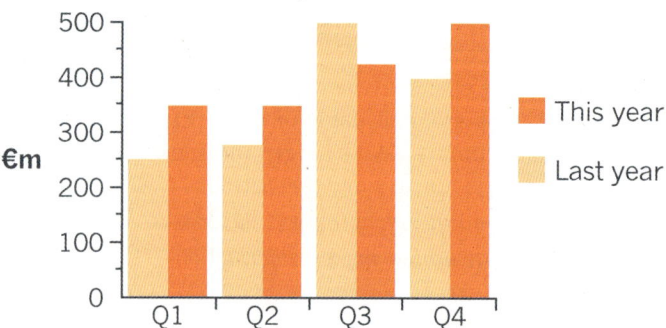

1 Look at soft drinks sales for last year and complete the presentation with prepositions in the list.

at   *to*   *by*   *from*   *to*   *by*   *to*

Last year sales started the year [1]____*at*____ 250 million euros. They rose [2]_____ 250 million in the first quarter [3]_____ 275 million euros in the second quarter. In the next three months, they then increased [4]_____ 225 million [5]_____ 500 million euros. Unfortunately they then fell [6]_____ 100 million euros [7]_____ a final total of 400 million euros in the last three months of the year.

2 Look at the sales for last year and this year and choose the correct words in *italics* to complete the text.

Have a [1]*look / notice* again at the figures for the third quarter of last year. Why did sales [2]*rise / decline* so dramatically? This was thanks to our new sports drink, Vitality. But then we had that problem with the contaminated drinks can, and our sales [3]*grew / dropped* in the final quarter to €400 million.

That contamination incident continued to affect our sales this year. As you can [4]*notice / see*, sales [5]*declined / increased* by €50 million in the first quarter. They then [6]*remained stable / grew* at €350 million for the next three months. However, since June our reputation has improved and you'll [7]*notice / look* that our sales have [8]*risen / fallen* every month, [9] *increasing / decreasing* to €500 million in the last quarter.

3 Are sentences 1–8 true or false for your country? Correct the false sentences.

1 House prices have fallen dramatically this year.
2 The price of petrol has risen in the last three months.
3 Unemployment dropped last year.
4 Average temperatures have grown in the last 30 years.
5 The retirement age has increased in the last ten years.
6 Food prices have remained stable in recent months.
7 Jobs in production are declining.
8 The number of university students has decreased slightly in the last 20 years.

Language at work

GRAMMAR REFERENCE

Present perfect (2) with *for* and *since*

Form
See page 117.

Use
1 To talk about an action that started in the past and is continuing now.
   I've worked for this company for ten years.
2 We use *for* with a period of time.
   She's had this job for a month/two years.
3 We use *since* with a precise date or point in time.
   They've been here since 2007/August/this morning.

Present perfect or past simple?

1 Note that *How long ...?* and *for* (+ period of time) are used both with the present perfect and the past simple.
   Present perfect
   How long have you had your present job?
   I've had it for six months.
   Past simple
   How long did you do your last job?
   I did it for five years.
2 Sometimes we use different verbs to describe the start of the action (past simple) and the action itself (present perfect).

Present perfect	Past simple
He's **worked** for this company since 2004.	He **joined** this company in 2004.
I've **been** here for an hour.	I **arrived** here an hour ago.
He's **known** her since January.	He first **met** her in January.
They've **lived** here for six months.	They **moved** here six months ago.

Name: Radka Bilkova

Qualifications:

2006	Degree in Sports Management from University of Portland, Oregon

Work Experience

2013–present	Alpurna Running – General Manager. Day-to-day management of four shops. Responsible for sales growth.
2010–2013	One Step Fitness – Assistant Manager. Responsible for developing new activities at club.
2006–2010	Sun Sports Clothing – Sales Assistant

1 Look at Radka Bilkova's curriculum vitae and correct sentences 1–7.
  1 I've obtained my degree in 2006. *I obtained*
  2 I worked at Alpurna Running since 2013.
  3 I've been responsible for sales growth since several years.
  4 I've been an Assistant Manager at One Step Fitness for three years.
  5 At One Step Fitness I've developed new activities.
  6 I worked as a sales assistant since four years.
  7 I've left One Step Fitness in 2013.

2 Complete questions 1–8 with the present perfect or past simple using the information from Radka Bilkova's curriculum vitae.
  1 How long / she / work / Alpurna Running ?
     How long has she worked for Alpurna Running ?
  2 When / she / join / One Step Fitness ?
     _____?
  3 How long / she / be / Assistant Manager / One Step Fitness ?
     _____?
  4 How long / she / be / a manager ?
     _____?
  5 Where / she / work / 2006–2010 ?
     _____?
  6 How long / she / be / responsible for sales growth ?
     _____?
  7 How long / she / work / Sun Sports Clothing ?
     _____?
  8 How long / she / be / sports and fitness industry ?
     _____?

Working with words

1 Complete the sentences and use the answers to complete the crossword.

Across

1 The __supply__ of gas in the world is large enough for 200 years.

2 One of the biggest causes of global warming is economic _____.

4 The governments of the world have agreed to take action to combat climate _____.

Down

1 People say education standards have declined because there is a _____ of good teachers.

2 There is a rising _____ for cheap, sustainable energy.

3 People in developed countries are eating too much – it's a serious _____ to their health.

4 When a country can't pay its debts, we have a serious global _____.

5 Population _____ is continuing and there will soon be 8 billion people on the planet.

2 Complete the text. The first letter of each word is given.

Population growth and economic development ¹a_ffect_____ the world's water supply in a very serious way. Experts ²e_____ that two-fifths of the people in the world already face water shortages. And this situation will get ³w_____. One study ⁴f_____ that by 2035, around 60% of the population will not have enough water to live on. It's a danger that particularly ⁵t_____ people living in the southern hemisphere.

The world is not going to ⁶r_____ out of water, but we need to work harder to save and share this precious resource.

Business communication

1 Put the words in the correct order to make complete sentences.

1 find / the / Is / likely / solution / to / government / a
  _Is the government likely to find a solution_____?

2 you / improve / think / will / the / Do / situation
  _____?

3 I / have / we / factory / close / won't / hope / to / the
  _____.

4 staff / support / will / The / decision / definitely / the
  _____.

5 the / likely / new / affect / Are / rules / to / us
  _____?

6 probably / decrease / before / Unemployment / won't / 2025
  _____.

7 future / free / have / unlikely / We're / to / time / more / the / in
  _____.

2 Rewrite sentences 1–6 with the words in brackets.

1 Will the manager listen to our demands? (likely)
  _Is the manager likely to listen to our demands____?

2 Will they find a substitute for oil? (likely)
  Are they _____?

3 The plastics industry is likely to be affected first. (probably)
  The plastics industry _____.

4 Food prices will probably rise dramatically. (likely)
  Food prices _____.

5 Standards of living are certain not to go up. (definitely)
  Standards of living _____.

6 I hope we'll develop renewable energy. (hopefully)
  _____ renewable energy.

3 Complete the extract from a radio interview with the words in the list.

hopefully   likely   ~~think~~   are   probably   will

A So, what do you ¹ __think__ are the most urgent effects of climate change to deal with?

B Well, water levels are rising and many coastal areas ²_____ likely to be flooded in the future. ³_____, governments ⁴_____ take more measures to protect communities near the sea. If they don't, a lot of people will ⁵_____ die.

A Are we doing enough to cut carbon emissions?

B I think there are positive signs. If governments, companies and each of us continue to reduce our carbon footprint, global warming is ⁶_____ to slow down as scientists have predicted.

Language at work

> **GRAMMAR REFERENCE**
>
> ## Future predictions
> ## will/won't
> ### Form
> See page 119.
> ### Use
> Use *will* to talk about something that you think is certain to happen.
>> *In the future more people **will work** from home.*
>
> Use *won't* to talk about something that you think is certain not to happen.
>> *Employees **won't stay** in the same job all their working life.*
>
> ## may/might (not)
> ### Form
> *may/might (not)* + verb
> ### Use
> 1 Use *may* or *might* to talk about something that will possibly happen.
>> *Office buildings **may look** completely different in the future.*
>> *Employees **might have to** share a desk with their colleagues.*
>
> 2 Use *may not* or *might not* to talk about something that possibly won't happen.
>> *In the future, people **may not retire** until they're 70.*
>> *Workers **might not use** their cars so much.*
>
> 3 *May* and *might* both have the same meaning and are used in the same way.

1 Rewrite the sentences with *will/won't, may/might* or *may not/might not*.

1 Perhaps / the CEO / visit the office this afternoon
   The CEO may visit the office this afternoon   .

2 I'm sure / we / finish the report today
   _____.

3 Perhaps / the manager / not in her office right now
   _____.

4 Perhaps your secretary / know when the meeting is
   _____.

5 I'm sure / I / not / get the job I applied for
   _____.

6 Perhaps / they / not give us a pay rise this year
   _____.

7 I'm sure / he / not go on any more business trips
   _____.

8 The staff / possibly / more motivated
   _____.

2 Complete the conversation with *will/won't, may/might* or *may not/might not* and the verb in brackets.

A Do you think you'll be working for the same company in ten years' time?

B I'm not sure. I [1] _____ *may look for* _____ (look for) a different job if I'm not earning much more than now. It depends on my promotion prospects, too. I hope I [2] _____ (be) a manager by then, and I certainly [3] _____ (feel) very satisfied with my job if I'm still in the same position. How about you?

A I don't think my company [4] _____ (exist) in ten years' time. There's a lot of competition from Asia and a lot of factories in our field here are closing. I'm not sure, but I [5] _____ (lose) my job in the next few years.

B Why don't you look for something else now before it's too late?

A I'm thinking about it, but I still haven't decided. I [6] _____ (apply) for a new job until I'm really sure my company is going to close. I've seen a lot of production jobs on the Internet, so I'm sure I [7] _____ (find) it difficult to change companies.

B Well, I'm sure the situation [8] _____ (improve) in your company. It [9] _____ (be) as bad as it seems at the moment.

A Yes, you [10] _____ (be) right. Let's hope so!

Working with words

1 Match 1–8 to a–h to make complete sentences.

1 Computers shortcuts usually allow you to _f_
2 I have to meet ___
3 I don't have ___
4 I'm a sales rep, so I spend ___
5 It's important to plan ___
6 You should allow ___
7 My train never arrives ___
8 If there's no agenda for your meeting, you ___

a yourself a ten-minute break every two hours.
b enough time to see friends.
c your day so you use your time well.
d a lot of time travelling.
e on time.
f ~~save time.~~
g waste a lot of time.
h deadlines in my job.

2 Complete the advertisement from Dream Holiday Planners with words from the list.

~~enough~~   run   leave   schedule   allow
spend   time   ahead   waste   save

> If you don't have ¹ _enough_ time to plan your perfect holiday, contact us. You can ² _____ precious time by allowing us to organize everything for you.
>
> Send us your destination, your interests and your budget and we will plan your holiday ³ _____ for you. We will ⁴ _____ you enough time on your holiday to visit the sights and relax. You will just ⁵ _____ your time enjoying yourself and not worrying about the small details.
>
> So, don't ⁶ _____ any more time comparing holiday offers online. And don't ⁷ _____ your holiday plans to the last minute and find you've ⁸ _____ out of time to take advantage of the good deals. Get your dream holiday booked ⁹ _____ of time. Just give us your requirements now and we'll send you your holiday plan within seven days. All you have to do is arrive at the airport on ¹⁰ _____.

Business communication

1 A customer is negotiating a new contract with a supplier. Put their conversation into the correct order.

a _1_   Sue   I'm afraid we have an issue with your quotation.

b ___   Franco   I think you'll find they sell very quickly. But at that price, we would need payment within 30 days.

c ___   Franco   Well, if you ordered 200 or more, we could offer you a price of €12 per unit.

d ___   Sue   OK, then. We have a deal. I'll email you the order right away.

e ___   Franco   OK. What's the problem exactly?

f ___   Sue   Yes, I think we could order that quantity. But what if we didn't sell them all?

g _10_   Franco   Great! I'll wait to hear from you.

h ___   Sue   What if we agreed to pay within 60 days? That would allow us to sell more stock before we pay you.

i ___   Sue   Basically, €15 per unit is too expensive. If we placed a big order, could you reduce your price?

j ___   Franco   Yes, I suppose we could accept those payment terms.

2 A restaurant ordered 50 ducks but the supplier sent chickens by mistake. Put the words into the right order to complete the conversation.

Restaurant   We / latest / delivery / your / have / with / an / issue
¹ _We have an issue with your latest delivery._

Supplier   dear / problem / the / exactly / Oh / What's
² _____

Restaurant   ducks / Basically / ordered / but / fifty / sent / I / me / chickens / you
³ _____

Supplier   sorry / chickens / Would / agree / to / keep / you / the / I'm
⁴ _____

Restaurant   I'm / that / I / accept / couldn't / No / afraid
⁵ _____

Supplier   ducks / be / we / Would / delivered / today / if / it / OK / the
⁶ _____

Restaurant   that / have / the / allow / Yes / me / for / weekend / them / would / to
⁷ _____

Supplier   them / OK / send / I'll / today
⁸ _____

Language at work

GRAMMAR REFERENCE

Second conditional

Form

Positive

1 *If* + past simple, *would/might* + infinitive
   If they **dropped** their prices, we **would (we'd) buy** their products.

2 The *if* part of the sentence (the condition) can also appear in the second part of the sentence (i.e. after the result). We don't use a comma when the result comes before the condition.
   We would (We'd) send them a catalogue if we had their address.

3 You can replace *would* with *might*. In this case *might* means *perhaps*.
   If they offered me the job, I **would** *accept it.*
   (I'm sure I would accept it.)
   If they offered me the job, I **might** *accept it.*
   (Perhaps I would accept it.)

Negative

If + past simple negative, *would not (wouldn't)* + infinitive
   If he **didn't love** *city life, he* **wouldn't live** *there.*

Use

1 To talk about things which will probably not happen and the results of these things.
   If there **was** *a new job in New York, I'd apply for it.*
   (But there probably won't be a job available.)

2 To talk about impossible or hypothetical situations and their results.
   If we **didn't** *have cars, the world* **wouldn't be** *so polluted.*

3 The second conditional is different from the first conditional. Both refer to the present/future but we use the first conditional for things that are more likely to happen, and the second conditional for things that are less likely or impossible to happen.
   First conditional: If I **have** *time, I'll call you.*
   (It's possible or probable that I'll have time.)
   Second conditional: If I **had** *time, I'd call you.*
   (But I probably won't have time.)

---

1 Complete the book review with phrases from the list.

might they do
could only read
they would give
would you think about
we would recommend

they could start
didn't know
~~you lost your job~~
found themselves

What would you do if you were 50-years-old and [1]_____*you lost your job*_____? If you [2]_____ where your next pay cheque was coming from, [3]_____ starting your own business? Journalist Matthew Colbert talked to twenty successful entrepreneurs who set up their own companies after losing their jobs in their fifties. He asked them what advice [4]_____ to people if they [5]_____ in the same situation. If [6]_____ their businesses again, [7]_____ things differently?

20 Lives That Began At 50 is a fascinating collection of interviews for anybody over 50 who's thought of starting their own company. If you [8]_____ one business book this year, this is the one [9]_____.

---

2 Choose the correct words in *italics* to complete sentences 1–10. Sometimes you need a first conditional form, sometimes a second conditional.

1 I *would* / ~~will~~ travel around the world if I *has / had* enough money.

2 What part of your job *do / would* you delegate if you *had / would have* an assistant to help you?

3 If they *need / will need* more help, they *'d / 'll* call me.

4 If you *were / would be* me, *were / would* you sign the contract?

5 If we *would give / gave* them more money, they *worked / might work* during their holiday.

6 We *'ll finish / finished* on time if the electrician *works / would work* faster.

7 He *wouldn't / didn't* work late if you *wouldn't pay / didn't pay* him so well.

8 *Would / Will* we receive the goods tomorrow if you *send / would send* them today?

9 If I *know / knew* the answer, I *'d tell / told* you immediately.

10 If I *don't / didn't* finish this report today, my boss *was / will be* very angry.

Working with words

1 Match 1–8 to a–h.

1 give _g_
2 promotion ___
3 improve ___
4 develop ___
5 take ___
6 set ___
7 achieve ___
8 motivate ___

a employees
b skills
c objectives
d a step back
e prospects
f performance
g ~~feedback~~
h goals

2 Complete sentences 1–8 with a word or phrase from **1**.

1 If you always arrive late at work, this won't improve your _promotion_ _prospects_ .
2 The best way to give _____ is to discuss the positive points about an employee first.
3 Doing training courses is a good way to _____ your _____.
4 I took a month's holiday this year. It really helped me to take a _____ _____ from my job.
5 Our boss doesn't _____ _____ for the team, so we don't know where we are going.
6 One way to _____ employees is to give them an annual bonus for good results.
7 It can be difficult to _____ your objectives if they're too ambitious.
8 I've just done a course on time management. It has helped me to _____ my performance at work.

3 Complete the conversation with words from **1**.

Anja How did your appraisal go, then? Was your boss happy with your [1]_performance_?

Jan It was OK. She told me I should [2]_____ my team better and give them [3]_____ on their work more often.

Anja Really? I mean, she's not great at doing that herself, is she?

Jan I know, but I can't tell her that. She said that I needed to get a business coach to [4]_____ my management [5]_____.

Anja And when do you need to [6]_____ these goals?

Jan Well, she said that if my results are better a year from now, my [7]_____ for promotion will be very good. And she's leaving at the end of next year!

Business communication

1 A manager is talking to a colleague about a staff problem. Put the conversation in the correct order.

a _1_ I only have three months to finish the new catalogue and two of my team have just left.
b ___ I'm not sure about that. I don't think they'd do extra hours for free.
c ___ You could offer them extra holiday in return for unpaid overtime.
d ___ In that case, how about offering the rest of your team paid overtime ?
e ___ No, that's out of the question. They'd need training and we don't have time for that.
f ___ Why don't you recruit temporary staff?
g ___ Yes, that might work. But I should check with my boss that we can do that.
h _8_ Well, I suggest you talk to Marina first and then you can make your decision.

2 Correct the mistakes in suggestions 1–6.

1 Why we don't organize a team-building event?
___ _Why **don't we** organize a team-building event_ ?
2 Maybe we should to set a time limit for meetings.
_____ .
3 How about ask Head Office for a solution?
_____ ?
4 We shall think about it and chat again tomorrow?
_____ ?
5 We could introducing a suggestions box.
_____ .
6 I suggest to discuss this with the Sales Manager.
_____ .

3 Complete responses a–f with a word from the list. Then match the responses to suggestions 1–6 in **2**.

~~idea~~   about   great   think   don't   let's   sure
might   question

a Good _idea_ . I'll call you after lunch. _4_
b I'm not _____ about that. I don't _____ people will keep to it. ___
c OK, _____ ask him what he thinks in our meeting tomorrow. ___
d Yes, that _____ work. Why _____ we try it and see if people use it? ___
e No, that's out of the _____. We need to deal with the problem ourselves. ___
f That's a _____ idea! What _____ going to the mountains for a weekend? ___

Language at work

Modal verbs (2) giving advice

Use

The following modals are used to give advice.

1 Use *must* or *mustn't* for something that is very important or necessary.

*You look ill. You **must** see a doctor.*

*You **mustn't** tell my boss I have a new job.*

(It's very important you don't tell him.)

2 Use *should* or *shouldn't* for something that is or isn't a good idea.

*You **should** stop smoking.*

(It would be a good idea.)

*You **shouldn't** drink alcohol at lunchtime.*

(It's not a good idea to do this.)

3 Use *could* for something that is a possible solution.

*You **could** speak to your boss about the problem.*

Form
Positive

There is no change in the form of modal verbs.

*I/You/He/She/We/They **must** make a decision soon.*

Negative

Add *-n't* to the verb. There is no *don't* or *doesn't*.

*You **mustn't** do that. (Not ~~You don't must.~~)*

*He **shouldn't** call so late in the evening. (Not ~~He doesn't should.~~)*

Questions

Modal verb + subject + verb

***Should I accept** that new job?*

***Could I ask** him to come later?*

When we give or ask for advice, we often include the word *think*.

***I think/I don't think you should** accept that job.*

***Do you think I could** ask him to come later?*

1 Match problems 1–7 to advice a–g and choose the correct modal verbs in *italics*.

1 Our competitor's new product is cheaper than ours *f*

2 Our salary costs are too high. ___

3 The new job is less interesting and it pays less. ___

4 Our restaurant is losing customers. ___

5 They've asked me to work abroad. ___

6 I'm stressed at work. ___

7 I've made a big mistake in the accounts. ___

a You *should / shouldn't* ask for language lessons.

b You *could / mustn't* change the menus.

c You *could / mustn't* work such long hours.

d You *mustn't / must* check the figures more carefully.

e I *think / don't think* you should accept it.

f You ~~*shouldn't*~~ / *could* reduce your price for the first three months.

g You *should / shouldn't* recruit any more people.

2 Aleksander is giving Natalia advice about writing a good curriculum vitae. Complete the email with *must, mustn't, should, shouldn't* or *could*.

Dear Natalia,

You asked for help with writing your CV. Here are some ideas to help you.

Obviously, you [1] *mustn't* forget your contact details (address, phone, etc.) and you [2]_____ include your education, work experience and skills. You [3]_____ add a photograph if you want, but it's not absolutely necessary.

It's a good idea to keep your CV quite short, so you [4]_____ write more than two pages. I think you [5]_____ also write short sentences, and use verbs with impact, such as, 'achieved my goals', 'improved my performance', etc.

And when you're describing your experience, don't forget that you [5]_____ start with your most recent job first.

Finally, you really [7]_____ check that you haven't made any spelling or grammar mistakes – and most importantly, you [8]_____ lie! At an interview, an employer can easily find out that you haven't told the truth.

Hope this is useful.

Best wishes,

Aleksander

Communication activities

Unit 1 | Talking point

1 Start on the Player A or Player B square.

2 Take turns to move one square in three possible directions.

3 On a blue square, you answer the question.
   Example: *Blue square: What's your name?*
              Your answer: My name's Carlo Fernandez.

4 On a yellow square, you give a question to the answer there.
   Example: *Yellow square: No, I'm American.*
              Your question: Are you British?

5 If your question or answer is correct, you move again like this ↙ ↓ ↘ and wait for your next turn.

   If it's not correct, you move one square like this ← → and wait for your next turn.

6 If you arrive on a 'Joker' square, you will hear a question from your teacher or on an audio file.

   The first person to answer correctly moves like this.
   ↙ ↓ ↘

   The other player moves like this.
   ↖ ↑ ↗

Unit 3 | Language at work, exercise 7

Student A

- Roland Moreno invented the smart card.
- He went to school in Paris but didn't finish his studies.
- He worked for a short time for different newspapers, then created his own company. He called it 'Innovatron'.
- He launched his invention on 25th March 1974.
- He had his first success in 1983 when France Télécom used smart card technology for its phone cards.
- He also invented a number of strange musical instruments, including the 'pianok', a portable piano you could put in your pocket.

Unit 3 | Business communication, exercise 5

Student A

You researched the Energypod, a bed that can be installed in the company. Read the notes and give a report on your research.

INFORMATION ABOUT ENERGYPOD

High-quality and easy-to-move beds.
Can be used anywhere in the company.

Aims

To find the best place for employees to have a 20-minute sleep.

To find out if a short sleep helps employees to be more creative.

Research process

Decide where to install them – in room next to canteen?

Order three Energypods for one-month trial.

Free coffee and biscuits for employees who use it.

Send questionnaire to all employees at end of month.

Interview employees who used it.

Results

Easy to sleep in (70% of users).

Too noisy next to canteen (35%).

20 minutes too short (43%).

Unit 5 | Talking point, exercise 1

Joanna Payton – Northwest Power

I didn't understand why my electricity bill was so high, so I went to their local office and spoke to Joanna. After five minutes, she saw that I couldn't follow her explanations (I'm a little deaf), so she offered me a coffee and sat down with me for half an hour to explain things more simply. At the end, Joanna said she was still surprised that someone living alone had so much to pay. She looked into the problem and discovered that there was a computer error and that my bill was in fact wrong. It took four months to resolve the problem, but it was Joanna who dealt with everything. She called me regularly and I never had to contact Northwest Power myself.

Shana Adams – Belvedere Hotel

I had a reservation in a small hotel near Brighton. I arrived at about 10.30 p.m., very tired and very hungry. I asked the owner, Shana Adams, if there was a restaurant still open nearby. She gave me an address about a 20-minute drive from the hotel, but when I got to the restaurant, it was closed. When I got back to the hotel, Shana was very embarrassed about her mistake. She asked if I still wanted to eat, and 20 minutes later she served me a delicious steak and chips with salad. She offered me a drink and chatted to me about my work for another hour. When I left, the meal she served me wasn't on the bill. She said that she enjoyed our midnight conversation so much that she didn't want to make me pay for it.

Conchita Diaz – Rialto Airport Hotel

We stayed at the Rialto Airport Hotel the night before our holiday. In the taxi to the airport the next morning, we realized that my daughter's favourite teddy, Kevin the Kangaroo, was still in the hotel room. I called the hotel, but they couldn't find Kevin and my daughter was very upset. When we arrived in Acapulco, I got a call from Conchita Diaz at the Rialto. They had just found Kevin under a bed. I was very angry because my daughter was still really sad. The same day, I received an email with a photo of Kevin sitting by the swimming pool at the Rialto. The message was 'Having a wonderful holiday!' The next day, it was a photo of Kevin at the restaurant, then Kevin at the gym, and so on for all ten days of our vacation. Now my daughter wants Kevin to spend every holiday at the Rialto.

Bartol Kukoc – Loc-Tite Security

Bartol's company manages security at our factory. After just 18 months with us, he knows all our employees by name, and greets everybody at the entrance with a friendly smile and a few words. He always asks me to tell him when important visitors are coming. When they arrive, he asks about their journey and chats to them about their country or home town. Last month, I completely forgot I had a visit from a VIP customer. I was in another meeting when Bartol called me. He said 'I have your visitor, Mr X, here. I told him you were stuck in traffic.' I then had to leave the company by a different exit. When I arrived at the main entrance ten minutes later, Mr X was showing Bartol photos of his holiday in Croatia.

Aaron Dyke – Joe's Superstore

It was just before the Christmas holidays, and there was a lot of snow in my father's home town. He's 89 years old and lives alone and I was worried that he couldn't go out to the supermarket. I called several stores, but either they didn't deliver to people's homes or they had too many other deliveries. Then I called Joe's Superstore and spoke to Aaron. 'No, we don't usually deliver, Ma'am, and we are just closing, but I'll speak to my boss.' Two minutes later he called back and took my order. My father has a special diet, so he suggested other products that would be good for him. When I wanted to pay, Aaron said it wasn't necessary. Half an hour later, Aaron was at my father's door with his groceries.

Unit 7 | Language at work, exercise 7

Student A

1 You have the schedule on Meghan's desk and your partner has the email from Arianna. Tell each other what information you have.

   Example: She's arriving …   She wants to …

2 Decide what to do with Arianna during her visit and who will do it.

   Example: We can take her …   Who's going to …?
              I'll do that.   We can both do that.

3 Summarize the details of the schedule.

   Example: So we're going to …   Then we're taking her …

VISIT SCHEDULE

Arianna Boyle – TFF

Wednesday 20th

6.35 a.m. Arrival, flight AH 216

???

11 a.m. Presentation of company (Meghan)

12.30 p.m. Lunch in company canteen
          (Meghan and CEO)

2 p.m. Visit company and meet
          department managers (Meghan)

4 p.m. ???

Evening ???

Thursday 21st

8.15 a.m. Departure, flight BK 165

Unit 10 | Business communication, exercise 5

Group A

1 Prepare a short talk on the advantages and disadvantages of taking the train to business meetings, compared with taking the car. Use these key ideas to help you.

   - Ticket prices
   - Distance
   - Productivity
   - Travel time
   - Carbon emissions
   - Tiredness

2 Work with a partner from Group B and give your talk.

Unit 11 | Talking point, exercise 2

A legal expert's view

1 The hospitality provided is very near in time to the price negotiations, but this is a regular event offered to a number of customers, not just one. **Verdict: Hospitality**

2 The businessman has probably chosen this moment to make his donation for a good reason. However, he hasn't contacted the university to talk about his son's application. **Verdict: Gift**

3 The hotel and dinner package is a way to attract customers to the event but there is no obligation to buy. The gifts are promotional products to advertise the company name and not of great value. **Verdict: Hospitality/Gift**

4 The dinner is an acceptable business expense for a supplier who wants to rebuild a relationship with a customer. However, the watch is a very expensive item. Maybe the supplier sent it by post to make it more difficult for the customer to refuse. **Verdict: Bribery**

5 The gifts are small and proportional in value to the service provided by the cleaner. However, three gifts in three months is too much, and it's not acceptable to follow these gifts with a request for a change in the cleaner's routine. **Verdict: Bribery**

Unit 12 | Talking point, exercise 1

1 Good for your reputation, and now you have a cheap source of recycled plastic. Score three points.

2 An important sales argument. Outdoor furniture needs to resist the weather – and vandalism! Score three points.

3 You earn a good reputation for promoting equal opportunity policies. Score three points.

4 Your web pages will mainly be read by potential employees or future customers. Not a very public way to promote your image. Score one point.

5 A good decision. You will have enough production space for the next two years and you can employ more local people. Score three points.

6 A good choice. Local salaries won't be too high because of the employment situation. Score three points.

7 Recycling is an important part of environmental protection. But in general, plastic isn't good for the environment. Score one point.

8 Your market share remains stable because your competitors have had to increase their prices, too. Score three points.

9 A good socially responsible gesture. It will also make you more popular with your local council customers. Score three points.

10 It's maybe not good for workplace diversity, but you'll be sure to have a good team. If you want the best, your wage bill may be high, though. Score one point.

11 You now have many problems with delays in delivery. Also, transport costs are rising dramatically. Is this really a low-cost solution? Lose one point.

12 You sell at a good price, but your association with the oil industry isn't good for your image. Lose one point.

13 Sales continue to go down because you've lost 40% of your sales force. Lose two points.

14 The safest way to prevent any more accidents. Your customers are very happy with your socially responsible gesture, and your ex-supplier agrees to pay half the cost. Score three points.

15 After six months, your customers are complaining that the quality of your furniture isn't the same as before. Lose one point.

16 The local council say they don't want another factory in their beautiful town. Lose two points.

17 Your customers are very disappointed – this doesn't solve the problem. What happens if somebody gets seriously injured? Lose two points.

18 The workers accept your proposal, preferring to work four days a week than to lose their jobs. Score three points.

Unit 14 | Language at work, exercise 8

Student A

1 Read questions 1–4 and answer them for yourself.

2 Ask your partner the same questions, using second conditional forms.

   Example: If you wanted to call a colleague at home, what would be the latest possible time to phone: 9 p.m., 10.30 p.m. or it doesn't matter?

3 Compare your answers and say why they are the same or different.

4 Then check your score on page 140.

---

1 You want to call a colleague at home. What's the latest possible time you would phone?

   a 9 p.m.

   b 10.30 p.m.

   c It doesn't matter

2 A customer asks you for a quotation by the end of the week. When would you email it?

   a Wednesday or Thursday

   b Friday

   c When you find the time

3 You're in a meeting which started at 9 a.m. It's now 1 p.m. Would you …?

   a suggest stopping for lunch

   b look at your watch every five minutes

   c not worry about it

4 Your friends and family advise you to slow down and work less. Would you …?

   a say it's not possible because there's too much to do

   b try to follow their advice

   c say you're surprised – your work isn't stressful at all

Unit 14 | Language at work, exercise 8

All students

Mostly 'a's Doing things on time is very important for you. You need to live in a 'clock time' culture.

Mostly 'b's You would probably be happy in a 'clock time' or 'event time' culture.

Mostly 'c's You're very relaxed! An 'event time' culture would be very good for you.

Unit 14 | Business communication, exercise 6

Student A

You work for Sigma Supplies. You have asked Pixel Printing to print your new catalogue for next year, but you now want to change the details of the order. Call the company, explain the situation and negotiate the new conditions.

	Original order	You now want
Number of pages	300	350
Number of catalogues	5,000	6,000
Delivery	By 15th Dec	By 15th Nov
Price per catalogue	€3.00	The same price

Notes

You think you should pay the same price per catalogue as you are increasing your order.

Pixel Printing is a high-quality supplier with reasonable prices.

Unit 15 | Business communication, exercise 6

Student A

Work with Student B. Each of you is going to suggest four ideas for improving motivation in your company. Respond to each suggestion, and decide on the three best ideas.

SUGGESTION

Hire a business coach for one day a month – available for all employees.

SUGGESTION

Redecorate all the offices and buy new furniture.

SUGGESTION

Introduce a 'Thanksgiving Day' – every Friday, employees must say thank you to three colleagues.

SUGGESTION

Organize more social events for employees in the evenings and at weekends.

Unit 3 | Language at work, exercise 7

Student B

- Martin Cooper invented the mobile phone.
- He studied at the Illinois Institute of Technology. He completed his Masters in 1957.
- He joined the Motorola company in 1954.
- He launched his Dyna-TAC phone on 3rd April 1973.
- He had his first success in 1983 when the first commercial mobile phone service started. The Dyna-TAC phone cost $4,000.
- He also invented other devices. In 1967, he created the first portable police radio system.

Unit 3 | Business communication, exercise 5

Student B

You researched the PowerNap company, which provides a 'sleep service' near your company. Read the notes and give a report on your research.

INFORMATION ABOUT POWERNAP

Five minutes' walk from company – gives employees a break from the workplace.

Aims

To find the best place for employees to have a 20-minute midday sleep.

To see if employees work better in the afternoon after a short sleep.

Research process

Rent a PowerNap bed for one month – 3 x 20 minutes per day.

Ask for ten volunteers to test the service.

Volunteers only pay 25% of normal price.

Complete questionnaire at end of each week.

Interview volunteers at end of month.

Results

Beds very relaxing (9 out of 10 people).

Good to have a break from company (7 out of 10 people).

Not good value: normal price very expensive (8 out of 10 people).

Unit 7 | Language at work, exercise 7

Student B

1 You have the email from Arianna and your partner has the schedule on Meghan's desk. Tell each other what information you have.

> **She's** arriving …   She wants to …

2 Decide what to do with Arianna during her visit and who will do it.

> **We** can take her …   Who's going to …?
> **I'll** do that.   We can both do that.

3 Summarize the details of the schedule.

> **So** we're going to …   Then we're taking her …

> … I only asked to come last week, so I quite understand that you can't be there all the time.
>
> You wanted to know what I would like to do or see. Well, it's my first time in your country, so it would be nice to try some local food. I don't eat meat, but I like fish. I'd also like to visit the area a little – I'm interested in towns and their history, but I'm also a nature lover. I also love all kinds of music, so if there's time to listen to a little local music, that would be great.

Unit 10 | Business communication, exercise 5

Group B

1 Prepare a short talk on the advantages and disadvantages of replacing all your company cars with electric vehicles. Use these key ideas to help you.

- Price of cars
- Running costs
- Distances
- Carbon emissions
- Speed
- Company image

2 Work with a partner from Group A and give your talk.

Unit 14 | Language at work, exercise 8

Student B

1 Read questions 1–4 and answer them for yourself.

2 Ask your partner the same questions, using second conditional forms.

> **Example:** If your boss invited you for Sunday lunch at 1 p.m., what time would you arrive – 1 p.m., 1.30 p.m. at the latest or 3 p.m.?

3 Compare your answers and say why they are the same or different.

4 Then check your score on page 140.

1 Your boss invites you for Sunday lunch at 1 p.m. What time would you arrive?
   a 1 p.m.
   b 1.30 p.m. at the latest
   c 2 p.m.

2 Your train to work stops between stations because of problems on the line. What would you do?
   a Get really irritable
   b Look at your watch
   c Read a book or listen to music

3 You have a three-day business trip that starts tomorrow. Would you …?
   a write a list of things to take
   b have a list in your head of what you need
   c have no list at all

4 You're in the supermarket on Saturday and all the checkouts are very busy. Would you …?
   a leave the items and go out without paying
   b find the shortest queue and hope it doesn't take too long
   c go to the nearest queue and relax – it's the weekend

Unit 14 | Business communication, exercise 6

Student B

You work for Pixel Printing. Sigma Supplies have asked you to print their new catalogue for next year. They will call you to ask for some changes. Complete the table below and decide what conditions you can accept or offer. Use the notes to help.

	Original order	Sigma now want
Number of pages	300	
Number of catalogues	5,000	
Delivery	By 15th Dec	
Price per catalogue	€3.00	

Notes

You are very busy in November.

For a print order of 5,000–6,000 catalogues, the normal price is €1 per 100 pages.

Sigma Supplies is a very good customer.

Unit 15 | Business communication, exercise 6

Student B

Work with Student A. Each of you is going to suggest four ideas for improving motivation in your company. Respond to each suggestion, and decide on the three best ideas.

SUGGESTION

Give annual bonuses to work teams or departments that achieve their objectives.

SUGGESTION

Start a 'Suggestions box' – the best idea for improving the company every month wins a prize.

SUGGESTION

Allow employees days off to do social work in the community, e.g. helping old people.

SUGGESTION

Introduce autonomous work teams with no managers.

Audio scripts

Unit 1

1.1

A Which company do you work for?
B I work for Assa Abloy.
A I don't think I know the name. What does the company do?
B We make locks and security systems. I'm sure you know some of our brands. Yale locks … or Chubb … or Vachette, for example.
A No, I'm afraid I don't. Who are your main competitors?
B The Eastern Company …? Ingersoll-Rand …? Master Lock?
A Well, I think you can see now that I know nothing about the security business. Where's the company based?
B It's a Swedish group.
A Oh, OK. Is it a very big group?
B Yes, it is. We have about 43,000 employees.
A That is big.
B And we have annual sales of more than €5 billion.
A So are you mainly in the European market?
B No, we operate in over 70 different countries worldwide. There are 150 different companies in the group.
A And which part of the company do you work for?
B Besam. B-E-S-A-M. It's a subsidiary of the main company. We specialize in automatic door mechanisms. Who do you work for?
A Microsoft.
B And what does your company do?
A We make … ah, that's a joke, right?

1.2

The Nestlé Company is over 150 years old. It was created in 1866 by Henri Nestlé, and the first Nestlé product was baby milk. The company still produces baby products today, but this is just one in a wide range of food and drink products, including chocolate and confectionery, bottled water, breakfast cereals and ice cream. It's a very successful company with an annual revenue of around 90 billion Swiss francs.

Nestlé is a truly global company. Its head office is in Vevey in Switzerland, but it manufactures in 447 factories around the world and sells on all five continents. It has over 300,000 employees. We talk to some of them today.

Nestlé believes that it is important to invest in its employees. Training is an important part of its philosophy. Last year, 80% of employees did training courses. We hear from a Nestlé employee who started on the production line and is now a senior manager. Nestlé also invests in people outside the company, giving money and help to local communities. The company offers education in nutrition, health programmes and gives free food. We talk to a health expert on how Nestlé products can improve your health. Finally, we look at Nestlé's role as a 'green' company. It protects the environment by using less water, less energy and less packaging. A supplier tells us how Nestlé helps him to conserve water in his agricultural business.

All this, and more, in Nestlé in Focus, right after the break.

1.3

A Our company operates in 165 different countries and it has 89 factories on all five continents.
B Sorry, can you say that again?
A Yes, sure. We're in 165 countries and we have 89 factories …
B Sorry, can you speak a bit more slowly? So that's 89 factories …
A In 165 countries. That's one-six-five.
B So you're everywhere in the world.

A Yeah, that's right – on all five continents. And we have 305,000 employees and annual sales last year of 17.8 billion dollars.
B Sorry, how many employees do you have?
A Three hundred and five thousand. Three-zero-five.
B And what are your annual sales again?
A Seventeen point eight billion dollars.
B Nearly 18 billion. OK.

1.4

Gianluca Excuse me. Is this seat free?
Carmen Yes, it is. Go ahead.
Gianluca Thanks very much. Can I introduce myself? I'm Gianluca Donatelli.
Carmen Nice to meet you. I'm Carmen Sanchez.
Gianluca Nice to meet you too, Carmen. Where are you from?
Carmen I'm from Argentina. But I live and work in Europe.
Gianluca And who do you work for?
Carmen I don't work for a company. I'm self-employed.
Gianluca Oh, really? And what do you do?
Carmen I'm a journalist. I write articles for consumer magazines.
Gianluca So why are you at this conference?
Carmen I'm here to research an article on Internet service providers.
Gianluca That's interesting. A friend of mine works for an Italian service provider. Can I introduce you to him?
Carmen Yes, of course. That would be nice.
Gianluca Roberto. Can you come here a minute? This is … sorry, what's your name again?
Carmen Carmen. Carmen Sanchez.
Gianluca Roberto. This is Carmen. She's writing an article on Internet service providers.

1.5

Gianluca What do you do?
Carmen I'm a journalist. I write articles for consumer magazines. What about you? What do you do?
Gianluca I'm a sales manager. Why are you here at this conference?
Carmen I'm here to research an article on Internet service providers. How about you? Why are you here?
Gianluca We want to find new customers in the European market.

1.6

Joker question 1 This Internet services company has its head office in Mountain View, California. If you are looking for information on the Internet, go to this company's page first. What's the name of the company?
Joker question 2 This car manufacturer is based in the UK, but it's a subsidiary of the German company BMW. It is well known for its luxury cars, but it also makes engines for the aeronautic and marine industries. What's the name of the company?
Joker question 3 This Japanese company specializes in audio, video and communications products. It has around 160,000 employees. One of its most well-known products is PlayStation. What's the name of the company?
Joker question 4 This American company has its head office in Seattle, Washington. Its products include the 737, 747, 767 and the 787. It's the main competitor of Airbus. What's the name of the company?
Joker question 5 This company specializes in tyres for cars, but it is also well known for its calendars. It's a competitor of Michelin and Goodyear, and it's based in Italy. What's the name of the company?

Joker question 6 This Northern European company produces mobile phones, multimedia systems and wireless networks. In the mobile phone market, two of its biggest competitors are Sony and Samsung. What's the name of the company?

Joker question 7 This French group is a world leader in dairy products, including yoghurts, cheese and desserts. It's the number two in bottled water, and it also produces biscuits. What's the name of the company?

Unit 2

2.1

Interviewer So what do you do, Simon?
Simon I work for a company that produces software.
Interviewer And which department are you in?
Simon I'm in the sales department and I'm a sales rep.
Interviewer So who do you work with?
Simon I work with a small team of reps. There are three of us. And obviously I have a lot of contact with my customers.
Interviewer So who are your customers?
Simon Our customers are international companies that work with producers and suppliers abroad. They use our software to calculate the cost of making a product in different countries.
Interviewer And how does this help your customers?
Simon Well, they know the production cost in each country. Then they choose the supplier with the best price.
Interviewer OK, I see. So what sort of problems do you deal with in your work?
Simon Hmm … I think the biggest problem is time – my company only employs 12 people, so there's a lot to do. As I said, I sell software, but I also train our customers to use it. I organize the training courses, and that's a lot of work. Five days a week just isn't enough to do everything.

2.2

1
So tell me, what do you do?
I'm a sales rep.
Who do you work for?
I work for a company that produces software.

2
I've not seen you at work for ages. What are you doing these days?
I'm travelling a lot more.
So that's why I never see you. What are you working on at the moment?
I'm working with our new suppliers in Hungary and Poland. We're setting up a new ordering system.
Sounds great.

3
Hi. What are you doing?
I'm just finishing this report.
Got time for a coffee?
Give me a minute.

2.3

1
A Technical Support. Aidan speaking.
B Hi, Aidan.
A Who am I speaking to?
B Sorry, this is Nadira. I'm trying to access my customer files, but the computer isn't accepting my log-in. The log-in details are still the same, aren't they? The first four letters of my name, N-A-D-I, then the last four of my mobile number: one three seven four.

A Yes, that's right. But you're not the first person to call me today! There's a problem with the server.
B Is somebody working on it at the moment?
A Yes, I am. But it's not easy, because I'm on my own here. Everybody else is having lunch. Try again in half an hour.
B OK, Aidan. Thanks.

2
A Good to see you again, Johann.
B Yes, you too, Anabelle.
A Are you staying here all week?
B Yes, I am. I'm giving a training course.
A So who are you training this time?
B It's a group of six people. They all work in telesales.
A Ah yes, I know Sonya and her team. So is it going well?
B Yes, they're making good progress. Do you work with the telesales team, then?
A No, I don't, but we have lunch together from time to time.
B Well, I'm going to a restaurant with them right now. Do you want to come?
A Sorry, but I always go to the gym on Wednesdays.

2.4

A My landline is oh-one-eight-six-five, double five-six, seven-six-seven.
B Sorry, double five-six …
A Seven-six-seven. If there's no answer on that number, he can try my mobile number. That's oh-six, two-five, nine-seven, eight-oh, double three. Those are UK numbers. If he's phoning from Germany, the code is double oh-double four.
B Zero-zero-double four. OK.

2.5

1
A Can you give me your name, please?
B Sure. It's Geoff Eccleston. That's E-double C-L-E-S-T-O-N.
A Eccleston. With a double C.
B That's right.
A And your first name, Jeff … is that J-E-F-F?
B No, it's Geoff with a G. G-E-O-double F.
A G-E-O-double F. OK.

2
A Can I have your name, please?
B Yes, it's Aliny Reis. That's A-L-I-N-Y …
A A-L-I-N-Y. And your last name? Reis, did you say?
B Yes, that's R-E-I-S.
A R-E-I-S. OK.

2.6

1
A Ackers and Shipton. How can I help you?
B Is Mrs Ackers there, please?
A Speaking. Who's calling, please?
B This is Simon Ilago from AOS – Ace Office Supplies.
A What can I do for you, Mr Ilago?
B I'm calling to offer you a special price on printers, Mrs Ackers.
A I'm sorry, I'm busy at the moment.
B Can I call you back tomorrow?
A Sorry, but I'm out of the office tomorrow. But thanks for calling. Goodbye.
B Er … you're welcome. Goodbye.

2
A BFC Consulting. Ralf Guterson speaking.
B Hello. Could I speak to Leo Keliher, please?
A I'm afraid he's out of the office at the moment.
B Could I leave a message?
A Yes, of course. Could I have your name, please?

B This is Natalie Kent, from NT Consulting. Could you ask Leo to call me back? It's quite urgent. He's got my number.
A Yes, sure. Could you tell me what it's about?
B Yes, I'm phoning to offer him some consultancy work.
A OK. I'll give Leo the message.
B Thanks for your help. Goodbye.

Unit 3

3.1

1 You loved the Okai Traveller 2. You'll really adore the Okai Traveller 3. There are even more high-tech features: we've added a totally new high-definition camera for perfect photos every time, and a high-speed G7 processor for super fast navigation. And that's not all: the Okai Traveller 3 now comes in a choice of six popular colours, from Sunset Red to Lagoon Blue. Visit our website to discover all the fantastic features that really makes the Okai 3 stand out from the Okai 2 and 1.

2
A Hey, you look great. Where did you get that outfit?
B At Priscilla's, just round the corner.
A Oh really? I love the material. It's really high quality.
B Yes, it always is. And you won't find this in the department stores.
A Mmm.
B Well, you know me – I like designs that are original.
A Yes, your things are always quite … original.

3
A So if you want a safe investment, I can recommend this savings account. It's an extremely reliable product.
B Sorry. What do you mean, reliable?
A Well, you earn a guaranteed 3% a year and you can close the account whenever you want.
B And can I check the account online?
A Yes, you can. And it's a very user-friendly site. If you have a moment, I can show you how easy it is.

4
A So how was Spain?
B Fantastic! Great place and amazing food. The accommodation was pretty good value, too. I'm glad we booked with Go South.
A So you'd recommend them?
B Yes, I would. They even pay you £10 if you write a review of your holiday. So you get a lot of helpful advice from people who used Go South before.

3.2

Welcome to our new series of Business Foundation, where we look at the entrepreneurs who have made our lives so different today. People like Jack Dorsey, co-founder of Twitter, who launched his popular social networking service in 2006. Or Tim Berners-Lee, who started the World Wide Web in 1991. Many people didn't know him before 2012, when the London Olympics celebrated his work.

Here's a question for you: when did mobile communications begin? That was in 1973, when Martin Cooper made the first mobile phone call using his new invention, the Dyna-TAC phone. And who was Roland Moreno? He invented the smart chip technology used in credit cards, passports and SIM cards just one year later, in 1974.

More on these people later in the series, but today we focus on Twitter, and its creator Jack Dorsey. We have Internet expert Neil Harris in the studio to tell us all about it. Neil, how did it all start?

3.3

Presenter Neil, how did it all start?
Neil Well, Jack Dorsey became interested in digital communications at a very early age. He was particularly interested in the communication problems of taxi drivers and delivery trucks. In fact, all companies with vehicles that needed to stay in contact in real time. When he was 15, he produced some communication software that is still used by some taxicab companies today.
Presenter That's interesting. So he started very young. Did he go to university?
Neil Yes, he did. First he studied at the University of Science and Technology in Missouri, then he went to New York University. But he didn't finish his degree, like many other high-tech entrepreneurs before him – Bill Gates, Steve Jobs, Mark Zuckerberg. The list is very long. Instead, he moved to Oakland, California.
Presenter And is that when he started Twitter?
Neil No, not immediately. In fact, he started a company to sell his communication software and he sold it online. But then he had an idea for a different type of communication service – one where you could exchange short messages with all your friends in real time. He found two partners who were interested, and started a new company with them. And then, immediately after, he created a simple, user-friendly website where users could post short messages of 140 characters or less. It took him just two weeks!
Presenter Oh really? So this was the beginning of Twitter as we know it?
Neil Yes, that's right. And Jack Dorsey posted the first Twitter message, or 'Tweet', on the 21st March 2006.
Presenter So what was the message? Something original and memorable, I hope?
Neil No, I'm afraid not. The first tweet was the words 'Just setting up my twttr.'
Presenter So not so original! And was Twitter an immediate success?
Neil No, not at first. A lot of people didn't see why the world needed another messaging service. And there were technical problems with the site in the early days – it wasn't very reliable. But in 2008, Barack Obama and John McCain used Twitter for the first time to communicate to voters in their Presidential campaigns. Today, everybody uses it: not only politicians, but also pop stars, sports personalities … and of course, you and me.
Presenter Neil Harris – thank you. We'll hear more about recent developments at Twitter … just after the break.

3.4

A Did you have a good week?
B Yes, it was great! I went on a trip for a change.
A Did you? Where did you go?
B We went to Monte Carlo.
A That's interesting! Why did you go there?
B It was a trade exhibition for high-tech communication devices. It was really exciting!
A Was it? I don't know Monte Carlo.
B It was my first time, actually. I really enjoyed it and the weather was fantastic.
A Oh really? It rained here all week. I think you went to the right place!

3.5

I'm here to report on our experiment with podpads at the Summerhouse festival last month. The purpose of our research was to find the best accommodation for visitors during outdoor festivals. We wanted to find out if people would pay to rent a podpad. We did this by interviewing 50 visitors to the Summerhouse festival. First, we offered a free night in a podpad to the 50 people in our research. Then we interviewed them about their experience. Finally, we spoke to the farmers who allowed us to use their land. We asked them for their opinion of the podpads and also of the company that installed them. We found that podpads were popular with visitors and farmers. The visitors were very happy with their accommodation and 75% of visitors said that they would pay to use them. The farmers also had no complaints. They commented that the podpads look attractive and they thought that the team who installed them were very quick and efficient.

So our research showed that the podpads were a big success. Our conclusion is that they are a great choice of accommodation for outdoor festivals and we recommend using them at our next festival.

3.6

1

I decided to buy this about three years ago, and now I use it all the time. I had so many books and no space in the house to put them. And when I went on holiday, I never knew which books to take with me. Now I can take my library everywhere with me. It's easy to transport, and I have about 300 titles to choose from. So I save space in my suitcase, and I also save money because e-books are generally cheaper.

2

I was never very good with maps. I could never remember the route, and stopped the car every 15 minutes to check the map again. But now the information is always there in front of me, so I save a lot of time. And it's reliable – if you take the wrong road, it will find another solution for you. And it always tells you what time you will arrive so I'm rarely late for meetings now. No, I can't live without it.

3

I bought my first one about 15 years ago because I had a problem with hot drinks! I often made myself a coffee and then forgot to drink it. So it was perfect for re-heating cold coffee! And now I have children, everyone in the family can use it. My children often make their own dinner in the evening if they're home early. It's easy to use, and it's safe – you don't want your seven-year-old daughter using a gas cooker!

4

My son didn't understand why I bought this. He said: 'Why don't you just look at your mobile phone or computer? Why buy a product that only does one thing? It doesn't play music, you can't contact your friends with it. It just tells you the time.' But that's what I like about it. I told him it was very user-friendly – you just look at it and you have the information in less than a second. Quicker than his phone!

Unit 4

4.1

A

In our department we do reports at the end of each month which show all the money going into and out of the company. We work closely with the Accounts Department, which gives us all the financial information we need. I have a meeting today with Anna Neves in IT, who's responsible for all our software. She's coming to show me a new program she wants to buy. She says it will help us a lot with all our financial reporting.

B

I organize all the transport from suppliers to our factories, and from our factories to customers. So we work a lot with Production, but also with the Sales Department. Today I have a meeting with Ralf Ehrling. He's the person in charge of purchasing for the whole company. He wants to use just three or four big international transporters for all three of our business units. He thinks it will cost less to have a small number of suppliers.

C

I'm in charge of recruitment, so I have frequent contact with all the different departments to find out their recruitment needs. I report to the HR Director, and I have a meeting with her today to discuss our recruitment strategy for the year ahead.

4.2

1

A So here on the first floor we have all the financial offices. This is the Financial Director's office just here on the right. He's not here today. He's working in Head Office.
B How often does he work in this office?
A Oh, he's only here about one day a week on average …
B Where does he come from? Isn't he American?
A Yes, he's from New York.

2

A This is our HR Manager, Carla Brookes. Carla, this is Istvan Sieliki. He's interested in doing some marketing work for us in Poland.
C Ah, that's good news. Nice to meet you, Mr …
B Sieliki. But please call me Istvan. Nice to meet you too, Carla.
C So how long are you staying here … Istvan?
B Just two days – today and tomorrow. So how many people work in Human Resources, Carla?
C There are six of us in all, but two people are part-time.

3

A We're now going into the new part of the company.
B When did you open this building?
A Just two months ago. I'll show you our new call centre. Our staff here take calls from customers all over the world.
B And are all the staff fluent in English?
A Not all, but a lot of them are taking English lessons at the moment.

4

A Can I introduce you to Alex Fenton? Alex is responsible for new business in Northern Europe. He's on the road most of the time, talking to new customers.
B Hello, Alex. So who chooses your sales markets?
D Well, we get information from a lot of markets and then the sales director develops a sales strategy depending on which countries are interested in our products.
B So which countries are interested in your products?
D Sweden and Denmark mostly. But there's some interest from Poland, too.
B Do you know the Polish market well?
D No, but I want to have a sales rep there soon. I'd be very happy to hear your ideas.

4.3

A There's someone who really wants to meet you. Dave Payton. He says he knows you.
B Dave Payton … oh yes, I think I remember him. Doesn't he work in International Sales?
A Yes, he does. That's right.
B I think I met him in Brazil. He travels a lot to South America, right?

A Well, not exactly. His market is more North America and Canada.

B OK, now I remember. He went to the trade fair in San Francisco, didn't he?

A Yes, that's right.

4.4

Jim Good morning. I have an appointment with Olivia Gonzalez.

Receptionist OK. Can I have your name, please?

Jim Jim Berman, from Trollberg International.

Receptionist OK. You need a visitor's pass. Can I see some identification, please?

Jim Sure. Here you are.

Receptionist Thanks. Can you sign in just here, please?

Jim Yes, of course.

Receptionist So here's your passport, and this is your visitor's pass.

Jim Thank you.

Receptionist Ms Gonzalez will be right there. Please take a seat.

Jim OK, thank you.

…

Olivia Hello, Jim.

Jim Hi, Olivia. Nice to see you again.

Olivia You, too. Did you have a good trip?

Jim Yes I did, thanks. My plane arrived on time. And my hotel's very nice.

Olivia That's good. And did you have any trouble finding us?

Jim No, but the traffic was bad. Sorry I'm a bit late.

Olivia No problem. Thank you for coming.

Jim Thank you for inviting me.

Olivia It's a pleasure. So let's go to my office. It's this way.

Jim After you.

…

Olivia So, here's my office. Please take a seat.

Jim Thanks.

Olivia Can I get you something to drink? A coffee or tea maybe?

Jim Yes, please. A coffee would be nice.

Olivia OK. And do you need anything else?

Jim Yes. Can I plug in my computer somewhere?

Olivia Yes, of course. There's a socket just there.

Jim And do you have a wi-fi connection here?

Olivia No, we don't. Just use this cable. You'll need the password. Here you are.

Jim Thanks.

…

Olivia OK, coffee's ready. Help yourself to milk and sugar.

Jim Great, thanks. I just need to check my email, then I'll be ready.

Olivia No hurry. Let me know if you need anything else.

Jim I will. Thanks.

Unit 5

5.1

1

I bought an expensive talking toy from an online retailer for my son's birthday. My son was very happy, but unfortunately Buzz Lightyear stopped talking after just two days. The only channel of communication was an email address to contact the company, so I wrote to them to report the problem. I was expecting a long wait. I certainly didn't think the response time would be so quick. The same afternoon, I got a phone call from the supplier of the toy, who was very polite and understanding. They sent me a replacement the same day, which arrived the day after. And in the package there was a £10 credit voucher for my next purchase on the site.

2

I saw a tablet computer I wanted in a store near my home. When I looked on the Internet, I saw that it was cheaper to buy it online, from the same company, and then go to the store to pick it up. So I did that, but when I tried the tablet at home, it was impossible to connect to the Internet. So I took it back to the shop to explain the issue. They weren't very helpful. They said they couldn't do anything because I bought it online. 'Yes,' I said, 'but from your website. And I came to your store to pick it up.' I asked for a replacement, or if not a refund, but they refused. They just gave me the phone number of the Technical Support hotline.

5.2

Why do people prefer to buy online? A recent survey asked this question to 15,000 shoppers in 15 different parts of the world. The first reason is probably no surprise to you. Online retailers offer the cheapest products. 55% of people chose online shopping because prices were lower. The second reason was shopping hours. Physical stores are of course limited by their opening times, but online stores have the most flexible hours: 24 hours a day, seven days a week. It's difficult to be more flexible than that. People also liked the fact that you can compare products and prices online. And it's true – it's not as easy to compare products in physical stores, especially if they're not near each other. Another reason was the number of products available. Some people buy online because Internet shopping offers a wider choice than in-store shopping. And finally, where do you prefer to get information about products? Some people think online retailers offer better information about a product. But only 11% thought this was a reason for buying online. Perhaps many of us still prefer to speak to somebody in a real shop.

5.3

A I get more professional advice in a shop than online. I think in general the staff in a store have a better knowledge of the products. That's very useful.

B I know the prices aren't as low as online, but it's the quickest way to get the product I want. I don't like to wait for a package to come.

C The most important thing for me is to see and touch the products. It's easier to make the right choice. But I still buy a lot of things I don't need!

D Well, it's less difficult to return or exchange items than when you buy online. With a real store, I can just walk there or go in the car. It's also the least expensive way because you don't pay for postage.

E Well, you see it in the news. The postal service isn't as reliable now. Delivery times are longer and a lot of packages are lost, so I prefer to buy in a shop.

5.4

A I'm sorry to say this, but the report you did for me isn't very good.

B I'm afraid I don't understand.

A It's not very easy for me to use these statistics. I'm afraid they aren't organized in the right way.

B Sorry, but I thought that's what you wanted.

A Well, actually, I told you to present the results by country, not by product. Sorry, but could you do it again?

B OK. Sorry about that. I'll do it this afternoon.

5.5

1

A Customer Service. How can I help you?

B Hello. Sorry, but I've just received a book from you, and I'm afraid there's a problem with it.

A Oh dear. Can you give me more details?

B Well, it's what I ordered – a biography of Nelson Mandela – but it's in Spanish, not English. I think I maybe clicked on the wrong button on your website.

A That's possible. Well, I'm sorry to hear that. We'll send you the correct version today. Can you return the other book to us?

B Yes, of course.

A And we'll credit £5 to your account to cover postage.

B Oh, thanks very much.

A Now, can you just give me your account details …

2

A Triple A Taxis. Good morning.

B Hello, this is Mrs Navarro. I booked a taxi to the airport for nine o'clock. It's 9.15 now and it still hasn't arrived. I have a plane to catch in two hours' time.

A I do apologize, Mrs Navarro. Let me check. The address is 7 Castle Street, right?

B Yes, that's right.

A OK, I'll look into it and get back to you right away. Can I call you on this number?

B Yes, it's my mobile. I'll wait to hear from you.

3

A Good afternoon, sir. What can I do for you?

B Good afternoon. I bought this music system six months ago. It's already been repaired once, and now it's not working again. I'm not very happy about it.

A Sorry about that, sir. This model is usually very reliable. What exactly is the problem?

B It's the same issue as before. It doesn't read MP3 files. I don't want it to be repaired again. I'd like a refund.

A I'm afraid we can't give you a refund now, but we can offer you a replacement. Do you still have the receipt?

4

A You know those customer files you prepared for me?

B Yes.

A I'm afraid they're not the right ones. I actually wanted the files for 2015, not 2016.

B Oh yes, I remember now. It's my fault. I'm sorry.

A Yes, sorry about that. I know it took you a long time to put them together.

B Don't worry. I'll deal with it now.

Unit 6

6.1

1

I was lucky. I only saw the advertisement for my job at the last minute. It was on the company's website, and the deadline was at midnight the same day. I only had about four hours to prepare my application. I sent it at about two minutes before midnight. I really wanted the job, but I wasn't really qualified for it, because I didn't have a Masters degree. So I didn't think I would be shortlisted, but I was. Why? Well, I was the last person to send my CV, so I was the first candidate on their list the next morning, and the first one they looked at. It's always useful to be at the top of the pile.

2

It all started with a job interview in another company. I could see that the person who interviewed me didn't like me. He wasn't interested in my answers. The company wanted a highly-skilled technician, preferably with three years working in the industry. I had the qualifications, but I wasn't at all experienced as this was my first real job. Anyway, I decided to go for a drink after my interview, and there I met one of my old teachers from technical school. He had a new job working for a company installing wind turbines. He was responsible for the recruitment of service technicians. I think you can imagine the rest. That was so lucky!

6.2

Interviewer So when did you start working in this field?

Naomi Well, I left university in 2009 and I got my first job immediately after that.

Interviewer And have you ever worked for a big organization?

Naomi No, I've never had the chance. But I've worked for three smaller ones, all with operations in Africa.

Interviewer I see. And have you been to Africa?

Naomi Yes, I have. I've spent some time in Tanzania.

Interviewer Oh really? What did you do there?

Naomi I was there to help with the construction of a new school.

6.3

Interviewer So when did you go to Tanzania?

Naomi Last year, in March. They asked me to go there for the start of construction.

Interviewer And how long did you stay there?

Naomi For four months. I came back in July, when the school was ready.

Interviewer So it went well.

Naomi Yes, we finished two months early. And we saved $10,000 on construction costs.

Interviewer That's great. So what other projects have you worked on?

Naomi I've done a lot of construction projects, but I've also helped to set up training programmes, giving local people the skills they need to manage their lives: farming, for example, or construction work.

Interviewer And have you ever managed a team?

Naomi No, not yet, but I've had very good bosses and I've learnt a lot about managing people. I know I'm ready to do this job.

Interviewer Yes, I'm sure you are. Tell me – why did you decide to work in this field?

Naomi My mother lived in Africa when she was a child. She's often talked to me about her life there. I wanted to discover it for myself.

6.4

1

A Have you had time to look at the product description I sent you?

B I haven't, but I saw a presentation of the product last month.

2

A Have you worked in any Latin American countries?

B No, but it's something I'd really like to do.

3

A Have you done the report on your trip to Toronto?

B No, but I'll send it to you before the end of the week.

4

A Have you ever used English in your job?

B No, but I've often spoken it on holiday. I have family in the USA.

6.5

A So here are the two options. We can either promote one of our existing engineers or advertise for a new project manager outside. I know we have some good candidates inside the company but I'd like to hear your views.

B I prefer to recruit internally. We have a lot of young engineers who want to progress in the company. I like the idea that we send them a positive message. They will see that there is a future for them here.

C Well, I understand that we have to give opportunities to younger employees. But are there really any good candidates? I'm not sure that our engineers have enough experience. Most of them joined the company just two or three years ago. I'd go for somebody with more experience from outside.

B Well, I think that would be a mistake. We don't want good engineers to leave to work for our competitors. And another disadvantage is that we don't have time to recruit outside the company. We need a project manager next month. That's not long to find the right person.

A Yes, and one other issue is the cost of finding someone. And then we will have to pay them a lot more. If we promote someone, a key advantage is that we save money … and of course we show our junior engineers that they are important for the company.

C OK, but we need this project manager for our biggest Japanese customer. I really think internal promotion is too risky. The Japanese prefer to work with more experienced project managers. No, we need somebody with more experience of managing big customers.

A Well, it's true that experience is an issue here. But then the internal option is attractive because it's quicker and cheaper. Let me think about this and we'll talk about it again tomorrow.

Unit 7

7.1

1

A Can I see your passport, please, madam?

B Yes. Here you are.

A I'm afraid your flight is cancelled.

B Cancelled?

A Yes, there's a technical problem. But there is another plane for Amsterdam an hour later.

B But I have a connecting flight in Amsterdam. I have another plane to Stockholm. I only had one hour between the two flights.

A Don't worry, madam. There are planes every hour to Stockholm, too. We can put you on the next one.

B But I'll be late for my meeting.

A I'm very sorry, madam. But we can offer you a free upgrade to first class.

B OK, thanks.

2

A Four people, sir?

B Yes, that's right.

A You only have three boarding passes here. Where's the fourth one?

B Oh no! I used the online check-in service at home. I didn't see there were only three.

C What's the problem now, Dave?

A And that suitcase, sir. That's hold baggage. It's too big to take on the plane. You need to check it in.

C Dave, what's happening?

B I'll have to go back. Can my wife and children go through the security scan now?

A No, I'm sorry, they can't. Just go back and explain the situation. Go to the priority check-in. It will be quicker.

B OK, thanks.

3

A Can you put your bags here, please?

B Yes, sure.

A I'm afraid I have to charge you for excess baggage.

B I'm sorry?

A This bag is 28 kilos. The weight allowance is 23 kilos per bag.

B Oh, I didn't know that. So what's the extra charge?

A $75.

B $75! OK, but can I have a window seat, please?

A I'm sorry, but the only seats I have are here, here and here.

B All middle seats!

A Yes, sorry about that.

B That's OK. It's not my day!

7.2

Fabrizio Hello, Emily. It's Fabrizio.

Emily Hi, Fabrizio. Great to hear from you. How are you?

Fabrizio I'm fine. How about you? Are you still working for ETI?

Emily Well, for the moment I'm still here. But I'm going to leave the company soon. At the end of July, probably.

Fabrizio Oh really! What are you going to do?

Emily I'm doing a one-year Masters course in Psychology. I'm starting in September.

Fabrizio Ah, that's great news, Emily. Listen, I'm coming to Montreal for a conference next week.

Emily Oh cool! How long are you staying?

Fabrizio I'm arriving on Sunday and leaving on Wednesday evening. Are you there? Can we meet up?

Emily Yeah, sure. I don't know my schedule yet, but I'll let you know. Can we talk about it later in the week?

Fabrizio Yes, sure. I'll call you again on Friday. Is that OK?

Emily Great. Speak to you soon, Fabrizio.

7.3

1

A Hello. Can you tell me the way to the station, please?

B Yes, OK. Turn right at the traffic lights. You come to a roundabout. Take the second, no, the third exit. You'll see the station in front of you.

A Great, thanks.

2

A Excuse me. I'm looking for the registrations office for the conference.

B Sure. Turn left at the end of the corridor, then go down the stairs. Registrations is the first or second door on your right.

A Thanks a lot.

3

A Excuse me. How do I get to the motorway?

B Er … let me think. Take the first left. Then go straight on for about a kilometre. After that, you'll see signs.

A Thanks very much. Oh, do you know where the nearest petrol station is?

B Yes, there's one on the road you're taking. You go past the supermarket … it's a big supermarket. The petrol station is just after that.

A Great. Thanks.

7.4

Emily Hello?

Fabrizio Hi, Emily. It's Fabrizio.

Emily Hi, Fabrizio. Are you calling about your trip to Montreal?

Fabrizio Yeah, that's right. I'm arriving on Sunday afternoon. When can we meet? Are you free that evening?

Emily No, sorry. I'm now flying to Toronto on Sunday. I have a meeting there on Monday. Can we find a different time?

Fabrizio Sure. I'm staying in Montreal until Wednesday. When would suit you?

Emily Well, I'm coming back on Monday evening. What about lunch on Tuesday?

Fabrizio Sorry Emily, but I'm having lunch with a customer. What's your availability later in the day? The conference finishes at five. How about Tuesday evening instead?

Emily I'm afraid I've got something on that evening. But I really want to see you. When exactly are you leaving on Wednesday?

Fabrizio My flight's at 21.45, so I'll have to leave for the airport at about seven.

Emily In that case, does Wednesday lunchtime work for you?

Fabrizio Yes, that's fine for me. I only have an hour for lunch, but I can miss the first session in the afternoon.

Emily Great. Let's meet outside the conference centre. I know a nice little restaurant nearby.

Fabrizio OK. The morning session finishes at 1.00. Shall we say 1.15?

Emily Yes, that suits me. OK, so that's quarter past one at the conference centre.

Fabrizio Yes, see you on Wednesday. It'll be great to see you again.

Emily You too, Fabrizio. Have a good trip on Sunday.

Unit 8

8.1

1

A Hello. Mr Roberts. I'm calling about your recent enquiry.

B Sorry, what enquiry?

A You phoned us to enquire about the external hard disks. The TR33s.

B Oh yes, that's right.

A And we told you we don't stock that product here.

B Yes, I remember.

A But I also said we could order them for you.

B Yes, but I wanted to find another supplier who had them in stock.

A Yes, exactly. And have you found somebody, Mr Roberts?

B No, not yet. I haven't had time.

A If you like, I can give you a quotation. If you agree with the price we quote, I can place the order with my supplier immediately. It'll be here in two or three days.

B OK, why not.

A So, we can supply the TR33 for €50 per unit.

B Erm … OK. Can I get back to you?

2

A I just have a few questions about the product.

B Yes, of course. Please go ahead.

A On your website, it says the guarantee is for three years.

B That's right. That's for parts and labour.

A And how soon can you deliver?

B Well, the order process is a little longer than usual, because we don't have it here in our main warehouse.

A So where does it come from?

B It's sent from China. But we can ship the product to you in the next 48 hours. It generally takes about 12–14 days.

A So can you give me a definite delivery date?

B I can confirm that very quickly. I just need to check with the warehouse first.

A That's fine. OK, I'll order now, but please call me back with a delivery date.

8.2

1

A So this is the call centre. This is where we receive all phone orders. First we check the stock position, and if the product is in stock, the operator just presses 'OK'. Like that.

B And the order is transferred automatically to the warehouse.

A That's right.

B That's very easy. And the products are shipped the same day. Is that right?

A Normally, yes. When orders are placed before 4 p.m., we guarantee next-day delivery.

2

A So you haven't received it?

B No. But when I tracked my order online, it said the goods were delivered yesterday. But that's not possible. I was here all day, and nothing came for me.

A Let me see … yes, delivery was confirmed by the courier at 9.15. Somebody signed for it.

B Not me.

A So it was sent to the wrong address. I'll have to check with the dispatch department. I'm very sorry about this. Can I call you back?

8.3

A So I think that's everything. What's the total price?

B €300.

A Does that include VAT?

B Yes, value added tax is 20%, so that's €250 before tax.

A And do you charge extra for delivery?

B No, delivery is free on all orders over €150.

A OK. Do you offer a discount for payment in advance?

B Yes, we can give you a 5% reduction.

A OK, that's good. What forms of payment do you accept?

B Credit card or bank transfer. Is that OK?

A Yes, fine. Can you send your bank details and I'll make the transfer immediately.

B Yes, sure.

A Oh, just one other question. On larger orders, is it possible to pay in monthly instalments?

B Yes, we offer payment in three instalments for orders over €750.

A OK, I'll note that for next time. Thanks.

8.4

A Hello. I've come to pick up a package.

B Yes, sir. Do you mind if I see this gentleman first? He was here before you.

A Oh, sorry, I didn't realize. No problem. Er, just one thing – would you mind giving me some small change for the car park?

B No, not at all. Here you are.

A That's great. Thanks a lot. I'll be back in a minute.

…

B Hello again, sir. So you wanted to collect a parcel?

A Yes, that's right.

B OK. Could I see your confirmation email, please?

A Ah, I'm afraid not. I didn't know I needed it. Is it all right if I just show you my driving licence?

B I'm sorry, but I need the order reference, you see.

A Ah. Well, I can probably find it on my phone. Let me see …

B Could I ask you to wait a moment while I serve this lady?

A Yes, sure. Go ahead.

…

B OK, so have you found the order number?

A Yes, I have the email here. The order reference is W-P-K-Y-F-14.

B Y-F-14. That's fine. And I need some identification, too, please.

A Certainly. Here you are.

B That's fine. So could you just sign here, please?

A Sure. Thanks very much. Oh, do you think I could have a bag? It's just started raining outside.

B I'm afraid I don't have one that size.

A OK, don't worry. I'll manage.

8.5

1

It's so quick and easy. Nearly everyone carries a phone with them now. But not everybody has a payment application on their mobile, and the people who have these applications have to update them regularly. And there are still problems with security, because phones aren't as safe as computers.

2

Not many people pay with it now, especially for more expensive items. And there are a lot of false banknotes, so you need a special detector to check that the notes are real. That's an extra cost when you start your business. But otherwise you pay no additional fees, and you have the money immediately.

3

More people are using this now as it's much faster. However, there's a limit to how much they can spend this way. In our store, anything over €30 still needs people to put in their PIN number. And some customers are a little worried that if they lose their card, anyone could use it!

4

Most people have them these days. And people can pay for something quickly and not think too much about the money they are spending. But it can be very expensive for us. With some card companies we pay up to 5% for each transaction.

5

It's a safe method because the payment isn't accepted if customers don't have money in their online account. And it's quick, because we receive the money immediately. This is particularly useful for international orders, where other forms of payment are slower. But the transaction fees are very high compared with credit cards.

Unit 9

9.1

1

Our problem is that it's very difficult to attract new customers. All the other providers are offering the same services at about the same price: Internet, free phone calls and TV access. With our new offer, we're trying to reach sports lovers. We're offering access to specialized sports channels for just €1 per day. So you pay for that day, and you don't have to pay for the whole month.

2

We are a small independent shop, so many people think we are expensive and don't offer much choice, compared with our main competitor. They are part of a national chain that has a big store in the same street as us. So every month we offer big discounts on 50 different products, like photocopier paper, printer ink or pens. We lose money on these, but it's a good way to attract people into the shop and increase awareness of our product range and prices.

3

We started our business two years ago. I think it was a mistake to open in a town where nobody knows us. But we now have about 90 people doing exercise classes. To attract more people we're offering our present customers one free month of classes for every new person they bring to us. And that word of mouth has started to work: last month, ten new people signed up.

9.2

1

We are promoting our sports channel service with digital advertising boards at football and rugby stadiums. We also have a lot of click ads on the home pages of online sports magazines.

2

To boost sales in our shop, we do a targeted email campaign to companies in the area twice a year. And we have a webmaster who's done a great job getting our website on to the first page of Google.

3

We promote our club on Facebook and Twitter and we invite comments from people who are already members. And once a month, in the summer, we run a free exercise class outside in the local park, where everybody can see us.

9.3

1

I know that companies have to advertise to sell their products, but you don't need to have big billboards everywhere. They're really horrible and they get bigger and bigger every year. I think the mayor of Grenoble was right to do what he did.

2

I think you need to have laws on advertising. You have to stop companies advertising products which are bad for you. In some countries, you aren't allowed to advertise cigarettes, for example.

3

I think some advertising laws are really stupid. In some countries, you are allowed to advertise alcohol on TV, but you can't do it before 8 p.m. The idea is to protect children, but most children watch TV until at least 10 p.m.

4

Some people say there's too much advertising online. But when we use the Internet, we usually don't have to pay to get the information we need. That's because many website owners make their profits from advertising, so we can use their websites for free. I agree that there are a lot of ads online, but you don't have to look at them.

9.4

A No, I don't see that at all. I think it's very useful to get targeted adverts about products that interest us.

B Sorry, but they store all that information on their website and we don't know—

A Can I just finish? This is an important point here.

B Sorry, go ahead.

A I mean, if you are a regular customer in a shop, they will recommend new products that you'll like, because they know you. It's the same with shopping websites.

B Can I just say something here? To use one of these sites, you need to accept cookies on your computer. But the cookies store all that private information about you.

A Yes, but they're doing it to help you find products—

B Please let me finish. And all that private information … they use it not only on their website, but when you're on other sites, too. So you see click ads for their products when you're reading a newspaper article online, for example.

A Yes, but you don't have to look at them or click on them. And sometimes the special promotions are very attractive.

9.5

Sonya So, we're here today to talk about Central Europe. We need to discuss our new marketing campaign.

Anton So, who's going to start?

Sonya Maybe you, Anton. Can you tell us about the advertising budget?

Anton Yes, OK. To support the new sales campaign, we have to spend more on advertising this year. Last year our spending in Central Europe was €28.6 million. This year we have decided on a budget of 37.5 million.

Edward Sorry, I didn't catch that, Anton. What was the last figure?

Anton Yes, sorry. Our budget for this year is €37.5 million. We want to spend the extra money on a big social media campaign.

Sonya Yes, that's definitely a good idea.

Anton OK, if we now look at the budget for Western Europe, we see that last year we had—

Edward Er, sorry Anton, but I think we're getting off the subject. Can we come back to that later?

Anton Yes, OK. But I really think we need to discuss Western Europe, too.

…

Edward OK, I think we've covered advertising. Can we move on to the next point?

Sonya Sure. Do you want to talk about sales now, Edward?

Edward Alright. Well, we forecast a 7% increase in annual sales for this year, and we are looking for a similar figure for the two following years. That's in the markets where we have a stronger presence.

Sonya Sorry, Edward, I'm not with you. Could you be more specific? Which countries are we talking about?

Edward I mean the Czech Republic, Poland and Hungary.

Sonya OK, thanks.

Edward Well, anyway …

…

Anton As I said before, I really feel we need to review the budgets for Western Europe.

Sonya OK, Anton, I agree, but I think we need to have another meeting about that. Edward, did you have anything else to say?

Edward No, I think that's everything. Can we sum up what we've agreed?

Sonya Sure. So Edward, you're going to prepare a detailed sales forecast, country by country, and Anton, you'll provide more details about the social media campaign. OK, thank you everybody for coming and …

Unit 10

10.1

1 We've got some rather unusual drinks machines in our office which recycle metal cans. They're called reverse vending machines. When you've finished your drink, you just put the can back into the machine and the cans are collected once a week. It's a great way to reduce waste and make us think about protecting the environment.

2 Someone in our company started an initiative to turn off lights. We have a lot of rooms that aren't used very often. Our electricity comes from fossil fuels, so every time you leave a light on, you're polluting the environment. We consume a lot less electricity now. You'd be surprised how much we save on our bill!

3 They've made two big changes in our work's canteen. Firstly, they don't throw away food at the end of the day. They keep it for the next day and sell it at a reduced price. Secondly, they've stopped using plastic knives, forks and spoons and they've gone back to metal. It's the same for cups and glasses. It's much better to have glasses you can reuse than plastic cups you have to throw away.

4 We've started a carpooling system in my office, and about half the staff do it now. At least two people travel in each car, which means we're reducing our emissions by more than 50%. It's nice to know that we're not polluting the air so much, and it's also nice to chat to colleagues in the car before and after work.

10.2

A It's clear to me that the electric bus is the only reasonable option. If we choose the bus system, the start-up costs will be much lower. Just €3 million per kilometre. To create a tram network, the infrastructure cost will be at least 19 million, maybe even 22 million.

B Yes, but you haven't included the cost of traffic management. For your bus system, we'll have to change the road structure because buses need to have priority over cars. It will cost us a lot more if we have to create special bus lanes. And don't forget that the trams have a much bigger capacity. They can carry up to 7,000 passengers per hour. For a bus, the maximum is 3,000 per hour.

A Well, I think your forecasts for passenger traffic are too high. If we don't have enough passengers, your system won't be cost-effective.

B The agency we used for the study has worked on transport systems in five major cities.

A Yes, but the study was done four years ago. Running costs are higher now. €7 per kilometre for the tram, but only €5 for the bus. What will we do if the system loses money?

B Well, I think we will lose money at the beginning. But this is a long-term investment.

A OK. Will you explain that to the public when their local taxes increase?

10.3

Teresa Hello, Guido. You said you wanted to talk to me.

Guido Yes, come in Teresa. I wanted to talk to you about the green initiatives proposed by Head Office. Which proposals do you think would be most effective?

Teresa Do you mean in my department or in the whole company?

Guido I mean in the whole company. Head Office wants us to cut our carbon emissions by 10% before the end of the year.

Teresa Sorry, did you say by the end of this year? I thought the proposals said by the end of next year.

Guido Yes, you're absolutely right. We've got until the end of next year. I've looked at the different ideas, and I think it would be really easy for us to keep the windows closed when the heating is on.

Teresa So, are you saying that we should tell people they can't open the windows anymore?

Guido Yes. At least not when the heating's on. Also, perhaps we should turn the heating off for part of the day.

Teresa What do you mean by part of the day?

Guido Just a couple of hours in the afternoon, between two and four, let's say.

Teresa Well, I suppose that would work. The office does usually get very warm in the afternoons.

10.4

Hello and welcome. I'm Christophe Jansen and I'm here to tell you about the advantages of going green. If you take action now, you'll be ready for the government's new environmental laws. I'll come to the new regulations later. But first of all, I'll give you a quick overview of my talk. We're going to look at the general benefits of a clear green policy and then discuss in more detail what it can do for your company.

Let's start with the subject of profits. If you turn off machines when you're not using them and turn the heating down in warm weather, you will reduce your energy costs significantly. We've calculated that you can achieve a 20% reduction, and this will significantly increase your company's profits. You have all the figures for your company in the document I've given you. My next point concerns your company image. An increasing number of consumers and business customers today will only buy from or invest in companies who help protect the environment. If you reduce carbon emissions, you will attract more business. And yes, that means even more profits! In addition, you will improve your reputation as an employer. People don't just want to buy from eco-friendly companies: they also want to work for them.

Finally, I want to talk about the importance of taking action now. As I said before, governments are going to introduce new regulations to combat climate change. Being prepared for these new regulations will save you time and money when they are introduced. Why money? Because companies that don't respect the law in good time will have to pay heavy fines.

So, to sum up, cutting carbon emissions is good for your profits … and for your reputation. But it's also good for your conscience. Do you want to be part of a company that is not making an effort to reduce global warming?

That brings me to the end of my talk. Thanks very much for listening. Now, are there any questions?

Unit 11

11.1

1

Last January, my employer, a big electronics company, held a corporate event for its top salespeople. I was lucky enough to be invited. The venue was a five-star hotel in Brazil and the package included all meals and day trips to places of interest. The only work involved was a two-hour convention on the first morning and the rest of the time we were free to enjoy the facilities of the hotel. But they also arranged a trip to the beautiful city of Salvador da Baía and we spent one afternoon riding quad bikes along the deserted beach. I had a great time.

2

The best corporate event I've ever attended was a visit to the opera in Italy. One of the big banks in Germany decided to entertain its VIP clients by inviting them to the opening night of *Tristan and Isolde*. The venue they booked was the world-famous opera house, La Scala, in Milan. The package included first-class plane travel, tickets to the opera, and a night in a luxury hotel. I accepted the invitation, of course, and flew to Milan two months later. The opera was wonderful and after the performance we had a tour of the building. The evening finished in the most exclusive restaurant in Milan, where we had a delicious five-course meal accompanied by the best wines.

11.2

1

A Excuse me, madam. Are there any other guests in your party?

B Yes, I'm still waiting for two people.

A Would you like some drinks while you're waiting?

B Yes, please. Can we have some mineral water?

A Of course. How many bottles would you like?

B Well, there will be 12 of us, so let's start with four bottles. And … er … I'll have something hot. Is there any coffee?

A I'm afraid not, madam. Just cold drinks. Apple juice? Orange juice?

B OK, I'll have an orange juice, please.

2

A Colin. Just a question.

B Yes, Francesca. Go ahead.

A How much time do we have before play starts?

B The first match is at two o'clock, so we have … er … an hour.

A Ah good. You see, I want to buy something for my children. They're big tennis fans. Is there a souvenir shop inside the stadium?

B Yes, there are several. Look, there's one just over there. Would you like me to come with you?

A No, that's fine. I'll see you back here.

11.3

Wimbledon fortnight is one of the most popular sporting events in the world. Last year, we received nearly half a million visitors. They come to watch the tennis, but of course, they also get thirsty in the Wimbledon sunshine! What's the traditional English drink? Tea, of course, but also coffee. 350,000 cups of tea and coffee are sold during the two weeks. And for those who prefer something stronger, there's champagne. We serve 28,000 bottles of it in an average year.

Our visitors also eat a lot of ice cream. 125,000 portions served every year. And what about the players themselves? What's their favourite food? Yes, that's right. Bananas. 15,000 bananas are served to players during the tournament – that's nearly 23 per match!

Wimbledon is like a small village, offering a number of different shops and other facilities: there's a pharmacy, there's a bank, there are souvenir shops. There's a museum, and there's even a library where you can read books or watch videos about tennis. There are also facilities for leaving luggage, but these are outside the grounds, so don't forget this if you arrive with a suitcase. And for those of you looking for hotel accommodation for Wimbledon, there isn't any accommodation inside the grounds, but on the Wimbledon website you can find details of companies who can help you find accommodation nearby.

A lot of people ask us how much money the players earn at Wimbledon. Well, the amount increases every year, but last year the total prize money was nearly £27 million. The top prize was £1.9 million, for the winners of the men's and ladies' singles tournament.

11.4

A So, Anita. What's good here?

B Well, you must try the Parma ham first. It's absolutely delicious!

A OK, that sounds good. I'll have the ham as a starter.

B Perhaps we can share the ham and order a salad, as well?

A Good idea, and then we can each order a main course.

B Right. What do you fancy?

A I'm not really sure. Er, what are the pizzas like?

B Well, they're not bad, but I recommend the pasta. It's excellent here – they make it themselves.

A Mmm, delicious. What are you having?

B I think I'll have the lasagne. What about you?

A I'll have the spaghetti carbonara.

B OK. What about dessert?

A I don't know. They all look good. What do you recommend?

B I think you'll like the ice cream. It's home-made, too.

A OK, I'll go for that.

B Me, too. Let's order then. Excuse me …

11.5

1

A So, here we are.

B Thank you very much for coming to the airport for me.

A You're welcome. Er … just before you go, some of us are meeting for dinner tonight. Would you like to join us?

B Thank you for the invitation, but I'm really tired. I'll just eat something in the hotel and have an early night. I'll see you tomorrow.

A OK, sure. Have a good evening.

2

A Please take a seat. Mr Idriss is coming down. He'll be here in a moment.

B OK … thanks very much.

A Oh dear. That sounds very bad. Would you like me to bring you a glass of water?

B Yes, please. That's very good of you.

3

A Hello. Anna, isn't it?

B Yes, that's right. It's my first day here.

A Hi. I'm Keith, from Accounts. Would you like a coffee?

B No, thanks. But I'd love a tea if there is any.

A Yes, there is. With milk? I like milky tea myself.

B Er … no milk. Thank you.

4

A Hey, Pamela. Did you know the Chinese State Circus is coming again?

B No, I didn't. They were fantastic last time we saw them.

A Yes, they were. Do you fancy going again?

B Oh yes. That would be great.

A Shall I get you a ticket?

B Sure. When is it?

A This Saturday. I only heard about it this morning.

B This Saturday? Oh no! Thanks for asking, Julia, but I'm not here this weekend.

Unit 12

12.1

1

It's not how they described it to me. At the interview they said that their target was to have 45% of management positions filled by women. But five years later, I'm still here in the same office and two men who arrived at the same time as me have been promoted above me. It's very disappointing – I really thought I had a big future here.

2

We've reduced the number of accidents in the plants by 20%. We haven't achieved our target of less than 100 accidents per year, but we're getting there. And we were encouraged by the big fall in serious injuries last year.

3

We've had a really excellent year, much better than we expected. We're the darlings of the stock market at the moment. If you want to buy shares in the company, I think you should do it now, before the price goes up too much.

4

The last three years haven't been very good. First there was that pollution incident in our biggest factory. Then there was all that media criticism for not using electric vehicles. It's been a very poor performance – things can only get better!

5

Well, it hasn't been easy in the last 12 months. The new CEO told us to reduce our costs by 10%. In the end, we only managed a 5% reduction. But then our sales increased by 2%. I think we've had a satisfactory year, but our CEO says our performance has been very average.

12.2

Raul When did you start selling here in Dubai, Lionel?

Lionel Well, we opened our first sales office in 2012. That's when I moved here.

Raul And how long did it take to get your foot in the market?

Lionel Well, we had disappointing results for the first two years. But since 2014, our business has increased by nearly 20%. The economy's really booming here.

Raul That's great.

Lionel What about you, Raul? How long have you worked here?

Raul I've been in Dubai for three years now.

Lionel Do you have a family here?

Raul Yes, my wife and children moved here last year. What about you?

12.3

1 one point three nine per cent
2 nought point oh three three
3 one hundred and two
4 seven thousand four hundred and sixty-seven
5 nine hundred and six thousand five hundred and seventy

12.4

It's 5.55 p.m., and here's the world stock market summary. In Tokyo this morning, the Nikkei closed at 20,235.73, that's 0.63% up on yesterday's closing figure. At first, the European markets responded well to the good news from Asia, but then fell again in response to the latest economic figures from the USA. At the end of the day, the FTSE 100 was 58.74 points down, at 6,561.21. The DAX also finished the day down, at 10,968.05. That's a fall of 0.17%.

At midday New York time, the Dow Jones was down by 343.13 points, to 17,596.35. And the Nasdaq was also down by 122.04 points to 4,958.47 – that's a fall of 2.4% since the start of trading.

12.5

Hello, everybody. We're going to look at the figures for vehicle production in the last 20–25 years.

Have a look at this graph. It shows the number of motor vehicles produced by the big four – the USA, Japan, Germany and, of course, China.

Let's start with Japan. As you can see, Japan is no longer the world leader in vehicle manufacturing. But production remained stable at about ten million throughout the nineties, and then rose in the first five years of this century. But between 2005 and 2010 it fell from 10.8 to 9.6 million. Since then, the Japanese market has started to grow again, and recovered to 9.8 million in 2015.

If we compare this with the USA, you'll notice that production rose at the end of the nineties. But at the beginning of the century, the number of vehicles decreased. Production dropped by about one million in the next five years. Then it declined dramatically to 7.7 million in 2010, dropping into third position behind China and Japan. But since 2010, US carmakers have made big improvements and the results have been very encouraging.

The performance of German carmakers has been more consistent than the USA or Japan. Production increased from 4.7 to 5.9 million in the period 1995 to 2015. And this strong performance has continued, thanks to Germany's reputation for high-quality vehicles.

So let's turn to China. In the year 1995, the country produced only 1.4 million vehicles. Ten years later, it was already 5.7 million, but the biggest growth was in the next five years. Between 2005 and 2010, it rose by two and a half million vehicles per year. Growth has been a little slower since then, but reached 23.7 million in 2015 and China will continue to dominate the world market.

Unit 13

13.1

Presenter Welcome to Energy Futures, and today energy expert Judy Collins is here to talk to us about the car industry. Judy, we're producing more and more cars in the world every year. How will this growth affect oil prices?

Judy Collins Well, Andy, industry analysts don't agree on this. Certain experts say the demand for oil will increase dramatically. Oil companies will have to find new sources of oil, and this will be very expensive. One report estimates that a 5% oil shortage could lead to a big price rise – maybe up to 400%. If that happened, we would have a very big oil crisis.

Presenter And this crisis would really threaten the automobile industry. I think about 60% of oil in the world is used to produce petrol for cars. Is that right?

Judy Collins Yes, indeed. But it's not only a question of petrol. Oil is also used to make plastics and other materials used in cars. About 20 barrels of oil are needed to produce just one vehicle. Some analysts have forecast that the car will become a luxury item once again, too expensive for most people.

Presenter But all these predictions seem very extreme. Is this really likely to happen?

Judy Collins No, I don't think so. I think there are reasons to be positive. Firstly, I think the technology is improving rapidly. Every year, new cars are using less and less petrol. Studies have shown that if we can reduce petrol consumption by 2.5% a year, oil demand will remain stable. We're doing this now.

Presenter So you don't think the oil situation will get worse?

Judy Collins No, I don't. Also, many new sources of gas have been found in recent years. Gas can be used as an alternative to petrol in vehicles, but also for heating and production of electricity. And we're not going to run out of gas because we have enough reserves for 200 years.

Presenter Well, that's a very positive message. Join us after the break, when Judy is going to be telling us about the latest technology in electric cars.

13.2

In 2030 people will work more flexibly and many jobs will be part-time. Traditional forms of management will disappear. More employees will work together in self-managed teams. Therefore, management positions might not be easy to find. In addition, it is forecast that working arrangements will be more flexible. More people will work from home, so colleagues may see each other less often. Companies will still have office buildings, but they will be smaller and won't be used in the same way as today.

In 2030, there will be a shortage of highly-qualified workers in certain sectors. Employees may not want to stay long with the same company, so employers will need to offer much better working conditions. Companies might provide leisure facilities for employees, like a gym and a bar area for social events. Many employees may decide to take career breaks. However, in the future, they will be allowed to rejoin the company with the same job and on the same salary as before. In general, companies will have to fight more to keep their staff, so employees will be in a much better position.

13.3

Jean So that's a quick overview of the teleworking scheme we're introducing from next year. I'm sure you have a lot of questions. Yes, Mansoor.

Mansoor Thank you, Jean. I wanted to ask about cost savings. You said that teleworking will reduce our running costs. Just how much are we likely to save?

Jean I can't estimate that very easily right now, Mansoor. It depends how many people choose to work from home. But we hope the new scheme will save the company at least €20,000 in heating, lighting and other office costs.

Rebecca So is our office building likely to close?

Jean No, the office is unlikely to close completely. However, the change will affect us because we won't need such a big building any more. We may look into the possibility of moving to a new building, or we might rent out some of the office space we don't need.

Ivan I have a question about motivation. Do you think people will be happy to work alone? They won't see their colleagues for long periods, and their only daily contact will be by phone or Skype.

Jean Our employees will definitely feel more motivated when they can organize their own time. Teleworking is a sign that we trust our workers to manage themselves. It probably won't be easy for some people to start with, but I'm sure they'll be happier working from home. And don't forget that this is a voluntary scheme – nobody has to do it.

Ivan And do you expect to see an increase in productivity?

Jean Yes, we do. Apparently, most companies report an increase of 10–40%. Hopefully, our teleworkers will have similar results.

Mansoor I wanted to ask about the employees. What advantages will they get from the scheme?

Unit 14

14.1

1

First of all, there's always one person who arrives late, and everything has to be repeated. And then certain people like to talk a lot, even about subjects that aren't on the agenda. To save time, we've tried introducing a one-hour limit, but it isn't enough. We always run out of time. Some of our meetings are more like two hours.

2

I have to write quality reports and send them to the quality manager at the end of each month. I know reports take a long time to do, but I never allow time for them. So then I have everything to do on the last day of the month. I always leave paperwork until the last minute.

3

The customer told us the product had to be ready by the end of March. Things went very well for the first two months. We even thought we could deliver ahead of time. But then in the middle of February, they asked us to change the design of the product. But they said the deadline was the same, the end of March. It was really difficult to get the job done in time.

4

I waste so much time answering calls. It really slows you down when your phone rings every 15 or 20 minutes. If it's customers calling, that's OK, but more often it's work colleagues. First, they send you an email. Then if you don't reply immediately, they call your office number. Thirty seconds later, they try your mobile.

14.2

A Hi, Silvia. So you're back from New York. How was it?

B Good. It's a great city to visit. And I met some really interesting people at work. But I'd go crazy if I lived in the USA.

A Why's that, then?

B Well, it's the pace of life there. Everybody's always running, running, running. No time to stop and think. Do you know what I mean?

A Yes, of course. So what would you do if they offered you a job there? It's quite possible. They're looking for new people all the time.

B Well, if it was only for a year or two, I might say yes. It would be good for my CV.

A But only for a short time?

B Yes. If they wanted me for longer, I wouldn't accept it. It would be too stressful.

14.3

1

A Can you finish the report by Friday?

B Well, I'm not sure. There's a lot to do on it.

A Well, within a week, then.

B I'll do it before the end of next week, I promise. Would that be OK?

A Well, I suppose so.

2

A When do we need to send the quotation?

B They asked for it as soon as possible.

A OK, I'll start working on it right away.

B Do you think it'll be ready on Monday?

A Yes, I think so.

B Oh, just one other thing – can you send me your results for June when you have time?

A Yes, sure.

14.4

Luca Hi, Hans-Peter. It's Luca. I'm calling because we have an issue with delivery.

Hans-Peter Oh, tell me more.

Luca Well, basically, we've got a lorry drivers' strike here. They're blocking all the major roads. I can't guarantee that we can deliver today's order on time.

Hans-Peter Oh no! We need those parts by tomorrow.

Luca Yes, I know. But I have another solution. Would it be OK if we sent them by train?

Hans-Peter Yes, that might be possible. But would they get to us in time?

Luca Yes, I've checked. They'd arrive at about 6 p.m. tomorrow.

Hans-Peter Six o'clock! But we need to start production mid-afternoon.

Luca Ah, I didn't know that. Well, what if we transported them by train to the border? Could you send a lorry to pick them up?

Hans-Peter Yes, I think we could do that. What time would the driver need to be there?

Luca The train gets in at … er, 5.35 in the morning.

Hans-Peter OK, good. That would allow us to get the parts to the factory in time.

Luca Of course, rail transport is more expensive than road. Would you agree to pay the extra cost?

Hans-Peter No, sorry, Luca, that wouldn't be acceptable. This lorry drivers' strike is your problem, not ours.

Luca OK, I understand.

Unit 15

15.1

1

Scott Hello, Thierry. Come in and take a seat.

Thierry Thanks.

Scott Now, this isn't easy for me to say, Thierry. Basically, I've been very disappointed with your performance this year in Eastern Europe. I was hoping for much better results in that region.

Thierry Well, I'm surprised, Scott. You asked us to boost sales and we achieved that. 3% on last year.

Scott Yes, but I really wanted to see 10%.

Thierry Well, you never told me that when we spoke this time last year.

2

Scott OK, everybody, we have ten minutes left. Can we talk about the South American market? Er … Freia, you were at the trade show in Mexico City last week. Can you tell us how it went?

Freia Scott, I didn't go to Mexico. I had to go to Spain last week. I told you about it in our meeting two weeks ago. Don't you remember?

Scott No, sorry, I don't. Never mind. Uhm … Roberto. Didn't you do a report on the South American market a few weeks ago?

Roberto Yes, but I didn't know we were talking about that today. I don't have the figures here. They're on my computer at home.

3

Scott Hi, Maria. Would you like one, too?

Maria Yes, please. Thanks, Scott.

Scott The sugar's right there.

Maria Thanks. So, have you finished looking at that proposal?

Scott Not yet. I've got to about page ten.

Maria It's just that I need your signature on it. I have to send it this evening.

Scott Sorry, Maria. I've got so much to read at the moment. The sales managers have just emailed me their monthly reports. I think I'll be here all weekend!

Maria Well, before looking at those reports, could you just finish reading my proposal, Scott? It's only about 15 pages in all.

15.2

First, think about where the appraisal will take place. If possible, you shouldn't use your own office, because employees sometimes find it difficult to talk easily. The next thing to remember is that this is a two-way conversation between you and the employee. So you mustn't do most of the talking, even if the person in front of you is very quiet or shy. If you know something about the employee's personal life, you could begin by asking them about their family or a recent holiday, for example. This will create a positive atmosphere.

Now, when you begin to talk about your employee's performance, you should start with positive feedback. You should look at their personal objectives for the last year, and let them say how they have achieved them. And if they haven't achieved them all, you must discuss why this hasn't happened and offer real, constructive solutions.

15.3

1

First, I think Marek should try to take a week or two of holiday and spend some time with his wife and children. It'll also give him time to take a step back and think about the reasons for his poor performance.

When he returns to work, he needs to work on his management skills. First, he must learn to manage his own work better. He should ask for training in time management and managing people. It might be an idea to hire a personal coach.

Then he really must talk to his team. He should set clear goals for them, and each person should know that they are responsible for meeting their own deadlines. If they can do all that between 9 a.m. and 5 p.m., that's fine. If not, they will have to work longer hours.

2

Klaudia is young and successful. Maybe her boss, the sales director, is afraid of her. Or perhaps he just doesn't want to lose his best sales rep. Klaudia should talk to him first because she needs his help to get a better job in the company. She could ask him what she can do to improve her promotion prospects. If it's a question of training, he should offer it to her.

Another possibility is to speak to the CEO. She shouldn't do this immediately because her boss won't be happy. But if her boss doesn't help her, she should tell the CEO that after five years in the same job, she would really like management experience. She could say that she would prefer to stay with the same company, but if it's not possible, she will leave.

15.4

1

A Thanks very much. I really enjoyed your talk. I learnt a lot from it. It was very helpful.

B Well, thanks for the feedback. I'm glad you liked it.

2

A Have you had time to read the proposal?

B Yes, you did a really good job. It's very clear and you made a lot of interesting points. Well done!

A That's good to hear. Thanks very much.

3

A I can see you worked really hard on this.

B Yes, but I'm not sure it's what you wanted.

A Well, not exactly. But you're on the right track. It just needs a few changes here and there.

B Not so bad, then. What do you think needs to be changed?

15.5

A Tony, can we talk about your team in more detail? Why don't we start with their motivation for the job?

B Good idea. Well, their main objective is to keep the rate of defective products at 1% or lower. That always motivated them before, but not now. I don't understand why.

A Do they know why that 1% rate is important?

B What do you mean?

A Well, do they understand the importance of quality for the company, and especially for the customer?

B Well, perhaps not. Not the younger members of the team, anyway.

A You could explain to them the value of their work in terms of customer safety, for example.

B Yes, that might work. So the idea that good quality can save lives?

A Yes, exactly. We'll come back to this, but let's talk about the different tasks they have to do. Would you describe any parts of their job as boring or repetitive?

B Let me think … well, they sometimes complain about the reports they have to write every Friday. But it never takes more than an hour, often less. It's just a summary of the week's quality issues.

A And what do they do with that?

B They email it to me, but I don't always have time to look at it.

A Ah, that's not good. You should always give feedback or show appreciation when somebody's done some work for you.

B Well, I'm not sure about that. It takes a long time to read all those reports. And it's not necessary to read them immediately – they're for future use if we have a quality issue.

A Then I suggest you just send each person an email to say 'thank you', even if you haven't read them. It's much better than no response at all.

B Yes, that's not a bad idea. It is nice to know that somebody has looked at your work.

A Yes, it is. Tell me, Tony, does the team have the chance to work on special projects sometimes? Something a little different?

B No, not really. Maybe that's part of the problem. Basically, they do the same things every week.

A One possibility would be to give them a new challenge. For example, what about introducing a team project to reduce the defect rate to … say … 0.5%?

B Zero point five? I don't think that would work. It's too difficult to achieve, but 0.7 or 8 might be possible. Yes, I think that could motivate them. My boss would be very happy too if we achieved it!

A All right, I think we have some useful ideas there. Shall we talk about how to put them into practice?

B Yes. Let's do that.

Irregular verb list

Verb	Past simple	Past participle	Verb	Past simple	Past participle
be	was / were	been	let	let	let
become	became	become	light	lit	lit
begin	began	begun	lose	lost	lost
break	broke	broken	make	made	made
bring	brought	brought	mean	meant	meant
build	built	built	meet	met	met
burn	burnt / burned	burnt / burned	pay	paid	paid
buy	bought	bought	put	put	put
catch	caught	caught	read	read	read
choose	chose	chosen	ride	rode	ridden
come	came	come	ring	rang	rung
cost	cost	cost	rise	rose	risen
cut	cut	cut	run	ran	run
deal	dealt	dealt	say	said	said
do	did	done	see	saw	seen
dream	dreamt	dreamt	sell	sold	sold
drink	drank	drunk	send	sent	sent
drive	drove	driven	set	set	set
eat	ate	eaten	shine	shone	shone
fall	fell	fallen	show	showed	shown
feed	fed	fed	shut	shut	shut
feel	felt	felt	sing	sang	sung
fight	fought	fought	sit	sat	sat
find	found	found	sleep	slept	slept
fly	flew	flown	speak	spoke	spoken
forget	forgot	forgotten	spell	spelt / spelled	spelt / spelled
freeze	froze	frozen	spend	spent	spent
get	got	got	stand	stood	stood
give	gave	given	steal	stole	stolen
go	went	gone / been	swim	swam	swum
grow	grew	grown	take	took	taken
have	had	had	teach	taught	taught
hear	heard	heard	tell	told	told
hide	hid	hidden	think	thought	thought
hold	held	held	throw	threw	thrown
keep	kept	kept	understand	understood	understood
know	knew	known	wake	woke	woken
lead	led	led	wear	wore	worn
learn	learnt / learned	learnt / learned	win	won	won
leave	left	left	write	wrote	written
lend	lent	lent			

OXFORD
UNIVERSITY PRESS

Great Clarendon Street, Oxford, OX2 6DP, United Kingdom

Oxford University Press is a department of the University of Oxford.
It furthers the University's objective of excellence in research, scholarship,
and education by publishing worldwide. Oxford is a registered trade
mark of Oxford University Press in the UK and in certain other countries

ISBN: 978 0 19 473880 4   (book)
ISBN: 978 0 19 473876 7   (pack)

Printed in China

This book is printed on paper from certified and well-managed sources

ACKNOWLEDGEMENTS

Back cover photograph: Oxford University Press building/David Fisher

*The authors and publisher are grateful to those who have given permission to reproduce
the following extracts and adaptations of copyright material:* p.8 The Nestlé brand
names and images are reproduced with the kind permission of Société des
Produits Nestlé S.A. p.58 Adapted extracts from "Using social media to target
your customers" by Howard Scott, www.marketingdonut.co.uk, 20 September
2010. Reproduced by permission of Howard Scott. p.77 Adapted extracts from
"Gifts and hospitality" 2 December 2015, www.rics.org/gifts. Reproduced
by permission of RICS. p.98 Adapted extract from 'Special Report: Coaches
can make you a real superhero' by Louise Armstead, www.thesundaytimes.
co.uk, 10 April 2005. © Louse Armstead, News Syndication, 10 April 2005.
Reproduced by permission of News Syndication.

Sources: p.7 www.assaabloy.com. p.20 www.biography.com.
p.26 www.hrbartender.com. p.37 www.thewowawards.co.uk.
p.46 www.tripadvisor.com. p.66 www.theguardian.com. p.74
www.wimbledon.com. p.78 www.riskybusiness.wordpress.com,
www.nielsen.com. p.86 www.dailymail.co.uk. p.91 www.marketing-schools.org.
p.91 www.toms.com. p.91 www.dove.us. p.91 www.boxtops4education.com.
p.95 www.newyorker.com. p.97 "The Secret Powers of Time" RSA ANIMATE,
www.thersa.org.

*The publisher would like to thank the following for their permission to reproduce
photographs:* Alamy pp.8 (Federico Julien), 11 (Derek Meijer), 17 (fStop
Images GmbH), 19 (bank/Mark Mercer), 46 (security/Oleksiy Maksymenko),
55 (Barrie Harwood), 60 (Roger Cracknell 01/classic), 96 (David Hare); Getty
Images pp.6 (Canary Wharf), 10, 12 (office, 1/Mark Scott, 2, 3), 13, 14 (A, B/
Jetta Productions, C), 16 (both), 18 (spectacles/RCWW, Inc.), 19 (shop/Betsie
Van der Meer), 20 (Paul Jeffers/Fairfax Media), 22 (camping/NTI, office pod/
Jim Rice/Fairfax Media), 24 (Bloomberg), 25 (Nik Wheeler), 26 (both), 28, 32,
38 (chairs), 40, 43 (building/Bloomberg, massage/Brooks Kraft), 46 (travelator,
man), 47 (Thomas Imo), 52 (men, box/Bloomberg), 54, 58 (market/Navya
Ponnuru, students), 59 (Nick Laham), 63 (girls/Ezra Bailey), 65 (café, solar),
66 (polar bear), 67 (C), 71 (speed camera, footsteps), 72 (canapés, F1), 74 (Neil
Tingle/LOOP IMAGES), 78 (bikes/Noriaki Maeda, volunteers), 81 (GlobalVision
Communication/GlobalFlyCam), 86 (wave), 88 (Thomas Barwick), 90 (Cultura
RM Exclusive/Frank Van Delft), 91 (shoes/Noel Vasquez, soap/Bloomberg,
box tops/Portland Press Herald), 92 (both), 94 (Andy Ryan), 98 (kitchen/
Hero Images, woman), 101 (man/Jetta Productions, woman), 104, 136 (AFP),
141 (Ted Soqui); Oxford University Press pp.6 (B, C (screen), D, H), 23 (satnav),
37; Rex Features pp.22 (sleep cabin/Action Press); Shutterstock pp.6 (A, C,
E, F, G), 18 (department store), 19 (laptop, tablet), 23 (background, e-reader,
microwave, watch), 27 (all), 31, 33, 34, 36, 38 (social media), 44 (both), 48,
51 (both), 57 (all), 63 (background), 65 (engineer), 66 (Upenski Cathedral),
67 (A, B, D), 68 (both), 71 (background), 72 (golf), 77, 80, 83, 84, 86 (drought),
87, 91 (background), 95, 97 (background), 103.

Illustrations by: Liza Whitney pp.32, 97.

Cover image: Getty Images/Maya.

Back cover photograph: Oxford University Press building/David Fisher

*The authors and publisher would also like to thank the following individuals for their
advice and assistance in developing the material for this course:* Beth Alexander,
Angelica Anastacio Molzahn, Clare Burke, Linda Cox, Louise Dixon, Simon
Drury, Justin Ehresman, Tom Evans, Jane Hoatson, Annie Kavaka, Christen
Kisch, Catherine Mayer, Sean O'Malley, Graeme Romanes, Rachael Smith,
Greg Steven, Edward Taylor.

*Although every effort has been made to trace and contact copyright holders before
publication, this has not been possible in some cases. We apologize for any apparent
infringement of copyright and if notified, the publisher will be pleased to rectify any
errors or omissions at the earliest opportunity.*